IN SEARCH OF SPIRITUAL IDENTITY

by

Adrian van Kaam, C.S.Sp.

DIMENSION BOOKS

Denville, New Jersey

Published by Dimension Books, Inc.
Denville, New Jersey 07834

Imprimi Potest: Rev. Philip J. Haggerty, C.S.Sp.
Provincial

Nihil Obstat: Rev. William J. Winter, S.T.D.
Censor Librorum

Imprimatur: Most Rev. Vincent M. Leonard, D.D.
Bishop of Pittsburgh

February, 1975

TABLE OF CONTENTS

FOREWORD

Many people feel dissatisfied with a mere ego identification in a functional society. They are in search of their deepest self in God. Christian spirituality can be seen as a discipline that guides this search for spiritual identity. The words of Scripture, the teaching of the Church and her spiritual masters, illumine this pursuit. They inspire attitudes enabling us to be more open to the call of our true self in Christ.

Spirituality explores these attitudes; it examines how we prepare for them, how they transform our daily life. This book proposes a framework for a science of Fundamental Catholic Spirituality that can facilitate this quest.

We realize that many people would be deterred from reading a book like this were it filled with footnotes and references for the sole benefit of a small number of readers interested in scholarly pursuits. We tried, therefore, to restrict our references to a minimum. Of the few we used, the main ones refer to St. Thomas Aquinas and St. John of the Cross, in tribute to our deep respect for the magnificent insights of these two giants of Catholic spiritual thought.

Students of spirituality will find here included an extensive selective bibliography of the author which may be helpful if they want to trace the gradual development of his thought. Information regarding his own books mentioned in the text can be found there.

Students may benefit also from a list of accomplished and current research at the Center for the Study of Spirituality. In each one of these studies in Fundamental Catholic Spirituality, they will find a vast number of references and an extensive annotated bibliography, both of which will prove helpful if they want to enter into the study of this discipline.

Chapters X and XI of this book deal with the issues and problems of research. The reader interested in this topic is advised to read first Appendix One that follows the last chapter. This appendix illustrates in an actual thesis proposal how this type of research can be concretely organized. A careful reading of this example may facilitate the understanding of the theoretical issues raised in the last two chapters.

While the reader may rightly feel that the theoretical considerations of Chapter X are beyond his interest, we would still like to suggest that he try to read at least Chapter XI, for there, in the course of the explanation of the research project, we try to develop an integrative view of some of the main points of the former chapters.

The pleasant duty rests upon me to express my deep gratefulness to my colleagues, Rev. Bert van Croonenburg, C.S.Sp. and Dr. Susan Muto, Ph.D., respectively executive and assistant director of the Center for the Study of Spirituality of the Institute of Man. Their numerous suggestions for improvement and simplification of the manuscript have been gratefully incorporated into the text. We are also indebted to the dedication of Sisters Margaret Gall, S.D.R., Dorothy Majewski, C.S.F.N. and Anita Carruthers, S.D.R. for their tireless assistance in the typing of the manuscripts, proofreading and many other chores that accompany the publication of a book.

Adrian van Kaam, C.S.Sp.
Center for the Study of Spirituality
Institute of Man
December 15, 1974   Duquesne University

I

FUNDAMENTAL CATHOLIC SPIRITUALITY

Over the centuries the study of the core of Western spirituality has been somewhat neglected, the essentials being hidden under their articulations in special spiritualities. Some Christians prefer to go to Eastern masters for enlightenment. Maybe they are unfamiliar with the fundamentals of their own tradition. Perhaps they are bewildered by the variety of exercises, devotions, styles, and ways of Western spiritual life. They may find it difficult to see how this complexity ties in with their own spontaneous experience of the life of the spirit. Their confusion may be compounded when representatives of each school praise their way as "the" way. So many possibilities are open to them over and beyond the essentials. It may seem to these seekers that Eastern masters present a more simple line of thought. They may be unaware that in the East complexity of spiritual ways is as prevalent as in the West.

In Catholicism it is not the fundamental but the special dimension of spirituality that dominates the landscape. How did this development come about? A bird's eye view of the emergence of spirituality may tell us.

* The source of Christian spirituality is the Lord; He is our Spiritual Master *par excellence*. He gently guides His followers through His Church, through Scripture, and through His Holy Spirit speaking in their hearts. His Church safeguards and unfolds His teachings contained in the Revelation.

7

Any great religion reflecting on its sacred writings—whether Scripture, Koran, Sutra's, Vedanta's—gives rise to two main streams of reflection: systematic theology and spirituality.

Systematic theology interprets intellectually the holy writings by means of cultural and philosophical concepts, categories, and frames of reference; it aims at an innovative development of the Church's authoritative presentation of the meaning of Revelation. It tries to formulate new possible interpretations which may or may not become object of the faith. Systematic theology also teaches in general that the faithful have to live a Christian life in accordance with doctrine as seen through the mirror of one or the other specific theology. Systematic theology proposes the moral norms of this Christian life.

The other kind of reflection is spirituality. In the light of Revelation and Doctrine, spirituality reflects on the experiences the faithful may have of an intimate self-communication of God; it studies critically the records of such experiences and the life praxis that accompanies them. Comparing such records, spirituality tries to make explicit the structures they have in common. Spirituality studies also the experiential and situational conditions and life praxis that guard, facilitate, foster, and deepen the readiness for such experiences. Spirituality focuses on what experientially happens to a Christian, who, already living in accordance with well understood Doctrine and Revelation, readies himself daily for the gratuitous elevation by God to a life of divine intimacy. Spirituality does not aim at an innovative development of the Church's authoritative presentation of the Revelation; it may aim at an innovative development of the practical ways in which man readies himself for the self-communication of the Sacred in his life.

In the beginning of a religion, systematic theological and spiritual reflection are not easily distinguished from one another. They are not yet highly developed and do not cover too much ground. A lucid mind can easily master both. That is precisely what happened in the Church Fathers. A thinker like St. Augustine writes both spiritual works like the *Confessions* and systematic theological treatises on complicated questions such as predestination.

Later, however, systematic theological and spiritual knowledge and methodology became too specified and elaborated to be mastered by one and the same expert, especially in view of the fact that each of these disciplines demands a different set of mind. These two nuances in approach to the same Church Doctrine began therefore to demand their own specialists and experts.

In Western Christianity this division of the labor of religious reflection took place along the line of the budding Christian schools or universities and the already flourishing widely spread monasteries. Theology in the strict systematic sense became the domain of the school and was accordingly called theology of the schools or scholastic theology. The study of spirituality became the prerogative of the monks and received aptly the name monastic theology. Later in history a more explicit study of the mystical dimension of the spiritual life was added. This addition was called mystical theology; it found its original formulations in the works of Pseudo-Dionysius, who seems to have been a Syrian monk. The study of this aspect of spirituality too found its main representatives in religious, most illustrious among them being John of the Cross and Teresa of Avila.

Both monastic and mystical spirituality—even if not broad enough for a present day formulation of the fundamental dimension of spirituality—were of a more basic nature than many of the special spiritualities that would develop later in various religious communities. The relative fundamentality of monastic spirituality was due to the simplicity of the beginnings of spiritual reflection; the spread of the monasteries in the known world of that time; the all pervading presence of a Christian culture; the daily interaction with Revelation and Church liturgy through liturgical ceremonies, singing and reading of the Office; and the absence of sophisticated scientific theories and clinical insights in regard to the nature of man.

Later in history new religious communities began to emerge that were not of a purely monastic nature. Conforming to the traditional division of reflective religious labor in Christianity, they shared with the monks the task to guard, expand, and promote spiritual reflection in Christendom.

These later religious institutions often responded to specific contemporary needs. The Dominicans, for instance, tried to counteract the influence of the Albigenses; the Jesuits were involved in the counter-reformation. More recent religious foundations specialized exclusively in particular enterprises such as foreign missions, teaching, nursing, or social work. Such specializations influenced their perception of spirituality.

Often the outlook of these institutions was circumscribed by a particular culture. National and regional cultures had begun to assert themselves in Europe at the time of these new foundations.

Another influential factor on these later communities and their spiritualities was that of more pronounced personalities who set the tone for the living of the life of the spirit. Personal and temperamental differences had, of course, always existed among people, but Western man had become more aware of them. He began to cherish, accentuate, and develop them. As a result this more pronounced differentiation started to play an increasingly active role in outlook, behavior, and spirituality. The founders of these later communities were more often than not pronounced personalities who put their own stamp on communities and their spiritualities. They tended to attract similar personality types who could continue and deepen the orientation of the spirituality given by the founders.

The subsequent specificity of each of these communities gave rise to a greater differentiation from the life of the secular clergy and the faithful. This mental and emotional differentiation fostered an increasingly particular development of the already special spirituality initiated by the founder on basis of the response of his type of culture and personality to a contemporary need. For example, the methods of meditation and particular exam of the French school of spirituality, elaborated in many French seminaries and communities, were further removed from the daily life of the laity than the more open-ended liturgical and scriptural inspiration provided by the monastic life.

All of these factors made for an unprecedented flowering of numerous special spiritualities such as the Dominican, Franciscan, Carmelite, Ignatian, Vincentian, Sulpician, Montfortan, Spiritan, Passionist, to name only a few, each one with its own distinctive characteristics and appealing to its own kind of person. The advantage of this development was the increasing availability of congenial types of spirituality for the increasing variety of pronounced personality types in which Western man had begun to differentiate himself. The disadvantage was the temporary stagnation of the development of an explicit formulation of the implicit core of all special and personal spiritualities.

This fundamental dimension is a necessary basis for the personal spiritual life. A person who would find no compatibility with any of the existing special spiritualities would need this fundamental spirituality too as a basis for his personal spiritual life. For what else is an authentic personal or special spirituality but a modulation of fundamental spirituality?

The discipline of Fundamental Catholic Spirituality roots itself in Catholic Doctrine; in the teachings of the recognized spiritual masters of the Church; and in the make-up of graced human nature. It takes into account the usual ways of life of priests, religious, and lay people; the normal means for spiritual life that can be offered to all their members—on a regular basis—by the average Catholic diocese, parish, and religious congregation and by a local religious community. It tries to discover and formulate the necessary and sufficient means, structures, conditions, and dynamics of a Catholic spiritual life lived within the common context of an average Catholic or Catholic-religious environment.

We can distinguish between fundamental, special, personal, and infused dimensions of spirituality. These are dimensions, not separate spiritualities, in the person who actually lives them. Special, personal, and infused spirituality are a modulated, personalized, and graced actualization of fundamental spirituality. A spirituality that would not include the fundamentals would be a false spirituality, hence not a spirituality at all. The one spirituality a person lives has thus fundamental, special, personal, and perhaps infused facets. What, however, is a lived unity in the individual can be distinguished by the intellect for the purpose of clarification. The student of spirituality can establish a special set of considerations for each one of the four dimensions that form together an indivisible mixture in the unique person who lives them. In this study, therefore, we will speak about the four aspects separately as if they were four spiritualities, keeping always in mind their actual unity in the person.

Let us begin with a consideration of the fundamental dimension of all Catholic spirituality. This will be followed by a reflection on each of the three articulations of the fundamental: the special, the personal, and the infused.

Fundamental Spirituality

Fundamental Spirituality deals with the natural and revealed necessary and sufficient conditions for the emergence of a spiritual life. If we know and live the essentials, we are less likely to get "hooked" on certain special forms that may be changed, for example, by a Chapter in a religious congregation or by new cultural-religious movements. Without the fundamentals, when the "specials" are changed or omitted, we may feel that our spiritual life is lost. Of course, this freedom from fixation on special articulations presupposes that we have assimilated the essentials not only abstractly but experientially. Many feel betrayed today because they were not initiated into the essentials in a living way. They fixated on what was "in" at the time.

Fundamental spirituality provides us therefore with

criteria for discovery and evaluation of fundamental insights, explicitly or implicitly present in all spiritualities and especially elaborated in special spiritualities.

For example, Ignatian spirituality is filled with insights that are fundamental and not just part of this special spirituality. The same is true with other spiritualities, such as the spirituality of the French School, the Benedictine, or the Carmelite spirituality.

Fundamental spirituality helps us in evolving a theoretical framework for the integration of findings and insights discovered in special, personal and infused spiritualities and in various other explanations of man's spiritual nature. The base of the fundamentals in human nature, its dynamics and conditions, may be touched upon, for example, in literature, medicine, arts, and sciences. In other words, we can select and reformulate ideas from specialized spiritualities and other sources and put these in the broader framework of fundamental insights we have already discovered.

Fundamental spirituality can be an instrument or tool of ecumenical dialogue with non-Catholic spiritualities. It is difficult to have fruitful dialogue with Buddhism, for example, if we present only the small details of the Montfortan school of spirituality for discussion and they present only the small details of some sub-sect of Tibetan Buddhism. But if both address themselves to the fundamentals, such as the need for quiet, repose, meditation, they may create space for ecumenical dialogue.

According to St. Thomas Aquinas grace builds on nature. To understand the fundamentals of spiritual life we must understand the nature of man. The fundamental dimension of the spiritualities of other religions must take into account the same human nature. This common ground facilitates fruitful dialogue. A fundamental approach can reduce accidental differences, highlight similarities and yet do justice to essential divergences that cannot be denied. Explicit awareness of the fundamentals of spiritual living has the function of reconciliation within the Church: it fosters oneness in essentials, diversity in accidentals; plurality in special and personal spiritualities, unity in fundamentals. When a person has a grasp of the essentials, he may be less passionate in his fight for accidentals. There can be reconciliation amid polarity and division. We must clearly oppose those who would throw out essentials—such as any form of prayer by saying, for example, that work in and by itself is already sufficient prayer. When a person, however, wants to do away with an accidental that is another story—for example, a person may have no personal devotion to the Way of the Cross. This is understandable. He may rightly omit this devotion unless the Way of the Cross is part of the special spirituality of his community. He must know even then that it is not fundamental but a special modulation of the fundamental.

Special Spiritualities

Certain personality types share aspects of their make-up with people of the same type. Other people again have cultural characteristics in common or love the same sort of activities. This sharing may be one of the determinants of the particular character of a religious community and its spirituality. We see also special spiritualities developing among lay people who are or feel alike in certain ways, such as married people, professional persons—nurses, doctors, teachers, lay apostles, socially engaged men and women.

Sharing the same culture may give rise to a special modulation of fundamental spirituality. Mexicans, for example, love exuberant spiritual expressions. This shared special cultural characteristic could color their spirituality; it may also be a first help for them on the way toward personalization of fundamental spirituality.

Special spiritualities may function as a bridge between the fundamental and personal modulations of one's spirituality. Essentials or fundamentals have to be lived by unique persons. They become necessarily personalized when they are lived concretely. A person may thus find nourishment and a beginning of personalization by participation in a congenial spirituality, developed, lived, and exemplified by people who share some aspect of his personal life.

Special spiritualities are authentic when they are articulations of the fundamentals and do not diminish or depreciate the latter. For example, the French School of Spirituality, the spiritualities of Ignatius, Francis de Sales, Francis of Assisi, the Carmelites or the Benedictines are special spiritualities. They are not identical with Fundamental Catholic Spirituality but a special articulation of it. If they were identical with fundamental spirituality, they would be useless as a bridge between the fundamental and the personal; they could not be distinguished either from the fundamental dimension of spirituality or from one another.

The authenticity of any special spirituality is not necessarily as well established as that of the spiritualities we just mentioned. What the latter have in common is a history of centuries in which they were tried out, purified, adapted, and approved of by the Church. We are more sure of their authenticity than, for example, the authenticity of a newly developing mode of spirituality that may or may not be authentic. Only time will tell.

Determinants of a Special Spirituality

What determines the character of a special spirituality? The personality of the man or woman who initiated a spirituality may be a prime determinant. We can readily see that Francis of Assisi was a different type from Ignatius of Loyola. This difference must be reflected somehow in their way of living the spiritual life.

Culture can be another determinant. For example, the Basque culture is different from that of Italian Umbrian. It may give rise to distinct emphases in the spiritualities initiated in such environments.

History can be a strong determinant. Living and growing old together, facing problems as a community, creates a certain mentality that influences the further development of a spiritual life style.

Also the work persons share, the common task, the questions it poses, the answers given in dialogue with one another can shape to some degree our spiritual way.

Importance of Various Determinants

In the beginning of a congregation or order, personality type may be called one of the important determinants. Mainly young adults may enter a new community; they are people who have thought of what they want and have experienced what they are like as persons. Usually those who join are, therefore, somewhat similar and temperamentally in tune with the personality of the founder who may still be alive or recalled by those who lived with him. Because of this similarity they feel similarly attracted by the same type of community spirituality. When a community exists longer and is well established candidates may enter rather young. Their measure of self-awareness is limited. They are less aware of the personality differences between them and the founder long ago or members of the community. They join because they may be interested in the work, in friends already in the community, in any number of other values they see in this life. As a result many long established communities are not made up of similar personality types.

The original shared culture too has become a smaller influence in those orders that have spread far from where they were founded. Moreover, that original culture itself may have changed considerably since their foundation. While present day shared culture still has a great influence on the members, the influence of the original cultural period that helped shape the special spirituality seems less influential than in the beginning of the community.

Another presently still important determinant is the history persons share together. We are making our own history all the time as we spontaneously live together and share similar experiences. We can compare this to a family. All families are basically the same—mother, father and children. But all families are still different because of their history. All the things experienced together make a history and make the family special. The same is true of what happens in a religious community or a community of faithful. The community is always creating its own history which gives it a certain style. This is true too of Christian communities that do not live the vowed celibate life but support each other in living a spiritual life in the world.

Another determinant is work. As shared personality and the original culture of the founder became less influential, work—next to shared history—became more and more influential especially in the Western world. The more recent religious communities chose usually a specific work, a special form of participation in the culture, as one of the reasons for their existence. Yet it is not wise to build one's whole spirituality on one inflexible form of cultural participation. If this work-bound spirituality is made to be the essence of spiritual life, there will be problems when this one type of work can no longer be done effectively, wholesomely, and graciously by the community as a whole or by a member of the community.

A community could promote a common enterprise while keeping its options open in case the existing work changes significantly and in case not all members of the community can do the common task reasonably and healthily.

In certain communities—religious or lay—since the 19th Century work rather than spirituality received the main attention. When this happens, if people can no longer do the work, they may feel they have lost their spirituality because they identified it unconsciously with the work of their community and with the special modulation of fundamental spirituality that this social or apostolic work might have given rise to.

Flexibility in inner attitude towards the work of a community does not mean that most people should cease being engaged in the main work of the community. It may be that all are engaged in the same task. Flexibility surely does not mean that everyone can do as he pleases, but that the community should not identify a special spirituality emerging from their work with fundamental spirituality.

The fundamental dimension of spirituality, to become real and concrete, has always to incarnate itself in special and personal structures, such as structures of prayer, recollection, reading, poverty, obedience. However, we can be accommodating in these special and personal forms provided the fundamental conditions are safeguarded. Fundamental spirituality thus creates room for dialogue about the concrete articulations of the fundamentals in personal and common ways of life.

For example, according to the basic requirements of all spirituality, no spiritual life is possible without a certain amount of recollection. If a person is talking, watching T.V., or reading magazines all day long, little recollection would be possible. We may try to specialize this fundamental need for inner silence by proposing a rule of silence, singling out certain times and places for silence, and so on. If a community cannot go along with this proposed special rule, its members don't have to cry out that no spiritual life is possible in the community. In that case they should try to live personally the basic conditions of recollection and inner silence in which they were hopefully initiated when they learned theoretically and experientially the fundamentals of the spiritual life.

Sometimes people tend to cut out special and personal modulations of fundamental spirituality. But because they do not know what the essentials contained in fundamental spirituality are, they may cut them out too and end up with nothing. If they have truly appropriated the fundamental dimension of spirituality, they can still, in any situation no matter how poor, live the essentials and embody the basics in new personal life attitudes and customs.

Special Spirituality of One's Community

How should members of a religious order or congregation approach the special modulation of fundamental spirituality typical of their community? Members of such a community should deeply know the community spirituality as distinguished from and yet related to fundamental spirituality. The explanation of the community spirituality should be explicitly linked to an explanation of the basic demands of all spirituality and show how such basics are particularized in this special spirituality.

This awareness of the essential root of the community spirituality can help members later—when particular ways may be changed—to fall back on fundamentals that are perennial. Out of these they may come to new personal particularizations of the fundamentals. They should respect the community spirituality in word, behavior, and inner attitude and honestly try to live up to it. Inwardly they may look for something else only after dialogue with the spiritual teacher or director.

For example, Father Libermann—one of the founders of the Spiritans—has a fine spirituality in tune with the fundamentals. This was presented to the novices in his congregation. But the wise director explained that people did not have to use Libermann's ideas and approach in each one of their meditations if they found they could benefit better by another Church-approved spirituality. Some people may be unable to live deeply some aspect of a community spirituality inwardly.

When some religious orders began, the initiates were older and often joined because the special type of spirituality appealed to their personal make-up, which they knew better because of longer life and self experience. Moreover, the new community spirituality was influenced by an own contemporary culture they felt at home with. This is no longer necessarily the case when a community has a long history behind it. Young people without much self experience may join without knowing sufficiently their own personality; they may not understand the original culture that helped shape the spiritual outlook of their community. As a result they may find themselves at odds with the community spirituality. Yet they should learn, respect, and live the spirituality of the community as well as possible. Usually most will be able to live the spirituality of their congregation inwardly. Even those, however, should come to know well the fundamental grounds of any spirituality whatsoever. For one thing, they may be less tempted to teach outsiders the community spirituality as if it were fundamental and necessary for all who want to grow in the spiritual life. They should realize that their community spirituality contains more than the essentials. They should never deceive outsiders by teaching their brand of spirituality as if it were only fundamental with nothing special added to it.

We can end our considerations of special spiritualities with two observations. We may often meet people who unwittingly try to combine various aspects of different special spiritualities. This is not bad if they keep clearly in mind the fundamentals. Otherwise they may be inclined unconsciously to gather a pleasant collection of superficial aspects by picking and choosing only what they like, a cafeteria type of spirituality. Taking only the "cream off the top," they may lose out on the "solid cake" of the essentials.

In light of the foregoing, we can now state the criteria of an authentic and effective special spirituality: it must be in tune with fundamental spirituality and capable of personalization by the appropriate personality type. From this perspective we can now make a similar point for the criteria of fundamental spirituality which would be its compatibility with Church Doctrine and its potentiality to be specialized and personalized by all—that is, specialized by specific groups of like minded believers into special spiritualities and personalized by individual faithful into a personally lived spirituality.

Special modulations of fundamental spirituality are not necessary for everyone. Many faithful move directly from fundamental to personal spirituality. They personalize the fundamentals spontaneously. This does not mean that they would not have profited from an appropriate special spirituality if they could have found one; it would probably have shortened the way in some cases, but not necessarily in all.

Personal Spirituality

Special spirituality developed with like minded persons can thus function as a bridge between the fundamental and personal modulations of one's spiritual life. Because such bridges are needed by many, the steady emergence of special spiritualities and the evolvement of the existing ones are important in the Church. A flowering of special spiritualities guarantees the availability of a sufficient variety of "exemplary" spiritualities for the many different kinds of faithful who could profit from them in their search for a personal spiritual life.

Personal spirituality is man's unique articulation of special or fundamental spirituality. For example, not all Dominicans are alike; even those who live the Dominican modulation of fundamental spirituality will necessarily live it in their own way.

There is no other avenue of spiritualization for the individual and the community than the personal way. A community of religious or lay people is only as spiritual as its individual members. We cannot spiritualize a community *en bloc*. Even if we speak to a group as a spiritual teacher, we must try to reach the individuals in that group. Spiritualization happens always in and through the person because the Holy Spirit only speaks in and through personal human spirits.

Think of the example of Christ. When He speaks as Spiritual Master, He speaks to a group, His disciples, but He speaks in such a way as to appeal to each one of them personally.

The same thing happens when we read a good spiritual book like *The Imitation of Christ* by Thomas a Kempis. It was written for many but in such a way that it can speak personally to each individual reader.

A danger for present day spiritual life could be that the need for the spiritualization of the person is played down or replaced by an attempt to spiritualize the community as a whole. The spiritualization of a group only takes place in and through the spiritualization of the persons who make up the group.

Presenting to others fundamentals of spirituality, we don't totally deny our personal way of living the fundamentals, but neither do we put our way so much in the forefront that it hides what is essential for all spiritual life. The personal way of living the fundamentals is linked with temperament, personal history, education, glandular system, and life situation. It should be clearly distinguished from the fundamentals. If the special and personal devotions, feelings, needs, and projections of a spiritual director or teacher have too much influence, they may become quasi-fundamental in the mind of the directees.

We don't have to deny our own personalization of spirituality, but we must prevent the quasi-universalization of it. We may show while speaking how we live the fundamentals or special spiritualities personally, yet we must make it clear that this is how *we* do it. There are countless other ways of living the same fundamentals well, some of which may be better for a certain personality. On the other hand, we should not dim or hide the fact of personalization itself because this factor is essential too for spiritual life. Paradoxically, the demand for personalization as such is one of the fundamental demands of all spiritual life.

Spiritual Direction, Personal and Special Spirituality

A spiritual director may be fond of a special spirituality or of his own mixture of certain special spiritualities that provide inspiration for him. The director also lives a personal spirituality, for all who truly live a spiritual life must personalize it. This personal spirituality has a deep and lasting value for him as a person, but what he must teach first of all are the fundamentals. For the members of a special religious or Christian community, he may add to the fundamentals an explanation of their special spirituality. However, he should never give the initiates the idea that they should personally and exactly feel as he does in matters that are his purely private predilections and prejudices.

Initiates in any religious or Christian community are vulnerable and sensitive. Their spiritual director or teacher is a person of great moral authority for them. If he proposes his personal style of living the fundamentals too enthusiastically, they may get caught in it without sufficient introduction to the fundamentals. Especially young people—closed off from the world with their spiritual teacher—are vulnerable. He becomes like an oracle to them. What he says could be taken by some as gospel truth. His moral authority over them makes it unjust to seduce them to accept blindly his special or personal way of living the basics, for—young, inexperienced, idealistic, anxious, and isolated as they are and eager to please him—they have no defense against his enthusiasm.

Sometimes the director's own way of living the basics will unavoidably come to the fore; this is fine but he must make clear that it is his way and not necessarily beneficial for everyone. Otherwise directees may become confused and end up being carbon copies of the director. He can only be careful in this regard if he himself knows clearly what is fundamental and what is special or personal in his style of spiritual life.

Immoderate promotion of the director's own style of life easily induces guilt feelings in initiates who cannot wholeheartedly feel at home in what seems to move him so deeply. They may be of good will, but his personal approach to divine intimacy may not agree with their personal life style, temperament, intellectual or emotional capacity, apostolic interest or vital make-up.

The worst case is the initiate who does not really benefit from a certain style of living the fundamentals but who, because of its acclaim by the director or others, compels himself to believe he benefits from it. He falsifies his own self-awareness. Slowly but surely he cripples himself as a healthy spiritual person. His spiritual life will become an exercise in pious self-deception. This false turn may mark a lifelong sequel of self-destruction begun in the time of formation.

This is not to say that, for example, the Slavery of Mary of de Montfort, the Way of the Cross, thirty day exercises and the devotion to the Child of Prague are not excellent. They most surely are and the Church approves of such things since they have proven to be inspirational for many. They offer fine possibilities for concretizing the fundamentals which have to be incarnated in some particular way. The more such possibilities are available in the Church the better. For it means that there will be a rich variety of occasions and opportunities for spiritual growth in accordance with the rich variety of temperaments and personalities that make up Christianity. If they speak to a person fine, but an initiate should not feel badly if such private or special predilections of his spiritual director don't appeal to him.

A director or spiritual teacher may ask how he can be honest if he is convinced about the value of some special or personal way of living the life of the spirit and then cannot promote it with unreserved enthusiasm. We would say there is no dishonesty about living on one's own an authentic special spirituality or having a personal spirituality, and over and above this, still to teach others the fundamental spirituality and its special modulation in the religious or Christian community concerned.

Why is there no dishonesty involved in living one thing and promoting another? We will give some reasons. It is not dishonest when the director believes that fundamental spirituality is essential, that any Catholic wishing to grow in Catholic spiritual life must adhere to it. He can honestly see and promote it as a primary necessity for all, in spite of his own predilection for a particular articulation of the fundamentals. He sees his own special and personal spirituality as only possible articulations of a basic Christian spirituality he lives implicitly.

The director can honestly respect the freedom of the initiates to find, over and above fundamental spirituality and its special articulation in their religious or Christian community, some special and personal modulation of the spiritual life that is meaningful to them. He leaves them free to find something appealing, warning them, however, never to drop any of the fundamentals. He is honestly and humbly concerned that they should never adopt blindly the personal way of living the basics that happens to tie in with the uniqueness and special work interest of their director.

If we look back at our own initiation into the spiritual life as priests, religious, or lay persons, we may recognize that some idea might have been communicated to us that was not fundamental, yet it was perhaps presented as if it were so. This can lead to trouble. For instance, some of these things might fall away later; then people may feel their spiritual life is over.

Take a case in which a priest, religious, or lay person called to initiate others into the life of the spirit is honestly convinced that a special way of living the fundamentals, not yet authenticated by the Church, is "it." Because of a person's life history, studies, experience, and the like, he may be convinced he should live personally a spirituality or devotion that seems to a significant number of Catholics at odds with the basic requirements of Catholic spiritual life. He may be attracted to something which is not well established as yet.

No matter what a person is convinced of, he should be humble and wise enough to realize that only he, with a limited number of sympathizers, see this truly as a Catholic possibility for spirituality in the future. He should have the humble conviction also that this limited number of people may be mistaken—that history may prove their experiment wrong even if they themselves will not live to see this event.

We may be deeply touched by a spirituality that is still doubtful. We are not yet sure if it is in tune with the fundamental requirements of all Catholic spirituality. It is neither condemned nor affirmed. We must be humble enough to say we feel it seems right for us but also history may prove us wrong; it is only an experiment we are engaging in. It would not be wise or just to expose initiates, religious, or lay persons to these views about which we cannot as yet be certain.

Infused Spirituality

Infused spirituality is the highest form of spiritual life. Beyond all possible special and personal articulations of his spirituality, man comes to utmost simplicity. His fundamental spirituality is modulated by God Himself. God as God is the main focus. In this union the person is overtaken by the Divine. The great masters of the mystical life such as Pseudo-Dionysius, Ruysbroeck, John of the

Cross, Teresa of Avila have described the fundamental experiences, dynamics, and conditions of this stage of the spiritual life. The mystic must regularly return to the fundamental norms explained by these masters. He must check his experiences with the Doctrine of the Church as made practical and directive in fundamental spirituality. For the danger of illusion is always present. So is the danger of not rightly responding to this ultimate gift of divine intimacy.

The important thing is to be clearly aware of what is special, personal, and infused and to know each as a modulation of the fundamental. We must always try to build on the basics. If we teach a special modulation of fundamental spirituality, we should never pretend that it is "the" Fundamental Catholic Spirituality; it is only one of its many possible articulations.

This book attempts to introduce the reader into the study of this field, its conditions, objectives, and main approaches. First of all we have to delineate further the meaning and scope of fundamental spirituality as the basic science of spirituality. This we propose to do in the following chapter.

II

THE SCIENCE OF SPIRITUALITY

The science of spirituality is a theoretical-practical science; it presents a theory about the praxis of spiritual living. To understand the practical character of spirituality, we shall first reflect on our everyday practical knowledge of spiritual living. This non-scientific knowledge that guides directly our daily concrete life is called by scholastic thinkers the knowledge of prudence.

Prudence is about my day to day life, how to act concretely in such a way that I live my own life rightly, personally, uniquely as well as in tune with the universal wisdom found in Church Doctrine, theology, philosophy, and spirituality. For example, all of us, to live a spiritual life have to be recollected. The science of spirituality can tell us concretely what man should do in order to be recollected. Nevertheless, each one of us may have to pay special attention to personal unique obstacles to recollection and find out how to deal with them effectively.

No science is possible about such immediate directive knowledge of unique spiritual living, for science is about universals. The fullness of an effective spiritual life demands not only a certain amount of knowledge about the spiritual life as taught in spirituality but also a certain growth in prudence that enables us to personalize uniquely what we have learned in the shared wisdom and theory of spirituality.

Personalization of Practical Knowledge

To understand the special place of prudence in the praxis of spiritual living, we may for a moment imagine the whole of our practical or life-directive knowledge in all its phases as a mighty stream or flood. This stream narrows more and more as it flows from the mountains into the valley, fertilizing the particular fields of the farmers there. The farmers may dig small canals and ditches to make sure that each individual field is watered in accordance with its particular needs. Similarly, the great stream of practical knowledge about spiritual life, starting on the high mountains of Catholic Doctrine, speculative-practical theology and philosophy, narrowing down in theoretical-practical spirituality comes down in the valley of daily life where people direct it through the channels and ditches of prudence to water their individual fields of spiritual living.

Prudence, then, directs my practical knowing about spiritual living to a knowing of the concrete singular act to be posited here and now within the shifting variety of contingent circumstances in which my daily spiritual life has to unfold itself.

For example, a seminarian once spoke of recollection and its importance for the life of prayer. He wanted to be practical about it. He pondered how to keep his mind and heart under control, but he had a problem. He was a gifted musician. In the chapel or in his room, during meditation or prayer, he easily became caught up with music, so much so that he could neither pray nor recollect himself sufficiently for prayer. He was faced with the problem of how to handle this.

First he had practical knowledge from his courses in

theology. God is infinite, omnipresent, indwelling as Holy Trinity in our graced souls. We must be present to this loving God. To foster this presence, we have to set certain moments of the day apart for meditative presence. To do so, we need to calm our desires and all the concerns and preoccupations they give rise to.

In a narrower theoretical-practical way, from courses in spirituality, he knew that he needed to calm his restless mind and emotional agitation by certain concrete means discovered and elaborated by Eastern and Western spiritual masters on basis of a penetrating reflection on their personal experience with themselves and others. But in the chapel near the organ he had to face how he, with his unique musical sensitivity, could make this universal wisdom work for him personally, how he could adapt it to his own personal situation, how he could personalize the wisdom of theologians and spiritual masters. Here he needed the knowledge that only personal prudence can give and that would grow by trial and error.

The speculative-practical knowledge of theology and the theoretical-practical knowledge of spirituality cannot tell us exactly in detail how to handle our personal spiritual problems. With the help of prudence, each of us must find concrete ways of living the spiritual life in the contingent circumstances in which we find ourselves.

To be effective in our daily life, directive knowledge has to be in touch with the particular acts of living that have to be evaluated here and now on the spot. The object of practical life knowledge is not only life in its grand design but life as minutely lived in daily changing situations.

When we are personally faced with a concrete singular act of consequence—what shall I do here and now in this crucial situation—each of us may come up with a somewhat different answer. We have to consider the particular meaning and consequences of such an act; we must take into account our personal make-up, our life history, our unique web of obligations to our family and others, the particular situations we are faced with. We need also to look at the life project we feel called to follow.

For instance, I may have decided to express my love for God by serving humanity as a good scientist. This personal option should affect my decision when I am asked to give a considerable amount of time to a charitable undertaking. To give so much time may interfere with my primary calling in life. Prudence may tell me that such a form of charity would hamper my concrete spiritual unfolding as a scientist who finds the Divine Will primarily in faithfulness to the life option God inspired him to make. All these particular elements enter into the knowledge of prudence. No theory of the spiritual life could tell us in a detailed way what precisely to do in such situations. The wisdom of spirituality would have to be particularized by prudence in each particular instance.

We conclude, therefore, that the immediate direction of my unique life within successive changing life situations cannot be an object of any science or scholarly discipline. Speculative sciences are always about universals and practical science is about general norms. Right knowledge that guides my life immediately is the knowledge of prudence. Prudence helps my mind to judge rightly and command what is to be done concretely here and now in this particular situation.

Prudence as Intellectual and Personal

Let us look now at another characteristic of prudence. The understanding of this characteristic will also help to clarify the nature of the knowledge of spirituality.

The virtue of prudence is both an intellectual and a personal virtue. Prudential insight can only be right and trustworthy when also the human will is rightly oriented. In practical life knowledge, the intellect does not function in isolation from the options of our will and its dispositions. The same is true for the knowledge of spirituality where rectitude of will is also crucial.

It is not enough for prudence to search intellectually for the right course of action. The human will too must be rightly directed. Otherwise the right course of action may never be discovered by the intellect. Rectitude of will is easily lost. Our vital strivings, passions, and desires affect our will, consciously or unconsciously, in many ways.

Let us give a simple example. Imagine I have to write an article. It is not enough that I have the intellectual insight that I should write it here and now. My will too must be rightly directed to this undertaking. This may be difficult because my vital needs and desires try to affect my will constantly even without my knowing it. Thus I might interrupt my work countless times for numerous reasons. I feel that I need to take time out for a coke, for chatter, for a walk in the garden, for a peek at the newspaper. Every time I do so, I will be inclined to justify or rationalize the need that takes me away from my task. My judgment is falsified by these needs. In this way my vital desires may vitiate my right judgment; my will does not have the necessary rectitude; it has lost its right orientation towards all kinds of disturbing vital influences that have not been worked through. We need to purify our will and its dispositions to secure the right judgment of what to do here and now.

Therefore, the judgments of prudence are true or false in relation to the direction my acts should take and in relation to the rectitude of my will.

We have examined what prudence is. The insights gained in this investigation help us to see better what a theoretical-practical science like spirituality is. To adapt the characteristics of prudence wisely to spirituality as a theoretical-practical science, we must first establish that spirituality is a theory of praxis and as such different from the immediate praxis of the virtue of prudence.

Spirituality as Theory

People today call only practical what is immediately practical here and now. The efficient cook is praised as practical. He may not have mastered culinary theories, but he possesses the practical magic that brings delicious meals to the table. He knows the art of cooking. The successful college administrator is lauded as practical. He knows how to handle prudently faculty, students, finances, and curricula.

When a commercial pilot learns to fly, he learns both theory and practice. The practical is about the actual flying. The theory includes general rules and principles of engine construction, signal reading, radio monitoring, and piloting—a whole practical science which by its very nature, however, remains theoretical. If it were not theoretical, it could not have a universal validity. The practice of flying itself is something different. There the novice pilot has to apply artfully theoretical rules to shifting flying conditions that are unique. They cannot be described exhaustively in any theory of aviation. Therefore, in the beginning a prudent instructor—who has mastered the art of flying thoroughly—controls and directs the fledgling attempts of the novice in this field saving him and himself in tight situations.

Similarly, the science of spirituality, like the science of aviation, is theoretical. Spirituality is not primarily a system of speculations about the "what" or the essence of the spiritual life; it is a theory about how practically to live the life of the spirit. Spirituality, therefore, in present day understanding could be called the theoretical science of how to live the spiritual life. This theoretical science emerged out of praxis.

Spiritual masters met with problems they sought to solve, experiences they tried to clarify, conditions whose impact they attempted to assess. These practical questions guided the development of their reflections on the spiritual life. The same experiences and questions showed up in people who appealed to them for help. They heard or read about other masters who had dealt with similar issues. They compared their answers with those they themselves had stumbled upon. Out of these threads of experience, comparison, observation, and reflection, they wove slowly over the centuries a practical theory of how to live the spiritual life—a theory that can guide our lives more directly than, for example, systematic theology does.

Systematic theology directs our spiritual life remotely; spirituality does so proximately; prudence immediately. We remember from the story of the musical seminarian that his courses in systematic theology were a worthwhile but less direct or remote aid in the solution of his problem of recollection; the courses he had taken in spirituality were more directly or approximately helpful; finally prudence helped him immediately on the spot to concretize in his unique situation what he had learned speculatively and practically in the study of systematic theology and practical spirituality.

Three Characteristics of Spirituality

The science of spirituality has three distinctive characteristics; it is theoretical, experiential, and practical.

This science is theoretical not only because it has to have universal validity but also because it develops by way of integration. Selective integration can only be achieved by means of a steadily developing theoretical frame. In the case of spirituality, this frame should be a kind of spiritual self-theory or personality theory. This frame of reference should be in tune with doctrine and prove most effective for the integration and explanation of all relevant data and insight provided by life, the arts and sciences.

Spirituality should be open to and studious of relevant experiences and experiments as reported in spiritual and other literature, in art, science, and medicine, and as observed in one's own life and the life of others. These experiences and insights can then be integrated by means of the theoretical frame of integration. Such is the experiential character of spirituality.

The aspect of practice comprises research into the question of how the experiences thus studied can be integrated within a spiritual self-theory, utilized in personal living, and made concrete in the initiation and direction of others in the spiritual life. \

The Object of Spirituality

On the highest level, spirituality speaks of the most eminent act of man, infused contemplation; it deals with the predisposing conditions for and obstacles to this act; it studies both proximate and remote means of preparation. Spirituality deals also with the incarnation of the spiritual life in man's daily world.

Man's most eminent act is the infused experience of things divine. This act is not possible by human power; it comes as a pure gift of God.

Spiritual masters like John of the Cross, Teresa of Avila, Pseudo-Dionysius, Ruysbroeck, the author of *The Cloud of Unknowing* discuss this highest state possible for humanity and the practical knowledge needed to respond rightly to this grace. This end stage of the spiritual life is one of passive detachment and infused experiential presence to the Presence. God is acting. Man cooperates.

Spirituality speaks also of our preparation for this infused experience and union. The nearest preparatory stage is that of acquired presence to the Presence. This is the stage of active detachment. Active does not mean that man moves without the assistance of grace. Grace is necessary in all stages of the spiritual life, but in this active stage grace refers to the ordinary grace granted all Christians who seriously follow the path of detachment and divine love; in this phase of the spiritual life the activity of man is far greater than in the end phase of infused union.

While this stage of active detachment and acquired presence represents a proximate preparation for that of infused experience and union, it can be prepared for in some ways. We could call this preparation remote. Remote preparation consists in the removal of natural obstacles and the fostering of facilitating conditions in our spiritual, personal, and vital life and in our daily environment so that grace may find less resistance in us. For the study of this phase of remote preparation, spirituality utilizes many data and insights of medicine, literature, the arts and sciences.

Lastly, spirituality is concerned with the incarnation of the fruits of either infused or acquired presence in daily life and world. To understand this last concern, we should realize that man is spirit in the deepest core of his being. This spirit-core tends to permeate other levels of his self. In and through this "inspirited" personal and vital self, the spirit goes out toward the world and others. This outgoing-ness is true for man's natural spirit even before it is transformed by grace. It remains as true for man's transformed or graced spirit.

Grace at the core of man's being transforms and elevates his free will. The spiritual will is then enabled to love God as He is in Himself. God pours into the human will His own divine love towards Himself. He wants also to show love to the world in and through His own love that elevated the will of the graced person. Grace gives rise to a love for people not for their merely human attractiveness or goodness but for their eternal calling in Christ. This love of God Himself in us, that flows out to others, is called charity. This gift of charity enables us to love others with the love of God Himself, for the sake of the image of His Son in all people, even if this image is veiled by greed, crime, and other distortions. The spiritual life always includes the living out of charity in accordance with our own unique make-up given by God. \

Spirituality and Doctrine

As students of spirituality, we never go far away from experience itself; we don't leave experience to speculate about it; we go deeper into it. Painstakingly, we describe and analyze what is happening; we strive to uncover the structure of the experience, its dynamics, its facilitating or hindering conditions for the spiritual life. We keep reflecting on it to come to theoretical formulations that hold true for similar situations. This reflection, too, keeps in touch with the experience it started from. At the same time the study of fundamental spirituality keeps rooting itself in doctrine, though doctrine is usually not the focus of attention of the student of spirituality.

Spirituality needs the light of doctrine. Compare this with reading. While reading, we are absorbed in sentences and their meanings; we do not pay attention to the lamp on our desk as long as it radiates its light, yet we could not read a letter without it. Similarly, spirituality needs constantly the light of doctrine. As long as it shines brightly in heart and mind, we don't notice this light. The moment it grows dim we hasten to rekindle its flame; we return to doctrine. The light is there all the time, but we don't focus on it.

Fundamental Catholic Spirituality is a practical extension of fundamental Catholic Doctrine about the spiritual life. The primacy of attention in this extension of doctrine is for concrete spiritual experience, its structures, dynamics and conditions. The practical extension of doctrine is thus based on experiences of self and others in regard to daily spiritual living in concrete situations.

Spirituality as Integration

The science of spirituality is complex because it has to combine the speculative and the practical: doctrine and experience. Experiences and the insights they provide have to be gathered from many sources that represent studies and reports on experience and its conditions—such sources as Scripture and literature, medicine, human sciences and spiritual masters, personal experiences of self and others, the expressions of experience in paintings, sculpture, architecture, dance and music. All such reports and expressions insofar as they touch on the life of the spirit are the object of the study of spirituality.

It is a difficult and complex assignment to gather this variety of insight and information into a consistent, well-articulated whole. St. Thomas says, therefore, that any practical science develops "modo compositivo;" that is, it emerges out of the "composition" of many other knowledges. In present day terminology we could say in the same sense that spirituality is an integrative science. It proceeds by integrating or synthesizing the insights of doctrine and experience as presented by a wide variety of sources.

Spirituality selectively gathers together what is already known spiritually, doctrinally, experientially, and scientifically about the life of the spirit. This gathering is done from new points of view that were not operative as such in the fields from which these relevant insights are taken. These new points of view—typical of spirituality itself—result from the theoretical-practical question of how to live concretely the life of the spirit. The material thus integrated, reorganized, and if necessary complemented by other theoretical and experiential insights can give direction to concrete spiritual living.

For instance, I may study gentleness as a facilitating condition for the spiritual life. I look at my own experience in this regard. I collect descriptions and insights from literature and human sciences about gentleness. I reflect on doctrine and ponder the observations of spiritual masters, writers, and scholars. Foremost in my mind, however, is the question; "Is this or that finding reported by them practically helpful for people who try to live the spiritual life?" This practical question is the criterion not only of my selection but also of the integration of my material.

Personal Growth and the Study of Spirituality

A practical discipline like spirituality is thus dependent on our insights into the meaning of human experience and praxis. We might recall here a problem discussed earlier when we spoke about the knowledge of prudence. We saw that rectitude of will is necessary to make right and prudent decisions in the particular individual circumstances of daily life. This rectitude of the will is necessary too for more general theoretical judgments concerning universal conclusions about God, man, life, and world, especially in the speculative-practical realm. Here, too, the disposition of the will is of great influence. In our case, rectitude of the will is needed in the person who studies, expands, or teaches the practical science of spirituality. Otherwise his own unclarified and uncontrolled vital and personal desires begin to color his formulations of spirituality. He begins to make wrong universal judgments about the praxis of the spiritual life.

Like prudence the practical science of spirituality is not merely an intellectual endeavor but also a personal effort. My spiritual insight can only be trustworthy when also my personal will is rightly oriented. A new insight that may affect my personal life strikes too close to home to leave it to my intellect alone. It is difficult to keep my "cool" when my life is at stake, when habits, customs, and ways of thought dear to me are threatened by my own judgment.

Let us give an example. Imagine I have suffered much oppression in my youth. Rage overwhelmed me. I could not dare to express my rage without endangering my safety. I repressed it; I buried it deeply in my unconscious. It became a hidden power unknown to me, poisoning my life of vital striving, secretly influencing the orientation of my will. Later in life, let's say I was introduced into a revolutionary movement. I don't understand why this movement grabbed me; all I know is that I felt irresistably drawn to it.

Spiritual life came to mean for me spending one's life for the betterment of the world's poor and oppressed. All other things, like prayer and sacramental life, grew from this self-gift of man to man. They support it and animate it. Deeply convinced that this way of spiritual life should be the way for all, I scorned critics who tried to point out that the praiseworthy battle for the oppressed cannot be the pivotal point of spirituality of all men. If any case can be shown in history of a person reaching spiritualization without being a revolutionary, the making of revolutions cannot be an essential condition of any spiritual life whatsoever. Evidently there are incidences of spiritualized people who were not revolutionaries, but I could not see it. I felt an irresistable inclination to justify or rationalize my stand.

This person's judgment, of course, was falsified by repressed anger that he did not recognize as such. His buried rage vitiated his right judgment when it came to studying spirituality; his will did not have the necessary rectitude; it had lost its right orientation due to a traumatic experience that had not been worked through.

This example shows that we need to purify our will and its dispositions to secure the right insights in the field of spirituality. Otherwise we come to wrong judgments about the praxis of the spiritual life.

The practical discipline of spirituality is thus in some way similar to prudence. Its effective study demands rectitude of will and the working through of one's inordinate strivings. Our vital strivings are never totally purified. Purification of the vital life is a never ending endeavor of the spiritual life. A not-worked-through element of experience may always affect the operation of the practical intellect and warp our judgment; hence, the student of spirituality, the spiritual speaker, writer, director has always to be cautious. Of course, this influence of the vital life is also operative in the speculative sciences. It may distort our speculative judgment too. Yet our vital life is more directly influential in a science like spirituality because a practical science affects more directly our lives as daily lived.

Another reason for caution is that a practical science like spirituality depends on reports of experience. Such reports are easily distorted by gross or slight exaggerations and diminutions, by emphasis on one aspect of the experience at the expense of another. All such distorted, inflated, or deflated recordings can affect the operation of the practical intellect of the reporter and the student who uses his reports.

　　The hallmark of a student of spirituality is wise caution rooted in humility. He should never be too sure of his opinions; he should maintain a healthy self-distrust and be wary of over-enthusiastic movements. Always on the lookout for possible onesidedness he humbly submits his own enthusiasms to the wisdom of the Church. He should work through his feelings and fantasies in meditative self-presence before God. Therefore, one cannot remain a trustworthy spiritual teacher or director without continuously trying to work through his vital feelings, fantasies, and strivings.

　　What has been said about this purification ties in with what happens in psychotherapy. St. Thomas could not know in as detailed a way as psychologists do today the power and extent of the hold of the unconscious on the vital strivings and their hidden impact on the will. For psychology and psychiatry as theoretical-practical sciences were not yet developed at his time. He had to go by the knowledge of speculative-practical psychology. This philosophical and theological psychology went deeper into the psychological life of man but lacked some clinical details known today about the precise working of the unconsciousness, repression, and defense mechanisms. Practical psychology later developed methods to clinically investigate and analyze the life of vital strivings; it showed how perception tends to be distorted when willing is influenced by unconscious strivings and defenses.

Spirituality and Catholic Doctrine

We need the light of doctrine for fundamental spirituality, but what about systematic theology? We benefit from systematic theology usually indirectly insofar as it has been assimilated by Catholic doctrine. Let us illustrate our point with an example.

Long ago there were two theories of grace. One maintained grace is inherent, a quality of the soul; the other said grace is only extrinsically added. The Council of Trent condemned the second view in response to Luther who held that grace does not change man inwardly. The declaration of Trent that grace inheres in the soul is doctrine now. Before this statement, it was just tentative theology. At present, it must be taken into account when we speak about grace in spirituality.

In other words, fundamental spirituality is indirectly linked with systematic theology insofar as theology is absorbed in doctrine. At times we may need to rekindle our knowledge of doctrine. One helpful way may be a return to the original theological formulation that has been taken up in doctrine.

Sometimes we may benefit directly from systematic theology. Often systematic theologians fill the gap caused in Western culture by the diminishment of spirituality as a central cultural and academic concern. Standing in for spiritual masters, their books become a mixture of systematic theology and spirituality. The student of spirituality can utilize the spiritual considerations of such systematic theologians. He should avoid, however, making a new systematic theology as such the exclusive basis of fundamental spirituality; for it would no longer be fundamental.

To give an example: Chardin spoke of the hidden power of grace. This power is transforming humanity inwardly and outwardly; after centuries of change, he says, we will experience the Omega point of earth, a humanity spiritualized and transformed by grace. Though a beautiful thought, it is not yet doctrine. We should thus not make it one of the fundamentals or essentials in which any Catholic should be initiated if he wants to develop a spiritual life.

Consultation of Systematic Theology

The student of spirituality consults systematic theological writings—if useful or necessary—in the light of the integrative method of spirituality. During this consultation he may be faced with various ways and styles of expressing the same doctrine. It is his task to discern which formulation lends itself more readily to the spiritual topic of his study or which is more compatible with the practical life and the spiritual enlightenment and inspiration this life is in need of.

For example, the scholastic theologians spoke of grace as a quasi-formal cause. This does not seem too inspirational a formulation for daily life. Neither is it too easily made clear. To use this formulation effectively, we would have to explain such philosophical ideas as what Aristotle teaches about causes and the like. Briefly, the formula is not too helpful for inspirational teaching about grace.

Other theologians speak of grace as man's presence to the Divine, as an encounter between God and man. They refer to the time before this encounter as God's courting the soul with actual grace. Then, moved by grace, the soul may say yes to God and be united with Him. This formulation seems to evoke more easily a longing for divine intimacy. The student of spirituality would probably prefer this explanation as more compatible with the purposes of inspirational spiritual teaching.

The Church needs the other explanation also for theological and philosophical dialogue. We, however, must try to choose from all formulations the ones that tie in best with the aim of spirituality, the fostering of experienced intimacy with God.

Informal and Indirect Consultation

A student of spirituality should consult theological writers informally and indirectly. This means that he should not make a theme drawn from systematic theology his formal theme as such. St. John of the Cross, for instance, brings out a few theological principles to clarify how God is present in the soul. He needs these principles, but he does not make them his main formal theme. If he were writing as a systematic theologian, he would have elaborated these principles much further theologically. In the same vein, he refers to speculative principles about knowledge. He mentions only as much as is needed for clarity on the nature of contemplative knowledge and then moves on. He brings in theological themes informally and indirectly. Spiritual masters refer to systematic theology only insofar as necessary; then they continue to develop the practical implications of such themes for the spiritual life.

People may get lost in systematic theological writings

when they try to make them the concrete guidelines for daily spiritual growth. For example, when a novice master emphasizes mainly systematic theological speculations, the novitiate may fail because the people never learn about the spiritual life in its daily practicality. Novices need nourishment for the spiritual life and not just a feeding of their intellect.

After this discussion of the interrelationship of systematic theology and spirituality, we may ask ourselves if the development of spirituality could possibly lead to a differentiation of the field of spirituality in various sub-fields. The following final section of this chapter will deal with this intriguing question.

A Speculative Question about the Future of Spirituality

How will the science of spirituality develop in the future? Admittedly, this is a speculative question. No one knows the future for sure. Only time can tell. Yet we should be concerned about possible developments of this science. Speculation about such possibilities helps us prevent aberrations from developing.

Speculation about the future of the science of spirituality may be aided by a comparison with a field allied to the study of the spiritual life, that of psychology or the study of the psychological life.

For many centuries all psychology was philosophical and theological. Philosophers and theologians gained a well-integrated insight into the psychological life, its essential structures, conditions, and dynamics. Gradually their picture of the psyche broadened. Philosophical and theological psychologists asked more and more detailed questions about psychological phenomena as they appear in reality. They began to develop methods to interrogate the psychological life empirically. They took into account the answers empirically and experientially obtained by integrating them into the philosophical and theological systems of thought they had developed. They tried also to apply this unfolding system of insights and data to daily psychological living.

This united effort was broken up about eighty years ago. The investigation in the realm of concrete appearances of the psychological life and of practical applications had mushroomed; it became difficult for one and the same person to be an expert in all dimensions of psychology. In the philosophy and theology departments, the specialist in the practical dimension of psychology concentrated increasingly on the less general, more directly practical aspects. Initially, he was wise enough to realize that the theories he developed as a result of his practical research had to root themselves in the far more basic and general insights developed by his colleagues. They, in turn, took into account the findings and theories he reported to them. They allowed these findings and theories to influence their study and formulation or reformulation of the general most fundamental structures and laws of the psychological life. For they too felt that their own field of deeper and general interests had expanded so much, demanded so much time and energy, that they were no longer able to engage themselves in all the practical research their colleagues were busy with.

On the whole, this division of labor in the one study of psychology proved to be a fortunate solution to the problem of an increasing workload. Unfortunately, human nature being what it is, tensions were bound to develop between two different types of specialists, both working within the same philosophy and theology departments, each group becoming more and more engrossed in the study of their specific aspect of this one field of study. Finally, the tension gave rise to a demand in some universities that those involved in the practical aspect of the study of the psychological life should have an academic department of their own. This demand represented the historical beginning of the recent development in the West of departments of empirical and practical psychology.

This emancipation of practical psychology was understandably accompanied by battles in which also the need for domination and prestige, status and material gain, played a role. For a long time the representatives of the dimension of practical and applied psychology and the representatives of the more general dimensions of psychology, the philosophers and theologians, avoided each other. Both groups of specialists suffered from this mutual neglect. The students of the practical aspect of the psychological life even went so far as to deny that their theories were necessarily rooted in philosophical or theological presuppositions. They denied that practical psychological thinking and researching is only a nuance of all psychological thinking and cannot be separated from man's overall philosophical and theological thinking about the psychological life.

In my book, *Existential Foundations of Psychology*, I tried to make a case for this basic unity of the study of the psychological life, to expound the weaknesses of practical psychology because of not making explicit its implicit philosophical or theological assumptions. Others took up the same cause. A few years later the American Psychological Association allowed the establishment of a division of philosophical psychology as one of its professional divisions. Such a development would have been unthinkable ten years ago. I could not have hoped that this would happen when I launched my then controversial plea for a new awareness of the philosophical rootedness of all psychological reflection.

One may gather from this story why we should be concerned about the admittedly speculative question regarding how the study of the spiritual life may develop in the future. We cannot *a priori* exclude the possibility that in the future a development similar to that of the study of the psychological life may take place. We should be on the alert to prevent a repetition in spirituality of the wrong turn the development of psychology had taken. From the beginning, we need to foster mutual respect for all aspects of the study of the spiritual life of man—doctrinal, theological, practical, and so on.

Let us frankly face, however, the possibility of a future subdivision of spirituality into the field of more general considerations of a systematic theological and philosophical nature and a sub-field of more concretized practical studies. One of the elements that gave rise to the emergence of a practice oriented sub-field of psychology was the sheer pressure of the work load; it became difficult for one and the same expert to master the total psychological approach. Is it so unthinkable that similar pressures may begin to affect those who want to master completely the total approach to the spiritual life of man?

Imagine an increasing development of the study of spirituality. How much would a student or expert in this field, or a spiritual director or teacher, have to master? All theology about spirituality? To know that well he would have to be at home in systematic theology. He should be familiar with all philosophy of the spiritual life, East and West, for the supernatural spiritual life builds on the natural spiritual life. Beyond the study of theology and philosophy, he would also have to research what the arts and sciences can offer as relevant contributions to a fuller understanding of the facilitating conditions of the spiritual life. Moreover, he would have to engage himself in direct experiential and empirical research. He would have to study and expand various self theories in order to develop one that could integrate all such scientific findings and insights while rooting itself in systematic doctrinal, theological, and philosophical presuppositions. This task of research, integration, and theory building would constantly expand because the arts and sciences are accelerating their growth.

On top of all this study, the expert in the total approach would have to be an expert in the application of all such insights and findings to practical life. He must know how spiritual direction should be given, how to engage in formation and initiation, how to be a spiritual master and teacher, how to set up programs for spiritual initiation. This whole area of applied spirituality makes him face a new array of questions about methods, attitudes, programs, skills, and information to be gained from the fast growing helping professions and sciences. The expert of all aspects of the science of spirituality would have to integrate into a unified system also all of this knowledge about the application of spirituality to life.

Is it so unthinkable that these practical aspects of the study of spirituality may in the future increase so much, demand so much time and energy that it would be rather difficult for a person to be an expert in all aspects of this study and to keep up with all developments in all areas? May not the same happen as in the development of the study of the psychological life? May not the person who is good at the mainly practical aspect of spirituality specialize primarily in that area, relying for basic insights on other scholars who specialized in the general speculative-practical aspects? Is it not possible that a sub-field of practical fundamental spirituality would develop—what Maritain would call a practical-practical science? We cannot answer this question, but we should keep in mind this possibility. For if it would ever happen, we must make sure that such a sub-field, while gaining relative independence, keeps rooting itself in doctrinal, theological, and philosophical foundations.

The subtle distinction between speculative-practical and theoretical-practical spirituality should never be understood as a separation; one flows naturally into the other. Systematic theology permeates spirituality at least implicitly, and practical spirituality does the same for systematic theology. Fundamental spirituality, even in its most practical form, is pervaded through and through by doctrine and theology insofar as it explains doctrine faithfully.

In general, it is infinitely wiser to fully admit and consciously utilize the dependency of practical psychology or spirituality on a more fundamental science than to let one's study become rooted implicitly in some foundational tenets without being critically aware of what necessarily happens.

We may add that this nuance between the practical and speculative-practical is less pronounced in more flexible, existential forms of the theological approach to the spiritual life; they shade easily and naturally over into practical spirituality. Yet even these less formal theological approaches are not exclusively practical. They don't deal continuously and painstakingly with the myriad physiological, psychological, psychopathological, and environmental details that affect the spiritual life. The wise management of these details is important. They bear on the facilitating conditions of the full spiritualization of man. Therefore, spirituality should study them carefully.

There is a history of the emergence of nuances in reflective thought and observation between speculative-practical and theoretical-practical spirituality. To comprehensively study and competently formulate and illustrate such fine nuances would be the task of the historian of theology, who is eminently equipped by background and type of attention to engage in this kind of research and speculative clarification. The practical spiritual director, researcher, and teacher is by nature and background usually less well disposed and trained for this task. Therefore, the historian of theology should be alert if and when this subdivision of the science of spirituality would begin to concretize itself as happened when the science of psychology found itself independent from—yet rooted in—philosophy and theology.

III

THE LANGUAGE OF SPIRITUALITY

Every science has a language of its own—a universe of words and meanings expressing most adequately the insights and findings typical of its own field of investigation. This language, that unfolds during the history of a discipline, is shared by its devotees; it is constantly updated and expanded. To master a science is, therefore, in great measure to master its language.

Spirituality too speaks its own tongue. The historical language of spirituality brings to life the experience and reflections of men and women who spent the greater part of their lives dwelling on the life of the spirit. To become a student of spirituality is to become fluent in that tongue. Fluency does not mean to repeat constantly and blindly traditional verbalizations; it implies that the student is at home with traditional expressions, draws light from them, resurrects their original meanings, and coins new words that do not betray the vision of the past while adding new insights and accommodating contemporary listeners.

There exists not only a common but also a private language of spirituality. Often people give words to their experiences in a language of their own. Some of them express a private experience undergone in solitude; others describe the shared experience of a group they belong to, such as a charismatic gathering. The latter could be called a semi-private experience. Private language is marked by a certain unawareness of the treasure of validated wisdom that universal spiritual language is.

Before going deeper into the nature of the common language of the spirit, we must distinguish it from the private one in more detail and ask ourselves about the relationship between these two.

The Language of Science

The language of science is universal, has undergone intersubjective validation, and shows an ordering or hierarchy of findings or experiences and their expressions.

Applied to the science of spirituality, spiritual masters such as Pseudo-Dionysius, Tauler, à Kempis, John of the Cross, Teresa of Avila, Ignatius, and Francis de Sales share a language that is somewhat similar. They are influenced by one another at least indirectly. There is among them some kind of intersubjective validation; they confirm many of each other's experiences and insights. Finally, they implicitly agree on some hierarchy of experience. They highlight experiences that are central; peripheral ones are described by them as peripheral—such as religious feelings, voices, visions, speaking in tongues.

The scholar of spirituality studies methodically the experiential expressions of the various masters, writers, and students in this field. He tries to establish a hierarchial system of universal spiritual experiences and insights, intersubjectively validated and clearly expressed in a universal language.

Private Language

In contrast, the private expression of spiritual experiences is not universal, not tested out as yet by the universal Church, its Magisterium, its recognized masters, writers, scholars, and students of spirituality. Private language may not be intersubjectively validated, that is, not yet compared critically with the experiences of spiritual masters and others in the contemporary and historical Church. Private language may not show a wise, universally acceptable ordering. The individual or group—excited by an exalted experience, no matter how peripheral in nature—may be overawed by its momentary impact. They may be unable to place it where it belongs in the hierarchy of experiences. Emotional experiences may be overvalued at the expense of the more quiet inner ones.

Conditions of the Common Language of Spirituality

The language of spirituality should be potentially universal, validated intersubjectively, traditionally, and doctrinally, either implicitly or explicitly.

When people claim spiritual experiences, it should be asked if they are the only ones reporting this awareness and its particular expression. How does it compare with similar reports of others? What does history, tradition, Church Fathers, Scripture, and spiritual masters say about this experience and the way it is verbalized? Is their language in tune with doctrine?

The language of the science of spirituality should be validated implicitly or explicitly. In certain types of scholarly studies the student may validate it explicitly. For other occasions, for example in a simple spiritual talk, the speaker may validate his language implicitly. This means he goes by his already assimilated knowledge of the language of the Church and its spiritual masters after his many years of study, reading, speaking, and experience.

The science of spirituality demands a language that is potentially universal. The universality of spiritual language shares in the universality of human experience.

Take the *Diary of a Young Girl* by Anne Frank. This diary has worldwide appeal yet its universality is different from that of a work by Kant, Hegel, or St. Thomas. The universality of Anne Frank's diary is one of human experience. It has a potential universality. This means that a significant number of people *can* experience what she went through if they put themselves in the same situation imaginatively.

To explain this potential universality further, we could look at a different kind of work, the writings of John of the Cross. He describes experiences we cannot prove by abstract arguments as we can try to prove some of the propositions of Kant or Hegel. Yet his experiences are considered to be universally true. One cannot demonstrate logically that what is experienced as the dark night of the soul is true in the way we can prove that one and one is two. His description of this experience is universally valid in that it can be had by other people if they would be in a similar situation.

Spiritual writers have intersubjectively validated the experiences rendered in St. John's lucid descriptions. They concluded that they are a universal possibility for baptized man, if God deigns to grace him in this way. We may surmise that a significant number of faithful—finding themselves in a similarly graced situation—might undergo a

dark night experience. Similar at least will be the fundamental structure of this experience. It is useful for the
student of spirituality to learn of the universal possibility
of such an experience happening under similar conditions.
It makes it easier for him to identify the experience when
he meets it in other reports or if it were to take place in
himself or others.

Limitations of Private Language

Private language is not necessarily wrong. The person
taken in by it unreservedly is as unwise as the one who
claims *a priori* it cannot be good. The only thing that can
be said in many cases is that this language, and the
experience it points to, is not yet sufficiently validated.
Therefore, caution is called for.

Wise caution neither paralyzes spontaneous expression nor fixates it prematurely as universally valid. Wise
caution puts the new expression in dialogue with the
existing and growing language of spirituality.

We must maintain in our mind a dialogue between
private expressions and those found in the great spiritual
traditions. New expressions should not be rejected *a priori*.
If valid, they may enrich the steadily unfolding language of
spirituality.

The important point is to put the expression in
dialogue. The problem is not just finding the right
expression but also finding the right place of that
expression. Where does it fit in the existing hierarchy of
spiritual expressions? Within the whole body of religious
experiences, how much weight can one wisely give to this
experience? Not all private language can become universal.

Much private language is inaccurate or poor language, even when referring to valid experiences that are potentially universal. The science of spirituality rejects such expressions as inadequate tools.

Think, for example, of a great mystic and fine writer like Meister Eckhart. In describing his experiences he seems sometimes to lean towards pantheistic expressions that might give rise to misunderstanding. Something similar might happen to private descriptions by other spiritual people. In some instances, private language may refer to spiritual experiences that are falsely assumed to be true experiences of Fundamental Catholic Spirituality. The subsequent process of validation proves them to be spurious. Usually the language expressing such experiences is not the language of the Church. Such private language cannot become universal either.

Private language may refer mainly to the latent residue of uniqueness that is at the root of any personal experience. To the degree that it symbolizes the unique only, it cannot be inserted into a potentially universal language for all. For example, some of the expressions of William Blake, an English Protestant mystic, do not have universal validity. They refer too exclusively to the totally unique in his experience. The totally unique can by definition not be communicated to others. We can only understand the unique insofar as it blends in with more universal aspects of the same experience.

Benefits of Private Language for Spirituality

In favor of a private language, we must say that the "stumbling" expressions of individuals and groups are worthwhile for the renewal, refinement, and development of the universal language of spirituality. For it is precisely the dialogue of less successful attempts to expression, progressively improving itself, that finally may lead to the right expression approaching most nearly the experience undergone.

Consider Julian of Norwich, an English mystic, able to express her spiritual experiences in English in a way more congenial to us Americans than the way chosen by some mystics in southern Europe. Her expressions are more in tune with our cultural setting yet well in line with doctrine, tradition, and the essential wisdom of the spiritual masters. In another instance of the same, T. S. Eliot expresses some of the ideas of John of the Cross in a new way. He revitalizes spiritual language, as it were. Ideally there should be a vitalizing inspirational dialogue between private and universal language.

Spirituality, as we have seen, is the theoretical-practical discipline of concretely living the experience of divine intimacy and our preparation for it. As we have seen, its main source is experience. Experience is initially a private event. We may have the same experience, at the same time, yet each of us has it personally. It is only the mutual expression in face, posture, behavior, or words that makes it public and may lead to a common experience. This latter experience can mark the beginning of the process of universalization of experience and its language. This beginning universalization can then go through the process of validation.

For example, all kinds of people come to Mass on Christmas night. The mood is set by the candles, the manger, the singing, the procession. These symbols were an expression of someone's experience far back in history.

Many people grew to like this expression and the mood it revealed; the mood was communicated from generation to generation in words and customs that survived their time and place of origin.

Liturgy, for example, could be called—from the viewpoint of spirituality—the celebration in symbols, acts, and words of validated experiences and expressions of the faithful who allowed themselves to be touched by the divine mysteries of salvation as celebrated within a community of believers.

In the beginning of Christianity, there were many small communities of faithful widespread in the Roman Empire, Asia Minor, and North Africa. They celebrated the Eucharist and each expressed their experiences in words and prayers. Our Canons go back to prayers that originated in such early Christian communities. Prayers arose from the experiences they all shared in. The community began to cherish the expressions of these experiences as given by some inspired individuals. The best prayers were repeated again and again. Some of them lived on in our traditional Canons.

The point is that even for liturgy *as* spiritual, universal language had to emerge from the private language of individuals and communities of faithful.

Diversification of the Universal Language
of the Science of Spirituality

To find the diversification of the language of spirituality, we must recall what kind of science Fundamental Catholic Spirituality is. Reflecting on this, we will discover the kinds of language to be used in spirituality.

Fundamental Catholic Spirituality is an experiential, doctrinal, theoretical-practical science of spiritual life. Spirituality is experiential; it is not, for instance, about the essence of the life of grace, about the speculative aspect, but about the experiential aspects of graced living. Spirituality is rooted in doctrine; it is doctrinal. It is also theoretical; it is a universal theory about the practice of spiritual living.

Each of these three aspects of spirituality—the experiential, the doctrinal, the theoretical—gives rise to a specific language, respectively a symbolic, a foundational, and a systematic-theoretical language. The experiential aspect of spirituality requires a symbolic language and symbolic concepts. This symbolic language can be metaphorical and relational. The doctrinal aspect of this science is due to the fact that theoretical-practical understanding of the spiritual life should be founded upon doctrine. Therefore, we speak here of foundational language—of certain concepts that help us found or root our knowledge of spirituality in the Doctrine of the Church.

In the science of spirituality, we are not only or merely becoming aware of experiences and relating them to doctrine; we also are reflecting on them; we become theoretical about them. We try to find the validity of an experience not just for one individual or small group but for all mankind. Then we work out systematically the results of our reflection, integrating them in an open, steadily unfolding and transforming system of concepts and tenets about the spiritual life, its conditions and dynamics.

For this type of organization, we need a systematic-theoretical language and concepts. An example of this would be our speaking of spiritual, personal, and vital self.

This language is not drawn from mere experience or from doctrine alone. The terms spiritual, personal, vital function as theoretical key concepts that in a systematic way help us organize a multiplicity of data and insights.

We will now speak briefly of the three types of language; then we will return to the subject of relational-symbolic language and expand on it. The latter is different from metaphorical-symbolic language and yet of great influence in the study and communication of spirituality and in the deepening of the spiritual life.

Symbolic Language

Experience in the realm of the spirit and in the realm of life is so rich it cannot be expressed adequately; we need symbols that point to the inexpressible. Thus a mystical writer may say God is darkness or God is light. No one takes this writer literally. His words are symbolically pointing to what God is.

Our Lord Himself, when He speaks as Spiritual Master says, "I am the vine, you are the branches." [John 15:5] The symbol points to the deep mystery of our unity with Christ through Baptism. The same life pulses in the vine and in the branches. This symbol of the vine and the branches has two aspects: the metaphorical-symbolic and the relational-symbolic. It shows the ineffable mystery of Christ's presence in grace; it shows also the mysterious relationship between Christ and the graced person.

The phrase "mystical marriage" is another example of symbolic language. It indicates the ongoing infused experience of at-oneness with God. This cannot be described or exhausted in functional concepts so we resort to a symbolic-metaphorical pointing to what cannot totally be expressed. This symbol symbolizes at the same time the mysterious relationship between God and the soul who received the grace of mystical union. It is, therefore, also relational-symbolic language.

Foundational Language

In reference to the doctrinal aspect of spirituality, we must speak of a foundational language; this refers to certain doctrinal expressions that we need to root spirituality in doctrine. Thus we say that the Christian spiritual life is rooted in the life of grace and totally dependent on it. The expression "life of grace" in our science is an expression of foundational language. Sanctifying grace as such is not open directly to experience. It is an ontological quality or habit, a change in the very depth of our being that cannot be experienced directly in itself. We know of its presence from doctrine.

Grace is not merely a symbolic word nor an experiential word; it is an ontological word about a change in our deepest self. There are many other foundational words; together they form a foundational language without which we would be unable to formulate a Fundamental Catholic Spirituality.

Systematic-Theoretical Language

To develop a science of spiritual experiential life, we reflect on experiences in the light of doctrine. We order the results of these reflections in a coherent way. We need for this ordering systematic and integrative concepts and language. This is what we call systematic-theoretical concepts and language.

Systematic-theoretical concepts are sometimes taken over from what may have been initially foundational and symbolic language only. For example, when we speak of the dark night of the soul, we realize these words at first meant to express symbolically a certain experience people went through on the way to union with God. Presently, because they cover so well a set of experiences, these words have become also a kind of systematic term. They are used now in any systematic approach that outlines the phases of the spiritual life.

Another example would be the terms purgative, illuminative, and unitive way—the traditional three ways of the spiritual life. These words originally were symbols expressing what happened in the soul. Gradually they received also a function in systematic-theoretical language and were used as principles for the organization of knowledge about the spiritual life. Here again we can see how sometimes words come to systematic-theoretical language from symbolic or foundational language.

A third example would be apophatic and cataphatic knowing of God. These are Greek terms from the Psuedo-Dionysius. The first refers to knowing God not by affirming perfections in the world, but knowing Him in unknowing, the way of negation. The cataphatic knowing means knowing God by affirming Him through what we know in creation. These concepts, too, help us to organize the science of spirituality in regard to a variety of ways of knowing God experientially that can be categorized under, respectively, the systematic concepts apophatic and cataphatic knowledge.

Relational-Symbolic Language

After this brief explanation of the symbolic, foundational, and theoretical language of spirituality, we shall now expand on one kind of symbolic language.

Relational-symbolic language plays a great role in spirituality. All language is relational. Take a simple word like "door." It can be understood only in relationship to a set of other words, such as inside, outside, going in, going out, opening, closing. When a child hears the word "door" for the first time, he will not know what it means. Gradually, he will hear the word "door" in different sentences, related to other words. These sentences express different functions of this word; it becomes clear for him. A child begins to understand a language by understanding the function of its words in relation to the other words he learns in the concrete everyday use of them within various sentences.

No word can be understood in and by itself. A word is itself precisely in its distinction from and its relation to many other words. In science, too, each word can be understood only in relation to all other scientific words. We gradually understand the meaning of scientific words when we see how they function in various ways in combination with one another within that science.

Take an original mystical writer like Ruysbroeck. When we read his works several times, at first strange words begin to light up with meaning. Any key word in the universe of Ruysbroeck's experience and language is related to all the other words he uses. We need, therefore, to grasp how words function in relation to other key words in his language.

A scientific word belongs to some autonomous

universe or sub-universe of words. For instance, spirituality is an autonomous universe of words different from that of physics. Think of the different meaning "dark night" has for a physicist and a spiritual master.

Interesting in this context is the reaction of some Swedish authors to Dag Hammarskjöld's diary, *Markings*. They quickly declared that Hammarskjöld must have been paranoid. They found in his diary grandiose tendencies, feelings of persecution, chronic depression. He maintained that he was at one with Christ and must suffer, perhaps be sacrificed like Christ. Not understanding the language of spirituality, they concluded he must have been clinically ill to imagine he was another Christ. Those who know the meaning of spiritual words knew what Hammarskjöld was talking about.

Symbols of Human and Divine Relationships

Some words can be understood only in terms of human or divine relationships. For example, the word "father" is freely bandied around in daily life. Yet the surface uses of this word are only a small tip of the iceberg of deeply rooted lived relationships. It is the latter that give words like father their real life meaning for the individual, a meaning that is always partly unconscious. Words speak differently to different people because of past experience. If a person, for example, never received caring attention from parents, the word mother or father would not speak to him in the same way as it would to those who received warm manifestations of parental love. For many people the word "father" is the crystalization of contra-dictory meanings dependent on how the persons experienced their fathers. Lived relationships color the word; hence there are many layers and meanings to this expression.

The faithful, too, call God their Father. Here the word father may have different meanings for different persons at various times of their life. During adolescence, when a person may be trying to free himself from authority, the word father may take on a forbidding aura. During that period, the word father as applied to God may not appeal to him because it is colored temporarily by other negative feelings.

After this general explanation of the word in its relation to life experience, it will be easier to understand what relational-symbolic means. When a word is relational-symbolic, we say that this word belongs to a specific symbolic order. A symbolic order is a specifically ordered world of meanings made up by a specific language. The terms that make up this "meaning-world" are bound to one another by many ties.

Think, for example, of words pertaining to the family as a specific world of interrelated symbolic meanings. Words such as father or mother do not mean merely this person who is father or mother. They also symbolize relationships such as those between father and son, and indirectly between brother and sister as being born from the same father. Indeed the word father symbolizes in and by itself a wealth of relationships.

Another striking fact is that these words not only signify a web of relations; they also create and foster these relationships experientially. Even before we begin to reflect on a relationship, language itself has already the power to give rise to a lived experience of it. We experience, for instance, a special relationship to our father. We were initiated into a living awareness of a particular bond between him and us by the word "daddy," spoken in a special way on numerous occasions and in various meaningful contexts. If appropriate words or other sign language, such as gestures or facial expressions were never communicated, we would never have experientially felt our particular relationship with him.

Because of this felt communication, we were also able to experience that in our culture the father should be more central in our lived relationships than, for example, our uncle who is the oldest brother of our mother. The latter is central in the experience of the children of certain matriarchal African tribes. The uncle's central position in the mother's family has been feelingly communicated to them. The role of father in our culture is pointed out to us symbolically by the word "daddy" as used in a variety of meaningful sentences. The experiential importance of a particular person, called "daddy," was brought home to us by naming him as special from the beginning.

Such is the power of the word to communicate to us symbolically a particular relationship and to make such relationships stand out in our experience for a life time. Spiritually we do the same. We name adoringly Father, Son, and Spirit because by so naming we render experientially "alive for us" special intimate relationships we have with the Divine as He reveals Himself to us.

We also begin to live experientially relationships that already exist factually. Relationships as such are not created by our words. We can say that they begin to acquire experiential meaning for us in and through the thoughtful and, in the case of spirituality, the prayerful repetition of words that symbolize these relationships.

The relationship exists whether or not we experience

it. For example, God is our Creator sustaining us independently from our naming, speaking, or saying He is so. We are always in a relationship of creature to Creator. Another example. As graced persons we are always in the relationship of being real participants in the Divine Nature itself, whether or not we know, say, or experience this relation. Again, God is our Father in a special way; we participate in the Sonship of Christ by Baptism. However, a baptized person may not deeply experience this relationship.

How do we come to the experiential awareness, for example, of our relation to the Divine Father? Certainly by hearing, reading, or speaking words that convey the lived meaning of this relationship. If we hear by the proclamation of the Church that God is our Father and if the proclaimer is really "proclaiming," that is, if his words carry and radiate an inner conviction, we may come to experiential awareness. Then the word has the power to foster in the listener the experiential acknowledgment of the presence of the already existing relationship, to bring this relationship to life experientially. We may repeat the words in growing love and adoration as they come more and more to life for us.

We can see an illustration of this power of language in the way some communities have had problems with the word "superior." For older members of certain communities with unpleasant past experiences, this word may have been loaded with unpleasant meanings. A far-away, cold authoritarian person is perhaps conjured up upon hearing this word, which may bring back a flood of painful memories. It is interesting that those who enter communities today seem to have less trouble with the word "superior," they have no past history of such partly repressed experiences.

The relationship with authoritarian parents also seems to fall into this same type of pattern and can affect a later relationship with a superior because of the negative relational meaning of "authority" for children of authoritarian parents. Since parents at present tend to be more relaxed in the matter of religious discipline, children may feel better in their relationship with their parents as representatives of religion, and so words about religious authority may carry less negative meanings.

Relational-Symbolic Quality of Myths

The relational-symbolic quality of language pertains not only to relationships between people but also to relationships between words that belong to the same group, for example, the words in myths, as myths are understood by theologians today.

A myth is a symbolic whole about a subject, such as creation. The important thing to realize is that the myth is not a symbolic whole because the words in the myth may have a metaphorical quality. It is called a symbolic whole because each term in the myth has its significance and meaning in the totality of the myth story and in its connection with the rites and social relationships that have developed around this myth. The myth story is a structure of relationships outside of which the terms lose their meaning.

For example, a number of religions have myths about the origin of the world. The myth in Genesis is inspired and true because God Himself revealed in and through this myth story that He created man and world. Each term in the myth is interwoven with and receives its meaning from the other terms. For a time, people did not realize this. Some scientists ridiculed Genesis. They took the terms out of the myth story and put them in another language universe, such as that of genetics, anthropology, geology, astronomy. The terms of Genesis lost their original meaning in these alien universes of language. Each term in Genesis is symbolically related to all other religious terms within the same story of divine creation and can only be understood within this structure of relationships.

We can apply the same principle to the functioning of words in a spiritual allegorical commentary on Scripture. For example, St. Bernard's spiritual commentary on the Song of Songs is filled with expressions that could be misunderstood when taken out of their mystical context and put into the context of philosophy, secular literature, or even daily chatter. Or take again the spiritual diary of Dag Hammarskjöld. Every word in his diary is related to other terms that make sense only in his particular world of Christian spirituality and mysticism. If his words are uncritically transposed into the language universe of clinical psychology, it is easy to see how his critics might say he was paranoid.

Relational Language and Self-Experience

Relational words initiate and foster the experience of the relations they imply. In human relationships such words also give rise to an experience of myself as different from others to whom I experience my relations. Relational symbols initiate and foster my self-awareness.

For instance, certain persons are identified with symbolic terms in a way that is experientially meaningful, words such as "mom" and "dad." The ontological relationship of father as procreator of the son is already existing whether the son likes it or not. But the word "dad"—as used in various sentences by him, myself, and others, at home and in my culture—introduces a living experience of what father means in my life. This lively use of the word father tells me simultaneously who I am in relation to him and others in my family and what I later must be if I would become a father in my own right. The word communicates to me, moreover, a lived experience of how my culture identifies me as son of a father. When a person says "you" to his father, he is at the same time saying "I." In this naming he experiences himself as different from, as standing over against, the person he calls "you." In the very saying, certain aspects of his own selfhood emerge experientially.

It is only this experiential happening that makes it initially possible for us to experience ourselves as an "I" related to a "you." Many lack this experience; they do not know their own identity experientially; they are weak and confused. To such people the word "you" was never spoken with love and respect. The experience of my "I" emerges out of this word "you," spoken to me in a respectful way.

In some European languages, one has a different word for "you" when speaking to parents and when speaking to brothers and sisters. The language differentiates the experiential variation of the relationships. The European form of "you" carries symbolically the particular respect due to a person who is somehow experienced as higher in the order of human relationships than, for instance, brother or sister would be. The different way of speaking to parents makes the relationship to them come alive in a different way than the relationship between brother and sister.

In religion, too, we formerly used the word "Thou," which symbolized the special quality of our experienced relationship to God as compared with our relationship to man. This quality is not denied in the word "you," but it is highlighted by using the particular word "Thou."

A specific relational word also fosters a lived experiential awareness of that aspect of reality. If we do not speak for a lifetime about an aspect of reality, that aspect may drop out of our experience.

A spiritual director, who would never speak in any way by word, facial expression, or gesture about the "you" of the person whom he directs, would not help him to become aware of his "I." The director must speak, but not too much. He must speak in a meaningful way in order to help the person experience the director's respect for his unique "you" in Christ and thus help him to grow in the awareness that he is called with a unique name by God in Christ as a divinized "you" and that he has to live up to this Christian identity.

In the area of spirituality, for many people relationships with the Holy Trinity may mean experientially very little. Religion for many may be just an outline of revealed truths and precepts. God did not become as yet a living "you" or "Thou" for them. God as a "Thou" has not been spoken to them in an alive language by a person to whom He really meant something personal, one who could express this meaning in a living language.

When the spiritual life is spoken of in a living language, it evokes the awareness that it is experientially meaningful to people who speak that way and, therefore, may possibly be meaningful for me. When spiritual life becomes experientially meaningful, then the secondary effects of the spiritual life, such as the living of the Beatitudes, begin to make sense also experientially.

The Experience of Living Words

Jargon is the use of empty words not rooted in experience. When experience fills our words, they are less likely to sound like jargon. We can see this in the lives of the saints. Some of them were poor speakers, yet people were spellbound by their preaching, for the saints spontaneously filled their words with their experience.

When a believer with conviction speaks to non-believers, the non-believer may see how alive, for example, is the speaker's I-Thou relationship to God as loving Father. The non-believer may not be able to personally enter into the relationship; yet he may realize that it means something to the speaker; he may wonder why and how this relation can be so alive for this person.

A believer may also speak to faithful who have had moments of religious experience at sometime in their life. Then his own faith experience, manifest in his words, can re-evoke in such faithful the lost awareness of the I-Thou relationship symbolized by these words.

Often speakers in their examples and stories try to adapt psychologically to their public; they try to be where their audience is. While this is commendable, it is not the primary point in powerful speaking. We cannot move people deeply just by clever stories and examples. We need to speak from inner conviction; if we can complement this conviction by examples and stories meaningful to the audience, so much the better. Today there is much concentration on the secondary points of psychological adaptation. What we need first or simultaneously is a deepening of lived spiritual convictions.

We can see this kind of conviction exemplified in the Curé of Ars. He was a rather ignorant, outmoded fellow, who did not have a rich flow of original language or a pleasant speaking voice. Still he attracted crowds of people, for he spoke with great conviction out of his I-God experience. People hunger for such vibrant testimony that can give rise to their own living relationship with God. For the same reason, it would be pernicious for spirituality if technical words would take the place of all spiritual-experiential words. A functionalizing of all words of spiritual language would affect spiritual life itself, for functional terminology, though important intellectually, is different from spirituality terminology.

Look at the rich symbolic language of the liturgy. It fosters the I-Thou relationship between the person and God experientially. Scholarly functional language, on the other hand, fosters intellectual understanding and analysis which, of course, is also necessary for other purposes at other times and other places.

Spiritual language in Scripture, liturgy, and spiritual writings helps us to keep alive our relationship with Father, Son, Spirit, the Blessed Mother, and the saints. As noted earlier, we cannot neglect a language for a long time without the relationships the language expresses dropping out of our lived experience. Then some people may feel tempted to leave the Church, religious life, or the priesthood because of the absence of these lived relationships.

Summary

Spirituality has its own language. That language diversifies itself in tune with the experiential-practical, doctrinal, and theoretical nature of the science of spirituality. These three aspects of spirituality give rise to respectively symbolic, foundational, and theoretical language. Symbolic language can be metaphorical and relational-symbolic. We have paid special attention to relational-symbolic language, which plays an important role in spirituality.

We concluded by saying that in relational-symbolic language one not only experientially discovers and affirms others in their relation to him, as, for example, in saying father or son, but he also implicitly affirms his own personal identity—his I as I.

This affirmation of personal identity by symbolic words plays a role especially in Christian spirituality. Christians are graced with special revelations about their identity in relation to the Eternal Father, the Divine Word, the Holy Spirit. Liturgical language reminds us of how we should relate experientially to God as a Person in an I-Thou relationship and how we must find in this relationship our personal Christian, revealed, eternal identity. We call this identity Christian because it is an identity in, with, and through Christ as Son to the Eternal Father. We are unique sons in the Son. We call this identity revealed because we could never know it if we were not proclaimed in Revelation as adopted sons of God, participants in the Divine Nature. We call this identity eternal insofar as we are called to live in eternity in this relationship to Father, Son and Spirit, and also insofar as from eternity we were meant to be unique participants in their eternal love.

We have also suggested in what ways spirituality keeps such living relationships with the Divine alive by benefitting with God's grace from the power of language. If we would never pray, go to Church, do spiritual reading, meditate, our lived relation to God and Christ would drop out of our experience.

Hence we may better understand the power of repeated words, for example, in the Jesus Prayer among the Russian Orthodox. Medieval authors too speak glowingly of the power of the name of Jesus. They see a special power of grace connected with that name. That special power is linked by these authors intuitively with the human repetition of the name of Jesus. They intuited the importance of keeping His name in mind and repeating it, for this repetition deepens their experiential relationship with Him.

We rely especially on the power of symbolic inner language when we approach Scripture not merely exegetically but spiritually. The spiritual understanding of Scripture is the main foundation of Christian spirituality. This chapter on the language of spirituality has prepared us well for the next one on Scripture and spirituality.

IV

SCRIPTURE AND SPIRITUALITY

Holy Scripture is a written record of God's Revelation. In and by itself it is not yet doctrinal, spiritual, apostolical-social, or ideological. Scripture can become any of these in and through our specialized attention. What fruitfulness the reading of Scripture will yield depends on what kind of attention the reader gives to it. Many approaches to Scripture are possible, not because the message is manifold in and by itself but because we have many ways of paying attention, each of which yields a different kind of meaning.

For example, as a moral theologian I become attentive to what Scripture says about Christian morality. The spiritual approach, on the other hand, helps me discover guidelines for spiritual living. In the case of doctrinal attention authorities of the Church, as enlightened by the Holy Spirit, read Scripture in such a way that it reveals truths that can be taught as doctrine for all the faithful. The faithful participate in that doctrinal attention when they look for the doctrinal meaning of the text.

Scripture can also be read to find support for some ideological outlook. A reader may try to see how the Gospel speaks, for instance, to contemporary philosophy or to present day social issues. Ideological reading can be useful at the right time. A person could harm his spiritual life, however, by concentrating prematurely or exclusively on philosophical and social meanings of the Gospel. He may then always read Scripture in service of some ideology and miss out on what Scripture may mean for his own spiritual life. This danger explains why spiritual masters like Pachomius, Basil, and Benedict warn against ideological reading. They insist that *lectio divina* should be in service of spiritual living. Many of their monks had been exposed to Greek philosophies. Some of them read Scripture mainly in light of the ideologies they knew instead of reading it also under the inspiration of the Holy Spirit in light of the needs of their own spiritual life.

Spiritual Reading of Scripture

Spiritual reading of Scripture seems somewhat different from a doctrinal or exegetical reading. One may do a doctrinal or exegetical analysis of a Scripture text without applying it to his personal spiritual life. This fact seems to point to some distinction between spiritual and doctrinal or exegetical reading. Distinction does not mean separation. A doctrinal or exegetical reading often shades over into a spiritual one. Ideally, a Scripture text should have been clarified doctrinally and exegetically before we ask ourselves what it might possibly mean for our personal spiritual life.

A reader can approach Scripture, having within the foreground of his mind either a spiritual or a doctrinal-exegetical purpose. In the latter case, he is explicitly and primarily interested in a doctrinal or exegetical analysis of the text; this dominant intent does not exclude openness to the possible practical meanings of the text for his personal spiritual life here and now. At this moment, however, such meanings are not his central concern. His first question is not, "Can I find in this text inspiration and practical application for my personal spiritual life?" but, "How can I most accurately analyze this text doctrinally and exegetically?" If he is a spiritual person, a spontaneous transition to a spiritual understanding of the same text will probably happen naturally.

In a mainly spiritual reading, the doctrinal and exegetical understanding of the text is presupposed and implied; it indirectly influences and enriches the spiritual reading. The central concern of the reader at this moment is not to gain or review this systematic and analytical knowledge. His question is, "Can this already doctrinally and exegetically understood text enlighten my personal spiritual presence to God at this juncture of my life?"

A distinction can therefore be made between a mainly spiritual and a mainly doctrinal or exegetical reading of Scripture. These readings should not be separated from one another; rather they should flow over into and sustain one another. What then distinguishes a mainly spiritual reading from a doctrinal or exegetical one?

The distinction between the two seems attributable to a subtle shifting of attention. The object of personal spiritual attention is the possible implications of a text for one's personal spiritual life. One asks, "Can this doctrinally and exegetically understood text be personalized by me in an inspirational-practical manner so that it stimulates and guides my personal and spiritual growth here and now at this moment of my life?"

Spirituality, as we have seen, is about the praxis of the spiritual life. This praxis is first of all an inner one, hence the name interior life. The growth of spiritual life is best fostered by the practice of graced spiritual acts such as adoration, repentance, faith, hope, love, humility, recollection, gentleness, simplicity—all virtues that foster intimacy with the Divine. Such acts must be inspired by Our Lord Himself. One way in which the Lord inspires us is in and through His word in Scripture.

The spiritual reader of Scripture focuses his attention on the already doctrinally and exegetically understood text in a manner that facilitates the possible emergence of inspirational-practical meanings for his personal life. Spiritual reading is an inspirational-practical approach to Scripture.

As we have said already, spiritual and doctrinal-exegetical attention do not exclude each other; they flow over into and sustain one another. Yet there is a subtle difference between these two ways. This difference is the cause of the development in Christian tradition of a special spiritual exercise called spiritual reading as distinguished from a mainly doctrinal or exegetical reading. When the study of the doctrinal or exegetical meaning is a central, explicit concern, it is difficult to come to the fullness of inspirational-practical understanding.

In the in-between moments of strict systematic analysis of the text, one can of course shift to moments of application of this text to practical spiritual life. The point is that at this moment of the shift one is momentarily no longer absorbed in the strictly systematic approach. Those already well versed and deeply immersed in doctrinal and exegetical reading are able to intersperse moments of learned attention with countless moments of prayerful practical attention to the possible meanings of the text for their own spiritual life. Such persons may not have to set aside a special time for spiritual reading. Not too many people, however, seem to be accomplished in this shifting of attention. They have difficulty in combining both kinds of attention and, therefore, need different times for a predominantly doctrinal-exegetical or spiritual reading.

Most people need a sufficient span of time to shift from a dominant systematic-analytical attention to a dominant inspirational-practical attention. This need for time seems to demonstrate again that the two types of attention, while related to one another, are not absolutely identical. If we ask people for experiment's sake to maintain simultaneously a systematic-analytical attention and an inspirational-practical one, the results of both ways are usually unsatisfactory, superficial, and confusing. Soon the persons experience mounting frustration and tension. They try to solve this tension either by leaving the task or allowing one type of attention to become dominant while the other type recedes in the background. It seems advisable therefore for most people to set apart a time which they devote regularly to a reading of Scripture that is mainly concerned with the inspirational-practical application of the text to their personal spiritual life. We should realize, of course, that not every inspirational-practical approach is in service of their spiritual life; it may serve other aspects of inspired Christian living.

The Inspirational-Practical Approach

The inspirational-practical approach may assume different forms. Scripture can enlighten me in regard to an apostolic enterprise I happen to be engaged in. It can inspire me to care for the poor. It may help me to develop an inspiring catechesis on how to live the Christian life.

The inspirational-practical approach may also make

me aware of the spiritual and mystical treasures of the text, thereby fostering in me the praxis of the life of divine intimacy over and beyond the general Christian life. This last inspirational-practical meaning of Scripture is kept alive in the Church by spiritual teachers and directors. The approach of the inspired teacher and director can be seen as one mode of the inspirational-practical approach. His calling is to let emerge for the faithful the meaningfulness of Scripture texts for their personal spiritual life. He reads Scripture in service of the praxis of spirituality, for the promotion of the ascetical-mystical life.

An example can be found in the spiritual writings of St. John of the Cross. In Book II, Chapter 6, Paragraph 5 of *The Ascent of Mount Carmel*, he writes as follows:

"That parable our Redeemer told in the eleventh chapter of St. Luke is noteworthy here. [Luke 11:5] He related that a man went to a friend at midnight to ask for three loaves [symbolizing these three virtues]. And He asserted that the man asked for them at midnight to indicate that the soul must acquire these three virtues by a darkness in its faculties regarding all things, and must perfect itself in these virtues by means of this night.

"In the sixth chapter of Isaias we read that the prophet saw one of the seraphim on each side of God, and that they each had six wings: with two wings they covered their feet, symbolizing the blinding and quenching of the affections of the will because of God; with two they covered their faces, symbolizing the darkness of the intellect in God's presence; and with the two remaining wings they flew, indicating both the flight of hope toward things that are not possessed and the elevation above all earthly or heavenly possessions that are not God." [Is. 6:2]

St. John wants to inspire people on their way to union with God. He is concerned that they be aware of the support of the three theological virtues, faith, hope, and charity, on their journey through the dark night of the soul. In light of this practical concern, he reads about the three loaves as symbolizing these three virtues. "Midnight" in this Gospel story means for the spiritual master the darkness that the soul suffers in its faculties if it is graced by God with this special emptiness and spiritual deprivation. He explains to his readers that such darkness is meant to help them acquire faith, hope, and charity.

When he reads Chapter Six of Isaias, he explains that the covering of the faces of the angels by their wings symbolizes the darkness of the intellect when faced with God. This passage is filled with other symbolic explanations. They all have in common that we are not obliged to believe them as if they were fundamental Church Doctrine. They share also the fact that they are not exegetical clarifications of the Scripture texts. They all are inspirational-practical explanations of these texts meant to enlighten and inspire the reader in regard to the praxis of faith, hope, and charity in the midst of the darkness of the intellect.

Spiritual animators and commentators like St. John have played a foundational role in the Church from the beginning of its history. They may be numbered among those called prophets in early Christianity. As we read in Ephesians 2:20, "You are part of a building that has the apostles and prophets for its foundations, and Christ Jesus Himself for its main cornerstone." Prophet means a person who is called to speak in an inspired way in the place of God. Insofar as spiritual masters express in an inspired way the mystical meanings of the word of God in Scripture, they could be called prophetic.

Prophetic speaking in the place of God can take many forms. For example, a person may be called to berate the Church in God's name about abuses. Most of these ways of speaking for God are not represented in an official function. The spiritual teacher of God's word, however, has a prophetic function that is often officially acknowledged. He may be appointed as spiritual director of a seminary or lay movement in a diocese by a bishop or in a religious community by religious superiors. Sometimes he is made a director of initiation, for example, in a novitiate. In the latter case, his duties, privileges, and responsibilities are clearly delineated in Canon Law. In regard to Scripture, his prophetic calling is to keep alive or to resurrect the inspirational-practical meaning of Scripture for one's personal spiritual life as lived alone or with like-minded people.

Scripture and Catechetics

There is a great need for teaching the inspirational-practical message of Scripture texts. Nevertheless, catechetical teachers should not give up their primary task, that is, they should not become exclusively inspiring witnesses for the possible inspirational-practical meanings of selected Scripture texts. They may do a certain amount of this inspirational work but not exclusively. Otherwise who would fulfill the eminent function of the catechetical teacher in the Church? Who would teach the faithful clearly and distinctly—yet in an inspiring and living way—what the doctrinal and exegetical meaning of Scripture is? Spiritual directors and animators—inspirers of the mystical meaning of the Word—refer informally to the doctrinal and exegetical meaning of the same Word. This reference would be useless if this doctrinal and exegetical meaning would not have been explained first formally, clearly, and distinctly by dedicated and capable catechists. How could the spiritual teacher foster safely the ascetical-mystical life if the moral Christian life of love and devotion were not taught and instilled in people by clergy and catechists to whom they were exposed in church, elementary school, high school, college, or C.C.D. classes?

I remember the girls of an elementary school in the parish of a certain European country. They were taught by well meaning catechists who had substituted for clear and inspired communication of doctrine experiential inspiration only. The girls had indeed developed a touching love for Christ, especially for Christ in the poor and in people in underdeveloped countries. They did not know, however, about the essence, meaning, and number of the sacraments, about the Ten Commandments, the commandments of the Church, the Holy Trinity. An eighteen year old boy who had finished Catholic high school in the same parish was well trained in transcendental meditation, in charismatic prayer, in ecumenical appreciation of all Christian churches. He was filled with Christian love for the socially underprivileged, but he had never studied the Catholic Creed, was not clearly aware of the doctrinal differences between Catholic and other Christians, and did not know about the acts of faith, hope, and charity nor about the Sunday obligation to attend Mass. He had never been to confession and did not know precisely what it was. He was dumbfounded when he heard in a conversation that adultery and abortion were not acceptable in the

Catholic Church. "Why?", he asked incredulously. "What has that to do with religion?"

A religious community could be faced today with candidates who are the innocent victims of merely inspirational catechists who have neglected their primary doctrinal duty. It should be clear that such candidates cannot be admitted to the novitiate before their lack of clear catechetical knowledge has been made up for by remedial courses in the pre-entrance program and in postulancy—courses about fundamental Catholic Doctrine that are truly catechetical and not mainly spiritual. Initiates cannot truly master Fundamental Catholic Spirituality without a firm, clear, and distinct formal grounding in basic Catholic Doctrine, to which the spiritual teacher always implicitly or explicitly refers and which he presupposes in them.

Interrelation of Spiritual and Doctrinal Reading of Scripture

We read Scripture spiritually to inspire and enlighten our intimacy with the Divine in Christ. While reading, we take implicitly into account the doctrinal and if possible exegetical meanings of the text. In that case, we do not have two mutually exclusive acts of understanding. The spiritual and doctrinal understanding influence one another naturally and spontaneously; they interpenetrate.

Take a text such as "We are to love, then, because he loved us first." [John 4:19] One reading of this text may yield a doctrinal understanding. By means of this approach, the reader knows what the text tells him. Even before he could deserve in any way His gracious love,

God's love granted him the undeserved life of grace. In His initiating love, He loved us first. Most people with some knowledge of catechism understand this meaning of the text, though it may not be understandable to a non-Catholic or a poorly educated one.

A reading of the same text may also yield an inspirational-practical insight. The reader dwells on the text for inspiration and practical guidance of his personal spiritual life. He may be struck by the message that he is submerged in the all encompassing love of the Divine, a love that holds him from eternity. He may sense this love of God for him so deeply that many images and feelings emerge. For example, he may feel like a little fish in the infinite ocean of love that was there before him and will exist after him. He feels carried by this overflow of divine love without any effort or merit on his part. The inner practice of loving surrender is rekindled and deepened.

This is one of many personally inspirational meanings that could arise from our spiritual reading. This personal spiritual understanding does not contradict the doctrinal one; rather it makes an inspiring practical application to one's personal spiritual life of a text understood already doctrinally and possibly exegetically.

Our doctrinal understanding is not always explicit. Our spiritual perception of the text may already be doctrinally or exegetically conditioned to such an extent that we thrive on its doctrinal or exegetical meaning implicitly and spontaneously. Our spontaneous doctrinal or exegetical understanding permeates naturally our spiritual understanding; there is a unity between them. Sometimes, however, these kinds of understanding need to be separated. Doctrinal or exegetical attention has to become explicit. We may even need a time, so to speak, of doctrinal or exegetical incubation before a new explicit doctrinal or exegetical understanding becomes second nature.

Occasions for Making Doctrinal Understanding Explicit

As students of spirituality, when reflecting on a specific topic in our field, we may focus on Scripture texts that appear to be relevant to this topic. We may find it helpful to make our implicit doctrinal light more explicit, to enhance its clarity, to update it. Therefore, we may study explicitly the doctrinal and possibly exegetical explanation of the text concerned.

This explicit study of the doctrinal and possibly exegetical meanings of the text raises the possibility of a temporary separation between doctrinal-exegetical and spiritual understanding. For example, we may make our implicit doctrinal-exegetical understanding explicit and bring the doctrinal meaning to the fore. We may have to do so, for doctrine is not stagnant; over the centuries it expands and is reformulated. Because of this expansion, we may need to update our understanding of doctrine and possibly of exegesis. We conclude, therefore, that our implicit understanding of the doctrinal-exegetical meaning must be made explicit sometimes.

At moments of updating our implicit doctrinal light, we may have an initial experience of a split between doctrinal-exegetical and inspirational-practical understanding. This initial experience of a split is hopefully followed by a period of doctrinal incubation. An integration must take place between the explicitly clarified and expanded knowledge of Catholic Doctrine in relation to the text and our spiritual dwelling on this text. When, after a period of doctrinal incubation, we will have assimilated the clarified and updated doctrinal and exegetical view of the text, this new doctrinal and perhaps exegetical knowledge will have become second nature. From now on, this assimilated view will automatically condition our subsequent spiritual readings of the text and its practical application to our personal spiritual situation.

In writing his sermons on the Song of Songs, St. Bernard's mind was already conditioned by doctrinal and traditional understanding. He would write nothing at variance with doctrine. Also his rich knowledge of traditional monastic commentaries entered into his spiritual understanding, implicitly and spontaneously. He looked at the Canticle from the concern of a daily seeking of intimacy with God. The words of the text then lit up for him in a new way relevant to his own spiritual life and that of the monks who shared his personal situation.

If St. Bernard had not been sure of doctrine, he might have first studied what the Church teaches. To master the doctrinal and exegetical meaning could then have been temporarily the main concern of St. Bernard. However, while focusing on this learned analysis of the text, he would probably not have burst out at exactly the same moment with poetic lively metaphors as he did while spiritually dwelling on the Song of Songs. Of course, in between the moments of strict systematic analysis, he could have shifted to the poetic, lyrical, and practical life approach. The point is again that the two moments of attention, spiritual and doctrinal, are not absolutely identical in spite of their deeper unity in an overall presence to God's words. They are two dimensions of one and the same attention that nourish and enrich one another but are sufficiently distinct to make it difficult if not impossible for both to be equally dominant at the same time.

Focusing on the doctrinal dimension of the approach to Scripture is important. In the recent past it may have been overstressed, sometimes at the expense of the personal-practical dimension of the Christian approach to Scripture. An unfortunate result of this onesidedness may be that people did not develop the attitudes necessary for a spiritual dwelling on Scripture. This lack may have dulled their lives somewhat. If people are only and always engaged in the doctrinal dimension of presence, and repress their need for the inspirational-practical dimension, they may be missing out on inspiration and guidance for their own daily spiritual life. They should not, let us stress again, neglect doctrinal understanding. We cannot live wisely either with only a personal spiritual understanding. We need both.

After the process of assimilation of new or unknown doctrine, our initially explicit attention to the doctrinal meaning of the Scripture text will recede in the background, will become implicit again. In the foreground of the attention of the student of spirituality will be the inspirational-practical life meanings of this doctrinally understood and accepted text.

We have spoken about the influence of the doctrinal on the spiritual understanding of Scripture. This applies also in reverse, namely, our spiritual understanding can influence the emphasis in our doctrinal understanding. In this latter sense our explicit approach to the text is spiritual. Only then do we make explicit the implicit doctrinal understanding of the text under consideration.

Consider, for instance, the experience of studying a

certain topic, such as contemplative prayer. We try to find appropriate texts on contemplative prayer. However, while looking at such texts, we may already experience a need for better doctrinal understanding. First of all, the texts that have been chosen and that we study doctrinally are already selected under the influence of our practical interest. We will choose a text about contemplation and then possibly look for a more doctrinal understanding of this text because our spiritual understanding has made us aware of the necessity or desirability of deepening our doctrinal understanding.

We may be faced with different doctrinal formulations. Again we will select the formulation most revelant to our spiritual understanding. For example, we may prefer a text of St. Augustine—assimilated in Church Doctrine—to the more analytical approach of St. Thomas and the other Scholastics. We conclude that our personal practical understanding influences the emphasis in our doctrinal understanding.

Review of the Preceding

We have seen that while engaged in a personal practical approach to Scripture we sometimes feel the necessity to make our doctrinal understanding of Scripture explicit. We do so in order to clarify or update our implicit doctrinal understanding. While explicitly clarifying and updating our doctrinal understanding, we may be faced with a variety of doctrinal explanations and with a variety of formulations of each one of these doctrinal explanations. While we are engaged in an explicitly doctrinal understanding, we keep in mind our central question as students of spirituality, "What meanings may Scripture yield to enlighten and inspire the praxis of the spiritual life?" This question keeps orienting our selection of doctrinal or systematic-theological formulations.

This implicit question is always operative in the student of spirituality; it was already influential in our selection of a specific passage of Scripture. We selected the text because we felt consciously or preconsciously that it might be revelant to the proximate direction of our spiritual lives. This same question is operative when we look at various doctrinal explanations and formulations of this implicit question. We spontaneously selected that explanation and formulation that seemed most helpful to our primary and central interest as students of spirituality: concrete spiritual living. As soon as we have made our selection, the period of incubation begins.

Characteristics of the Period of Incubation

The incubation period has the following characteristics. First we experience a decrease in attention for the selected doctrinal meaning as such. This selected doctrinal meaning becomes gradually more implicit while we slowly assimilate it in our mind. We slowly return to a more explicit attention for the many possible inspirational-practical meanings of the text. We become aware again of the possible applications and elaborations of the text in service of concrete daily living.

For example, we select out of the Gospel text for Sunday the passage that says it is easier for a camel to pass through the eye of a needle than it is for a rich man to enter the Kingdom. We ask how this text speaks to us in an

inspirational-practical way. Could the Kingdom of God
refer also to the kingdom of grace and its flowering in
contemplation? Could the riches that interfere be understood also as a clinging to our own ideas and images which
makes it impossible to enter the kingdom of contemplative
presence?

    If we are doubtful about the meaning of Kingdom,
we can look it up in exegetical commentaries. We will find
that there are different meanings of this term, one of
which may tie in with our personal practical reflections.
Then, on basis of this exegetical understanding, we give a
possible inspirational-practical meaning of the text.

    The choice of this text, out of all the texts of the
Gospel of that Sunday, was already in service of spiritual
practical understanding, as was our selective look at some
exegetical explanations. We could restrict ourselves to an
exegetical explanation of the same text and simply recite
and develop various possible exegetical meanings of the
word kingdom. Then the listeners may receive much
important knowledge but less immediate practical enlightenment or inspiration for their spiritual life.

    The priority of dignity and certitude always belongs
to the doctrinal explanation of the text. We could
therefore consider the spiritual understanding of the text
as a particular application of its doctrinal meanings. Recall
the text "...because He loved us first." [1 John 4:19]
This has a doctrinal meaning which tells us of the absolute
initiative of God's grace. We know that meaning already
and perceive it implicitly in the reading. Then the text is
further developed as to what it means for our daily life,
that is, we give a particular application of the doctrinal
understanding to our daily spiritual living. This practical
application of the text to life is not the same as further

development in the doctrinal direction. The particular development of the doctrinally understood Scripture text is evoked, guided, and structured by our attention to the questions, problems, and dynamics of concrete spiritual living.

To illustrate this use of the text let us again quote St. John of the Cross, Book I, Chapter 2 of *The Ascent of Mount Carmel*:

"The appetites weaken a person's virtue, because they are like shoots burgeoning about a tree, sapping its strength, and causing it fruitlessness. The Lord says of such people: *Vae praegnantibus et nutrientibus in illis diebus*! (Woe to them who will be with child in those days, and to them who will be nursing!). [Mt. 24:10] Being with child and nursing refer to the appetites which, if not cut off, gradually grow. Their growth will be costly, like the growth of sprouts around the tree, for they debilitate the soul's strength. Our Lord consequently advises us: *Let your loins be girt.* [Lk. 12:35] The loins here indicate the appetites. The desires are indeed like leeches, always sucking blood from one's veins. This is what the Wise Man calls them: *The daughters* (the appetites) *are leeches always calling: give! give! give!"* [Prv. 30:15]

In this case the question that guides the spiritual reading of St. John is the practical problem of dealing with one's desires and appetites in order to become more ready for union with the Lord. He reads Scripture to find motivation and inspiration for people to overcome these appetites. The Scripture text he uses yields a meaning that goes beyond the doctrinal and exegetical one. St. John makes sure that the meaning he finds is not at odds with Church Doctrine but beyond that his concern is to inspire and guide the soul in its detachment from desires that interfere with the growth of its spiritual life. He probably would not have found such explanations if these practical questions about the spiritual life would not have been with him for a long time. Such practical questions are the source of a spiritual reading oriented toward the praxis of spiritual living.

Out of our remembrance of daily living, questions and issues emerge. They may stimulate us to apply Scripture texts as explained by doctrine or exegesis to our personal spiritual life situation here and now. In the light of these questions, we may read masters like John of the Cross to find how they have applied Scripture in response to similar questions.

Practical applications of a doctrinally and exegetically understood text are thus structured by implicit or explicit questions of daily spiritual living. The doctrinal meaning can also be developed itself, not primarily from the viewpoint of daily spiritual living, but rather from the viewpoint of doctrine in dialogue with other doctrines.

The student of spirituality, *as* a student of spirituality, should consult systematic theological and exegetical explanations of Holy Scripture occasionally, informally, and indirectly. This means that *as* a student of spirituality he should not make the theme of systematic theological or exegetical explanations of Holy Scripture his formal theme as such.

Doctrinal Approach as Defining Approach

The necessary doctrinal approach to the meaning of Scripture is primarily a defining approach. "To define" comes from the Old French *definer* and from the Latin *definire.* It means to limit, to determine, to explain, to terminate. In the Latin *definire* we find two words: *de,* which means totally, complete; and *finire,* which means to bound, to limit, to terminate. *Fines* in Latin means borders. In English we have the word finish or end.

We can, therefore, derive the following meanings of defining: to state or set forth the meaning or significance, as of a word or phrase; to explain the nature or essential qualities of; to determine or fix the boundaries or extent of; to make clear the outline or form; to fix or lay down definitely; to be a distinguishing feature of; to characterize.

This description of defining helps us to see more clearly what the doctrinal explanation does. The doctrinal approach to Scripture, as we saw earlier, aims at an exact locating of its fundamental meaning, a fixing of the boundaries of what safely can be believed, a determining of the extent of possible meanings, a distinct outlining of the fundamental truth to which the Scripture text is pointing. The Magisterium defines or circumscribes the limits within which what is revealed in Scripture can be safely and surely experienced, lived, elaborated, and applied. If we search for faith experience outside these boundaries, we are out of bounds; we are extra-*fines,* outside the faith as defined by the Church.

The student of Fundamental Catholic Spirituality respects deeply and is grateful for this delineation. He respects this outlining of the boundaries of the faith experience by the Magisterium. He realizes that the Scripture text contains—within these limits set by Church authority—an inexhaustible reservoir of potential inspirational-practical meanings—inexhaustible from the viewpoint of divine mystery and from the viewpoint of the application of these meanings to countless believers in countless life situations.

Focus of the Inspirational-Practical Approach to Scripture

The focus of spirituality is not on doctrinal delineation but on practical penetration, that is, on a personal penetration of the already doctrinally and exegetically understood text which yields applications to and inspiration for our personal lived spiritual life. In the light of faith and the gifts of the Holy Spirit, the spiritual reader tries to penetrate practically an already doctrinally and exegetically delineated text fully accepted by him as such. The student of spirituality goes deeper and deeper into this delineated Scripture text in the light of the Holy Spirit at work in him and in the light of his life situation as lived in faith.

What we have said of these two approaches can be illustrated in a comparison with drilling for an oil well. One of the most important aspects of drilling is the exact locating by geologists of the places where oil may be found. This locating is done before work on the well begins. Then the spiral drilling starts, going deeper and deeper into the earth, until the hidden treasure of oil gushes forth.

Doctrinal definition gives the exact location in the sense that this text can basically have only this fundamental meaning. This established significance of the text can then be applied in many practical and inspirational ways to the personal life of the spiritual reader. The spiritual reader dwells on the text, drills and spirals, so to speak, until the treasure of applied meaning springs up.

The Tension of Spiritual Presence to Holy Scripture

The spiritual reader of Scripture may find in himself a polarity between what he has already discovered and his longing for the not-yet discovered. He reaches out for the mystery the already discovered is pointing to. He feels the tension of a reaching beyond the pointing expression to the not-yet expressed and the Eternal Inexpressible. This tension gives to the personally lived expression of Scripture the qualities that distinguish it from the doctrinal definition. This expression is not definite or defining. It does not set boundaries. Spirituality communicates that its practical-inspirational expressions—as distinguished from its theoretical expressions—are provisional, inadequate, partial in relation to the reader, pointing to a boundless meaning which cannot be defined in an exact way.

Flexible Spiritual Reading

There are many ways of harvesting the spiritual meaning of a text. We feel most inspired when we bring the whole of our lives to it. It is the marriage between text and life that keeps Scripture alive for us. We bring to it what we are and, because we are also graced by Baptism, the Holy Spirit may be influencing our prayerful presence. To be able to bring the whole of life to the text implies that the reader can flexibly move between doctrinal-exegetical and spiritual reading. The essence of paralyzed Scripture reading is the freezing of this act into merely informational and doctrinal patterns with no application to life whatsoever.

We need to transcend a merely intellectual and informational attitude. This maxim sounds simple enough, but some people never manage to escape a merely doctrinal or exegetical orientation; they feel unable to read, reflect, and speak in a way that is spiritually nourishing. Yet the potential for creative spiritual presence to a Scripture text is universal. We may not all have the same potential, but each of us has some.

The problem is not the absence of potential but the masking of one's potential for creative spiritual reading because of anxiety or because of an upbringing in a functional society which did not foster an attitude of creative listening. This anxiety or ignorance makes the person cling to only a doctrinal or exegetical approach. He feels he cannot go wrong as long as he only quotes, repeats, or slightly paraphrases the explanations of authorities. It is advisable to do so primarily, but not exclusively.

The lack of creative flexibility in Scripture reading is never due to the doctrinal or exegetical approach as such, but to the anxiety that drives people to stick to that approach exclusively. At present, there may be an over-reaction against the doctrinal approach. Some consider it the cause of inflexibility and uninspired preaching. It is not the doctrinal approach which is at fault, however, but the attitude with which insecure people engage in it, never daring to move beyond it. They are overanxious; they feel they must be absolutely sure they are correct; they cannot risk the slightest mistake. Terrified by the possibility of risks, they stick to a doctrinal or exegetical approach rigidly in all circumstances. They cling to it desperately, never gaining spiritual freedom; they cannot become inspiring spiritual teachers and directors.

A flexible wise person can be both inspirational and

deeply careful about being correct. We have to realize that the measure of our spiritual reading ability is bound to our flexibility and freedom. This freedom includes the freedom to grow through spiritual experience and life experience; the freedom, within the limits of doctrine, to change spiritual views and expressions with changed or changing life situations; the freedom to let oneself be influenced by doctrinal statements.

Reflecting on these marks of the inner freedom of the spiritual reader, we may wonder about the freedom to let oneself be influenced by doctrinal statements. Because of traumatic experiences with representatives of authority, some people have lost the inner freedom to listen to authority. They react in a stereotyped unfree way, driven by unconscious fear, resentment, and hostility. Such imprisoned persons feel that doctrinal statements take away their freedom. If we are truly free inwardly, we can listen in a relaxed way when the Church speaks forth its fundamental truths with divine authority.

When we read in a flexible relaxed way, we are able to cultivate a spirit of prayerful receptivity. When our minds are receptive and open, we may receive insights and experience that come from the Spirit as gift. If we are too rigid, arrogant, and clever, too walled in by our intellectual acquisitions, we may close out the Holy Spirit.

Ways of Receiving the Word

Direct inspiration by the Holy Spirit, like a sudden flash, is exceptional and we must be cautious of those who claim it too easily. The Word may grow in us and be made known to us in Spirit-guided reflection on the Scripture text or any other holy text. This is the normal way of receiving the Word. The term "grow" is important here. Growth is a slow process, taking place over months and years. We are speaking here of growth through reading regularly in a recollected way. Gradually the Holy Spirit may make Himself felt and speak in the text.

The Word of the Holy Spirit may ripen in us as the fruit of a special keenness of hearing. Through the life of spiritual presence to God, we may develop a keenness of hearing so that when we open Scripture the words may light up with inspirational-practical meaning for us. We could compare this keenness of hearing with that of a mother for her baby. Before having her baby, the mother may sleep soundly through the loudest noise, but after the baby is born he only has to rustle in his crib and the mother is awake. Her keenness grows and ripens in loving attention and presence. Her loving care permeates her senses so she hears with new ears.

When we, with God's grace, live in love for Him, we too will develop a new ear. Then, when we open Scripture, certain texts may "jump out" at us immediately. We become keen of hearing to the extent that we are truly given to God as the mother is given to the baby she loves.

The initiative for inspiration rests with God alone. We cannot force it or compel it; we can only wait in loving attention. Inspiration does not necessarily mean the infusion of bright or new ideas. What comes to the spiritual teacher may be old ideas; inspiration means that these ideas come alive for him in a new way because of the Holy Spirit. Inspiration is God's speaking to the heart. To keep open to the Spirit, we should keep ourselves in an attitude of receptivity. Receptivity is not an overnight acquisition. It implies a growth in personal readiness and openness; it means being awake and ever on the watch for the Word of God that might speak on the occasion of reading Scripture. We say "might speak," for we cannot force this speaking. It could happen and we must be ready.

This receptivity is preserved by a gentle life style, inner stillness, and recollection. We cannot listen if we are not gentle—if we are excited, excessively worried, over aggressive. Inner silence, recollection, and gentle living limit the obstacles to receptivity.

While we cannot force divine inspiration, we can hold ourselves in readiness; we can put ourselves at God's disposal. On the other hand, we can also refuse ourselves to God. We may not want to listen. When we do not like to hear what the Holy Spirit is saying, we escape His word by refusal to listen.

We may become inspired if we read Scripture devoutly and reflectively over the years. Gradually, in and through Holy Scripture reading, we may feel held by God in Christ. This spiritual knowledge of Scripture can be won only by a total commitment. We must put our whole selves into the venture, centering our lives around the Word of God.

Conclusion

Our reflections on Scripture and spirituality have made us aware of certain psychological conditions that can facilitate spiritual reading. We realized already that these conditions are helpful not only in regard to spiritual presence to Scripture but also in other kinds of spiritual presence. In this chapter we only touched upon such conditions. We want to go deeper into them in the following chapter on the psychodynamics of spiritual presence.

V

PSYCHODYNAMICS OF SPIRITUAL PRESENCE

We are always experiencing ourselves and the world in various ways, few of which we are aware of in daily life. These ways influence one another continuously; their mutual interaction colors our mood and manner of presence. One way of experience flows over into the other; one cannot be understood without the other.

Any experience we have reverberates in our total style of life. That is true too of spiritual experiences. They may transform the rest of our experiences. Our life of presence as a whole is spiritualized insofar as it is colored by spiritual experience and vice versa. Our spiritual presence is permeated by other dimensions of our human presence to the world. For example, spiritual experience can be distorted by remnants of feelings that are forgotten or repressed. Hence, we must examine how various psychic forces of experience past and present shape dynamically our spiritual experience, what we could call a psychodynamics of spiritual presence.

The interwovenness of the various dimensions of presence makes it difficult to discuss any one of them in isolation from the other. It seems best to first introduce these dimensions with an explanation of their name, function, and special relationships to each other. After this overview we will relate some of them more explicitly to spiritual presence.

Provisional Preview of the Dimensions of Presence

Our presence to reality is constituted by five dimensions; they are the natural and the divinely illuminated supraconscious, the infraconscious, preconscious, and conscious dimensions of presence.

In this summation we note especially the terms *supra* and *infra* conscious. They are not found in self theories that do not start from the principle of the fundamental spiritual nature of man. In our self-theory both the supra and the infra conscious are unconscious. This means that my presence on these levels is not available to my actual awareness; neither can I make these levels available at will. Other self theories usually use the word *unconscious* to identify only what we call here infraconscious.

The word *infra* means "below" or "under;" *supra* means "over," "above," "beyond." We wholeheartedly agree that there is a storehouse of experiences below our usual consciousness, experiences that have been repressed but still exude a powerful influence on our conscious life. We also believe that we have another storehouse of experiences that go far beyond our daily actual consciousness, that can uplift, even divinize our conscious life. They too are not directly available to consciousness. They may have been "refused." Refusal is the term we use for the peculiar kind of "upward repression" of which we may be the victim when we dread the demands of the spirit. Because this presence to the beyond transcends our usual consciousness we call it *supra*conscious.

The infraconsciousness binds us to the body; the supraconsciousness to the great beyond. Our conscious presence to reality is influenced by both. The more the messages of both sources are repressed and refused, the less integrated we are and the more we suffer anxiety, indecision, and enslavement to elaborate defenses of repression and refusal.

Supraconscious Presence

To be human is to be spirit in the flesh. Our spiritual life finds its rootedness in our fundamental or spirit self and its anchorage in the vital drives of the body, the vital self. This spirit self is already an openness to what is beyond us, to the whole of all that is, the Holy. Any spiritual presence finds its core in this intuitive pre-presence to the sacred, the eternal, the infinite. The term pre-presence signifies that this intuition is not necessarily a conscious one. When the infinite announces itself to our awareness, we may be terrified by this immense beyond; we may be frightened too by the demands it may make upon us. We may flee from this experience by a refusal that bans this announcement of the beyond from our awareness once and for all or so we hope. This radical refusal has an effect somewhat similar to that which repression has on our infraconscious drives.

Divinely Illuminated Supraconscious Presence

We are not only natural spirits; by Baptism we are graced spirits. The gifts of the Holy Spirit illumine our supraconscious presence to the Holy. The light of faith enables us to be open in principle to the God of Revelation, of redeeming love; to experience how He relates to us intimately as indwelling Trinity; to sense what

He asks of us personally. The Holy Spirit speaks in us as Jesus promised. Our spirit self is elevated to a divinely illuminated spirit self. Natural supraconscious presence is thus not destroyed but elevated by the Spirit. The enlightened supraconscious does not lose its natural powers and characteristics. On the contrary, they are deepened immensely by the Spirit Himself.

As the natural intuition of the spirit can be refused, so also can the supernatural gift of intuition of the "Revealed Beyond" be refused out of dread. We may not want to hear what the Spirit calls us to nor what He reveals to us at the occasion of a sermon or meditation, of sacred liturgy, Scripture reading or reading of the spiritual masters. Here, too, our refusal can be as radical as the repression of infraconscious experience. Our flight from the Light will give rise to elaborate structures of refusal; they support our forgetfulness of the Spirit. Maybe that is what Jesus meant when he told us that the sin against the Holy Spirit cannot be forgiven. [Matthew 12:31–32] Our radical refusal to be touched by the Spirit makes it impossible for us to experience the need for and the fact of divine forgiveness as long as we persevere in our refusal.

In both cases, the refusal of natural and supernatural tending to the beyond does not go away; it keeps haunting us. The denial of our spiritual pre-presence does not take away the powerful aspiration linked with this tending. It is an aspiration for all that is, for participation in a beyond that generates and encompasses us. This refused aspiration returns as a totalizing tendency that has lost its true object. We feel impelled to totalize frantically all kinds of little beyonds that we have made absolute, such as status, money, honor, success, popularity. We do not know how to overcome these fixations on earthly concerns that wear us out, for we have lost our openness to the original source of all totalizing tendencies: the refused tending toward the absolute and the subsequent aspiration for the Eternal.

Infraconscious Presence

Our infraconscious modes of presence are rooted in the drives, feelings, and passions that emerge from our vital make-up. As a result of life experiences starting in early childhood, these drives are oriented in certain directions. For example, the drive to escape danger may have become a drive to stay away from authority. In this case the child may have experienced authority as dangerous and over-powering. These drives and their orientation are often repressed. Nevertheless, they keep influencing our conscious life indirectly. They have a stereotyping influence on our thought, feeling, and behavior. Dominated by our repressed drives, we keep monotonously reacting in all situations as if they were still the identical situation we reacted to as children in panic and anxiety. Infraconscious modes of presence are thus not free and responsive. From this viewpoint they could be better called modes of reaction. We call them modes of presence insofar as they co-constitute our overall style of presence to life.

As the supraconscious modes of presence are rooted in the spirit self and point to the future, so too the infraconscious modes are rooted in the vital body self and point to the past in which these drives received their reactive directions. Among these reactive directions are ones we could call quasi-spiritual. Quasi-spiritual orientations are anxiety driven spiritless reactions to religion as misapprehended in childhood. We will refer to these reactions when we deal in more detail with the infraconsciousness.

Infraconscious modes of presence are not capable of being openly and directly communicated because they are unconscious. We cannot talk about them in clear and distinct terms. Take a compulsive religious person, unconsciously driven by repressed anxiety to identify the enjoyment of personal leisure time with lack of virtue. He cannot talk of the anxiety and guilt that are the source of his warped judgment for he is unaware of them. He may be only slightly aware of feeling uneasy or somewhat embarrassed when he enjoys himself, but he is not conscious of the deep lasting terror behind these feelings.

Infraconscious spiritual anxiety may give rise to a rigidity that betrays itself in movement, in facial and verbal expression. This spiritual rigidity is far more universal than the more obvious quirks spiritually minded people may develop. In certain cultural periods a stern religious outlook may become so universally accepted and contagious that it may be taken for granted even among clergy, religious, and lay people striving after a spiritual life. We may then get the stereotype of the stern, sour spiritual director, teacher, or student.

Preconscious Presence

The preconscious modes of presence are the opposite of the infraconscious ones. The latter are repetitive, monotonous reactions, basically always the same. The neurotically submissive person, for instance, says "yes" to all commands no matter the person who gives them or the situation in which they are given. The infraconscious rebel reacts as repetitiously; his life comprises a stilted "no" to any command, no matter the circumstances.

By way of contrast, the preconscious is the source of playful interaction with reality. It is marked by a rich interplay of flexible operations and free associations. What is preconscious is available to consciousness, unlike the infraconscious drives that are repressed and may tyrannize us, unable as we are to become aware of them without special help.

We could say that the preconscious surrounds consciousness, that our actual consciousness floats in the preconscious like an embryo in the womb. The other levels of consciousness—infra and supra modes of presence—have access to the consciousness in and through the preconsciousness provided that the preconsciousness is allowed to playfully be itself and is not suppressed by our conscious life or taken over by the infraconscious.

The preconscious functions as a bridge between the conscious and the unconscious levels of presence. It provides an ideal meeting place for lightning quick interactions between all modes and modalities of presence; it is the most free and creative part of our experiential life.

The preconscious could be compared to a busy airport. Planes from far and near fly swiftly in, while others take off in all directions. All of them report to the control tower from which they receive their flight orientation. Our conscious personal presence, with its strong rational power, is the control tower; the planes are drives, aspirations, and experiences, each with their own historical and present orientations coming in from the infra and supraconscious regions of the far and near past; the preconscious is the lively airport itself.

The preconscious not only receives the flights from the infra and supraconscious. We all have countless experiences which are neither filtered through the personal conscious process of rational attention nor through the unconscious processes. Much of what we see, hear, feel, sense, or do affects us without our clearly knowing it. We could not live sensibly if we would be fully conscious of every experience we have. We would be overwhelmed and destroyed by the sheer amount and complexity of our experiences. Much of these experiences have to remain peripheral knowledge. This knowledge is not necessarily repressed; therefore, it does not become infraconscious. It just falls outside of our focus of attention. It remains present preconsciously. The preconscious modes of presence are functioning constantly. They constitute our global experiential life. We can thus say that in the ideal case our conscious presence is surrounded, nourished, and stimulated by our lively preconscious presence. This preconscious presence in turn is surrounded and nourished by the world to which it is present in its own playful way and by infra and supraconscious presence.

The strength of the preconscious lies in the fact that it receives simultaneously an incredible variety of insights, experiences, and data; it combines and utilizes them creatively with the speed of lightning; it gives rise to new insights which conscious thought could not reach in and by itself. The preconscious is the source of creativity, of quick solutions, of fast and flexible adaptation to changing situations. Our slower paced conscious study, thought, and observation must prepare the work of the preconsciousness; afterwards it must check and control the results of preconscious associations. For the preconscious has no critical acumen or the potentiality for logical thought.

To be creative and alive, also spiritually, we must allow our preconscious free play within the limits of doctrine and reason. The unconscious and conscious modes of presence must be included in the totality of our presence to the world. But if either the conscious or the infraconscious take over totally, our experiential life will be paralyzed. We may still be functioning in the intellectual or managing realm but it will be impossible to be inspired and inspirational, alive and creative as spiritual directors, readers, students, teachers, or animators.

Preconscious presence—if not interfered with unnecessarily by conscious or unconscious modes of presence—can function freely in every human being. Preconscious presence is not circumscribed by the formal restrictions of doctrinal language or of the technical language of systematic theology. This presence is continuously nourished by nonverbalized or only partly verbalized experiences. This lack of conscious literal restriction enables the preconscious to use the symbolic process in an allegorical, poetical, and figurative way.

For example, if we dwell meditatively on a religious text, we may find ourselves becoming less literal, less exact; our preconscious presence comes to the fore; life experiences, not verbalized and clearly delineated at the conscious level, begin to speak in and through the text. They give rise to symbolic imagery. Flexibility of imagery, thought, and feeling is made possible by the free continuous and concurrent action of our preconscious presence during reading, reflection, and self-expression. We say "continuous", for while we do spiritual reading, reflecting, and expressing consciously, the preconscious modes of presence should go on unceasingly, giving rise to apt associations in consciousness.

This preconscious presence is "concurrent" because it should not take the place of our conscious presence. While we are consciously present with rational understanding and reading skill to Scripture, liturgy, and spiritual texts, our preconscious presence works concurrently at the same time. This concomitant preconscious presence fosters the association of such texts with life.

Our preconscious presence is thus rooted in a spontaneous, lightning fast, ever changing confluence of life experiences and unconscious modes of presence. Within the preconscious these countless elements influence one another during the ongoing play of free associations. The results of this creative interplay must be then checked by the critical powers of the conscious ego.

Take, for instance, the description by the mystics of the inspirations they received. Before the mystic expressed himself on the conscious level, these inspirations received in the supraconscious may come to consciousness through the preconscious. In the preconscious, other life experiences and infraconscious influences tend to associate themselves playfully with supraconscious experiences. They may transform or even distort the message. The mystic may communicate a message which, in its final expression, is excessively personalized and may even be distorted because of other powerful experiences in his preconscious personality that cling to the inspired message.

Conscious Presence

The tip of the iceberg of human presence, so to speak, is the conscious aspect of this presence. The conscious dimension of presence is a power center of rational control, management, clarification, and direction. It centers and guides our overall presence. However, it is always in danger of paralyzing by over control the vital and imaginary dimensions of our experiential life. It risks also to be enslaved by the stereotyping powers of the infraconscious. The power of consciousness can also be distracted, disturbed, and sidetracked when it does not keep on top of the playfulness of the preconscious on which it thrives for its creative aliveness.

The conscious ego should keep wise control not by blunt imposition but by patient listening to all the other modes of presence, by taking into account what is happening in the person. Consciousness asks itself if ideas and feelings emerge from the infraconscious or supraconscious, from the flesh or the spirit. If from the spirit, it examines critically if this spirit is enlightened by the Holy Spirit. If information emerges from preconscious and unconscious presence, consciousness checks if the information is accurate and correct, if insights are true, logically consistent and can be distinctly conceptualized.

In the creative phase of spontaneous association, the preconscious modes of presence prevail. In the stage of formulation and judgment, consciousness should take the lead. Conscious presence provides the necessary checks and balances. The latter are crucial. For the preconscious presence, from which creative conscious insight emerges, is most vulnerable. Preconscious presence is wide open to the infraconscious modes of presence; they often distort the preconscious ones; in and through an unchecked preconscious they may even warp our conscious judgments.

This rational checking and objective self-criticism is far from easy. It presupposes the ability to take distance, to view one's spontaneous experiences as though one were a third person looking on from a distance. The problem is that our preconscious experiences are so spontaneous, representing all kinds of peculiarities that are typically our own, that we feel naturally at one with them; we feel that such experiences are truly us, the "real me," as we like to say.

Our conscious presence helps us to realize that our preconscious selves are not our whole selves, that we are our conscious selves also. However, people with a weak conscious presence seem unable to take the necessary distance to scrutinize their feelings and opinions rationally and realistically.

The same necessity holds for spiritual experiences, even for those seemingly coming from our divinely illuminated spiritual presence. It is not enough that spiritual reading and reflection are rooted in preconscious creative presence. We must check out consciously what we have experienced in our inspirational reading or meditation. We may have to check these experiences in contact with the conscious critical presence of others who can strengthen and enlighten our self-critique. The more inspired we feel, the more we need conscious checking and validation. An abundance of inspiration implies an abundance of preconscious presence. An abundance of preconscious presence means always a concomitant increase in vulnerability for infraconscious stereotyping modes of presence and for capricious preconscious associations. Even the purest inspiration coming from our divinely illuminated supraconscious becomes easily distorted when it arrives in the bewitching cauldron of preconscious presence.

Yet we must watch for the opposite exaggeration. An

exclusive reliance on conscious modes of presence gives rise to rigidity in the spiritual life. The conscious modes of presence are anchored to specific concepts in the rational mind by precise and literal relationships. For example, when we look at a text of Scripture, liturgy, or a spiritual master from the viewpoint of defined doctrine or systematic theology, we may find its meaning expressed in concise concepts and words exactly delineated by the conscious rational mind. This anchorage of conscious knowledge is necessary, but we need to go beyond it; spiritually we need room to relate the text to life experiences not yet conceptualized or exactly formulated. If we stay with only rational concepts on the level of conscious presence, we may find little profit for our spiritual lives.

If our religion affects only our conscious self and becomes nothing more than a collection of customs and concepts, we may become like a dead and labeled butterfly, pinned in a box for display. We may cause no trouble, but we will be far from inspirational for ourselves and others.

As present, we may sometimes face the opposite problem. Some people may just want to live a preconscious life. In overreaction to the rigidity of an almost exclusive conscious presence to self and world, they try too eagerly to lessen the clarity and alertness of a well educated and continuously updated consciousness. They forget we need the conscious modes of presence badly to check our preconscious presence. Many today weaken their ego functions and, on top of this, don't work through their infraconscious modes of presence. Many want only to sense, to be creative, to feel playful, alive, on an emotional "high." This anxious hunt for playful feeling

also signals a stereotyped reaction evoked by infraconscious modes of presence such as resistance to authority,
rules, and regulations; repressed erotic needs; obsessive
overreactions against the tyranny of rational consciousness
over the creative preconscious in past personal or communal experiences.

As we have seen, we need not only the creative
playfulness of the preconscious but also a well trained
conscious mind that checks and controls its creative play,
if our experiences and opinions are to remain in tune with
reason, reality, and Church Doctrine.

Infraconscious and Spiritual Presence

After this overview of the dimensions of human
presence, we can relate some of them more explicitly to
spiritual presence. Already in the overview, we hinted at
this relationship but did not go into detail. The deepest
source of the spiritual life is the divinely illumined
supraconscious presence. This is the fountainhead of all
spiritual living. The incarnation of this inspiration in the
total self depends mostly on the other dimensions of
human presence. The dimensions of presence that are most
influential in regard to the incarnation of spiritual presence
in human presence are the infraconscious and the preconscious. The first can paralyze the incarnation of spiritual
life; the latter can revitalize it. Both need the control of
the conscious rational and realistic dimension.

During spiritual listening, reading, or meditation there
can be in subtle, almost unnoticeable ways, a shift to
infraconscious connotations. The infraconsciousness is the
principle of stereotyping, of paralyzing the incarnational

movement of the spiritual life. Many always listen, read, meditate, speak, and pray with their infraconscious mind. They keep mentally and emotionally grinding out the same thing. For example, a person like the Pharisee in the temple may always end his prayers and reflections with thanking God that he is not like other people.

Listening, reading, and meditating on the infraconscious level can also initiate such blindly compulsive drives as work drives, prayer, perfection and guilt drives, all rooted in the infraconscious. Anything related to such compulsions can set them off when one reads a spiritual book or hears a spiritual talk. Thus if a person is compulsively lazy, he may read about the gentle life and agree that relaxed gentleness is indeed his favored virtue. He feels reinforced in his obsessive tendency to dawdle always and everywhere. In spiritual talks and writings, in personal prayer, he finds only a highly selective and inflexible meaning, monotonously repeated. For example, someone who comes from a rich family may have developed early in life an infraconscious anxiety, guilt, and shame about being rich. In compensation he may have become compulsively involved in the cause of the under-privileged. This excessive overreaction is infraconscious. He may feel compelled to find in Scripture and other spiritual talks and readings only meanings that strengthen and justify his own obsessive preoccupation with material poverty.

The infra modes of presence anchor us rigidly to infraconscious conflicts, objects, and impulses we cannot accept in ourselves. As a result, they have been made inaccessible to our conscious reflection. They elude the corrective influence of our conscious, preconscious, and supraconscious experiences. Such repetitious infra modes of presence evoke continually the same stale reaction to what we read, hear, and reflect upon, also spiritually.

Consider a person who as a little child lived in a Jansenistic milieu. He was overwhelmed by an atmosphere of anxious righteousness and pious rigidity. Thoughts, words, and feelings in his family were not liberated by a relaxed trust in God, by the joyful hope to be redeemed, loved, and esteemed by Him. Rather life was burdened by countless fearful questions, such as, "Did I do the right thing? Did I do it perfectly well? Am I in sin? Have my sins been truly forgiven? Did I give into temptations, bad thoughts? Am I saved or condemned?" The child was too young to work through the resulting experiences—experiences, for example, of God as a tyrant ready to put him in hell if he were not one of the chosen. The "Divine Tyrant" was experienced also in the imagined or real little tyrants called parents, clergy, teachers. All this was a part of his experiential life, but he never dared to face it. He may have felt that this way of life was unreasonable, even repulsive, but he would not dare to become aware of this feeling for fear that if he did, God might destroy him. All these experiences were repressed, yet still present as a lasting inner feeling, endlessly repeated.

Later the person might become a rigid adherent of religious customs, prim and precise in all things. He will read Scripture in a stereotyped, anxious way, hearing God speaking in the texts as a stern taskmaster ready to punish and condemn.

It is also possible that an equally repressed reaction of revolt may prevail in the infraconscious. Not worked through, it evokes an overreaction nourished by unconscious anger and resistance; the person might become anti-authority in an unreasonable way. He may read many Scripture texts as condemnatory of authority.

True spiritual orientation is free and insightful; our spirit self, freely and with insight, orients itself to the Divine and to spiritual values. But the religious orientations we pick up as small children from parents, family, neighbors, teachers are not yet freely chosen by us after personal prayerful reflection.

We can see an example of this in an experience of a missionary in Africa. He was amazed that the children seemed afraid of him. Then he heard that their mothers used to instill fear in their children, threatening to hand the child over to Father if the child misbehaved. The religious symbol "Father" took on a special anxiety-evoking meaning.

Infra symbols are sterile and repetitive. For instance, a memory trace, present in some tense inflexible Christian, tells him that "to be leisurely is to be imperfect." That conviction may be so deeply buried that it is unknown to him. But the same sterile response of guilt, shame, fear, and embarrassment repeats itself monotonously in every personal leisure situation because of this unknown underlying conviction. If such a person catches himself relaxing, he may feel guilty; he attempts to conceal what he is doing or tries to justify his leisure by saying that he was just relaxing because he had a headache.

A person may be able to live with these anxious attitudes and repressed conflicts for a long time. In all too many cases, however, he may have a breakdown in middle age. He may, for instance, feel strongly tempted to leave marriage, religious life, the priesthood. He may show neurotic or psychosomatic symptoms. Such infraconscious quasi-spiritual attitudes need to be worked through. As long as they are not available to consciousness, they maintain their sterile, repetitive, and non-creative influence. An attitude that, on the contrary, has been made available to consciousness can be adapted creatively to a changing situation.

One possible way to discover some of these unconscious attitudes to a degree is through doing spiritual reading and having to communicate what is read and one's first reaction to the reading. This may mean writing our experiences in a spiritual journal. This exercise may be helpful, for such records of experience may reveal some of these unconscious attitudes by use of certain repetitive expressions and interpretations.

Another example of this problem can be seen in a person who complains he cannot pray or does not dare to enjoy spiritual reading. There are many possible reasons for this problem. One of them may be that in his youth he received the idea that what was pleasant, easy, interesting was not virtuous but only what was unpleasant, difficult, or boring. It can be deeply ingrained in a person that what is good and holy always entails some hardships or unpleasantness. This becomes for him a quasi-spiritual maxim. If this person finds spiritual reading easy and enlightening, he may feel unconsciously guilty, thinking perhaps, "This is too nice to be really sanctifying." He may feel himself driven to read on so as to move away from a pleasing passage. This is not a conscious response but rather stems from an infraconscious reaction.

For the same reason sometimes, people do not make the transition from discursive meditation to the prayer of quiet. In the prayer of quiet, they feel they are doing nothing, just sitting there and enjoying it. They feel this cannot be good; they must be doing something. This is another example of how infraconscious modes of presence can interfere with the spiritual life.

All people are influenced in some way and to some degree along these lines. Certain prevalent infraconscious modes of presence are often shared by many in the same cultural period.

Emergence of Deeper Anxiety and Guilt Feelings

Infraconscious modes of presence may give rise to feelings of guilt and anxiety when we begin to read and meditate playfully, creatively, in a relaxed way, giving the preconscious a chance to operate in our spiritual life. Even if we overcome these initial blocks and start to meditate, respond, speak, and reflect spontaneously—even when we are able to let down our guard and approach Scripture more freely—we may suddenly be faced with unexpected strong infraconscious feelings. An unknown guilt, terror, or rage may emerge.

If we have never allowed threatening experiences to affect us, if we have only read and spoken in a rigid functional way, we may find that when we initiate a more creative presence repressed experiences will emerge. Denied experiences will come to the fore. We may be faced with temptations, images, feelings, and thoughts that scare us. We may find that we are enraged about people we did not dare to see in an unfavorable light during our life of emotional repression.

We can see this rage exemplified in the timid clinging wife who comes home from therapy and explodes to her husband. For the first time she may discover that he abused her need to please him and that she does not like what she suddenly finds out. She does not know how to cope with an experience never admitted before and so bursts out in anger.

We must move slowly, gently, and gradually into the way of spiritual experience and not be surprised by the anxieties that may emerge. For the same reason, there may be anxieties in a Christian community when someone suggests reading a text of Scripture and sharing each one's experience of it. People fear speaking of their experiences. We should be cautious in fostering such a threatening process and preferably keep it on a voluntary basis.

Possible Blend of Freedom and Fixation in a Person

A spiritual person may be more or less free from inordinate guilt, anger, and anxiety. We must add to this, it may be that he is free from these inordinate affects in most dimensions of the spiritual life yet hampered by any or all or these affects in other areas.

Many spiritual people may seem to be balanced persons, but if we touch on certain areas they may manifest fanatic, stereotyped, or otherwise exaggerated reactions. The more they strike people as balanced in most areas of life, the more others may be inclined to take as also balanced what they express unwisely without catching the exaggerated quality of their judgment or its expression.

Consider persons with a hang-up about authority. If there is anything in Scripture or spiritual writings about authority or obedience, they tend to get inordinately excited. They start to read Scripture or other spiritual literature in a way that seems to say to them that authority is not meant to be taken seriously. They read Scripture, therefore, onesidedly.

Others will freeze in such areas as chastity or social engagement. From this will result a onesided, fixated, repetitive reading, listening, and reflecting. They may be balanced in other areas, but if we touch that one sensitive area they may go off in strange directions.

As soon as we come to an area in which the person is affected by infraconscious fixations because of traumas in childhood, we will find an inability to spiritually read or meditate in an open flexible way.

Therefore, if an initiate in the spiritual life, in spite of his best attempts, is unable to flexibly read Scripture or other spiritual authors or to hear what the novice director is saying, we may suspect that this block is deeply seated on the infraconscious level. It is so deep it affects all free associations; the person either misreads the text or rigidly sticks to only its doctrinal or exegetical meaning.

Infraconscious and Spiritual Communication

Infraconscious needs, conflicts, affects, or defenses distort spiritual communication. These infraconscious forces alter what we hear or read in the spiritual text. They may alter the spiritual message in the act itself of our spiritually communicating what we have set out to say.

For example, we may start out with a little spiritual message but, in the act of communicating it, we may get worked up; instead of saying what we have to say in a wise, moderate, compassionate way, we may become upset and angry. We should ask ourselves why this happens. We may find something deep inside ourselves which makes us want to use our spiritual message as a club over the heads of others. We may discover a hidden infraconscious anger that turns our message into a weapon. We may plan to be sweet but, before we know it, our sweetness is poisoned. We would be wise to ask ourselves why we constantly seem to upset others with our spiritual tidings.

Preconscious and Spiritual Presence

The preconscious shaping of our spiritual presence goes on from earliest infancy to old age, most of the time without our conscious knowledge. We began gathering spiritual experiences already when we were children. Our "lived" spiritual experience came first of all from our environment: the way the family prayed at table, the way mother lit a candle before a statue, or the parish priest said Mass, or a sister spoke about Christ. Their devout manner affected us, not on the level of reasoning but preconsciously. It is precisely this preconscious experience that may come to life again later.

The preconscious shaping of spiritual presence, insofar as it fosters our spiritual life, implies opening ourselves also as preconscious human beings to spiritual influences. We take on a receptive attitude of relaxed spiritual reading, keeping a spiritual journal, and so on.

We can now understand what may happen if we try to replace this preconscious process by intellectual processes only; for instance, if we pretend that courses in systematic theology are the only and exclusive way to spiritual aliveness. Such courses can have a fine influence on our spiritual life, provided we look at their content also from an inspirational-practical viewpoint. At the moment that our preconscious presence prevails, there is a less immediate impact of the doctrinal or systematic theological outlook. A process of spontaneous association begins to complement our doctrinal insights. We begin spontaneously to associate fragments of Scripture, liturgy, spiritual reading, religious talks, and meditative reflection with fragments of experience; they meet in our preconscious.

For example, we read the psalm text that speaks of the God who saved us, who is our hope and who is at our right hand. The preconscious may associate that text suddenly with a memory trace of childhood. We may think of a child holding his father's hand. The father seems so big to the child; his right hand holding him seems wonderfully protective. There is an increase in life meaning as a result of the spontaneous association of this text with a life experience, such as the loving remembrance of holding father's hand as a child.

It is the preconscious that enables us to make such creative associations between, on the one hand, the fragments of Scripture we are dwelling on, and, on the other hand, relevant fragments of life experience. Once we are in this process of creative spiritual reading, we should not interrupt it by attitudes that interfere in an untimely way with our life approach to inspired texts.

One such interfering attitude is an incessant conscious critique. A person may feel tempted to remain on the intellectual level during his spiritual reading or meditation. He asks himself anxiously or curiously, "How does this idea fit into systematic theology? Is my experience of the Lord in tune with the exact formulations of doctrine?" Or he may shift his attention constantly to the exegetical footnotes in his Bible. Such questions are excellent at other moments, but at this moment of prayerful dwelling, they should be postponed. It is advisable to study also the footnotes at another time. Once we have a general idea about the doctrinal meaning of a Scripture text and have assimilated it carefully, we should engage in spiritual reading and meditation without returning explicitly to conceptual explanation and factual information. Incessant intellectual critique interrupts the creative flow of preconscious associations.

Sometimes people ask why it is so difficult for persons well trained in religious studies to be spiritually inspiring. Part of the answer may be that they were not as well initiated into "lived" spiritual thinking. In preparing a talk they may stay with doctrinal and systematic theological concepts memorized well by them. Occasionally they may be surprised by a spontaneous flow of experience, but they flee quickly back to mere intellectual considerations and thus interrupt the preconscious flow.

On the other hand, there is no logic in our preconscious presence to counteract patterns from the infraconscious. For this reason, we need to check the preconscious associations always consciously by means of doctrine, reason, and reality testing.

The checking process is difficult and must be done carefully. We have just seen that it is impossible to dwell spiritually and prayerfully if we attempt simultaneously to maintain a watchful critical scrutiny of what we are reading, experiencing, feeling, and thinking. This watchfulness would interrupt the process. The best thing to do, especially when preparing a talk, is to set down impressions, put them aside, and let time elapse before returning to them. Only after such a delay may we return to our spiritual self-expressions with an ability to scrutinize them objectively, with lessened attachment and personalized defenses. It is not possible to be wisely self-critical at the moment of personal spiritual experience or immediately thereafter.

Think of what happens when we are freely reading Scripture. We are taken up with the spiritual experiences welling up in us spontaneously but also with the infraconscious processes and hang-ups that mix with them in countless hidden ways. We feel really at one with our experiences. Therefore, we express them. However, others react negatively to our expression and we feel personally rejected. Later other experiences intervene. In the meantime, we are at some distance from the original experience. Less identified with the experience, we can feel less defensive about it as persons.

When we are too close to our experiences, it is better not to speak out on the spot. If we are wise and cautious, we intuitively realize the need for carefulness; we may speak out spontaneously only in a situation where we can trust others such as when we are with personal friends. We must thus check out consciously what we have experienced in our free inspirational reading or meditation.

We check out our experience of the divine message under four aspects:

(1) The doctrinal aspect: is my experience and its expression still in tune with Church Doctrine?

(2) The rational or sensible aspect: is my experience and its expression compatible with what is reasonable, with common sense, with reality as we know it?

(3) The intersubjective aspect: is my experience validated by recognized others who have had similar experiences in the Church; is it at least not positively invalidated by them?

(4) The aspect of communicability: can my experience and its expression be communicated to other human beings and make sense?

Inspiration and its conscious validation must alternate; both are necessary. Certain people exaggerate or live exclusively on one or the other pole. They are either always "checking" or always "experiencing."

The great art of the spiritual master, director, or teacher is to play both roles wisely in a balanced way. We will find to our discomfort at times that there are some who are always inclined to checking and who don't want to talk of experience; others will want to talk only of their experiences. We must be a buffer between the two extremes. Such balance may seem difficult, but gradually it may come naturally as, with the aid of divine grace, we become more relaxed persons.

Preconscious Spirituality and Anxiety

Anxiety may operate on a preponderantly preconscious level. Anxiety on this level—unlike anxiety on the infraconscious level—will not block all associations; it will give rise to selective blocking: inhibitory in certain directions and exaggerating in other compensatory areas.

In novices, juniors, seminarians, or lay people who read, write about, or discuss Scripture, we will find some who are flexibly able to associate freely. Others simply freeze and fall back on doctrinal, exegetical explanations without spontaneous associations with their experiences. There may be in them a deep-seated anxiety on the infraconscious level. In some this anxiety has already entered the preconscious. Then it leads to inhibitory effects in certain directions and exaggerating ones in other areas.

We find three kinds of people who in three kinds of ways react to anxiety. First we have those who become paralyzed by infraconscious anxiety. They stick to the conscious doctrinal level of Scripture exclusively. Other people, suffering from preconscious anxiety, try to overcome their inner turmoil by over-production. We can see this solution, for instance, in the hostess whose preconscious anxiety, instead of paralyzing her—as infraconscious anxiety could—causes her to ramble on endlessly. We can see the same practice in the anxious preacher who keeps adding sentences to his sermons and never seems to know when to stop. Lastly, there are the people who, as a result of preconscious anxieties, experience an irresistible pressure to distort the spiritual material. An example is the person who hears and reads always and only that he is condemned because of his human weakness and on the verge of meeting punishment. No confessor or director can take away his propensity to distort even their words in this regard.

Transition from Conscious to Preconscious Presence

Let's begin with an example of this transition. In remote preparation for a spiritual homily, a priest might take the text of the Gospel, read it meditatively, and then take a walk, meanwhile dwelling on the text in a relaxed prayerful mood. Often something will happen. An interesting idea, story, or image may emerge. It is important for him to write it down. Some ideas may not at first seem to be related but over a period of time such ideas will gather and surprisingly begin to fit together.

In this way we may come to a new ensemble of relevant texts and experience fragments. An important point to remember is that such associations, which might happen at propitious times, tend to be forgotten unless they are written down.

The miracle of spontaneous association may happen to us at any time—while driving, riding the bus, doing the dishes, taking a walk, waiting in an office or store. Such flashes can be the starting point of investigation in the light of doctrine; they present us with a goal for renewed reflection and study.

We may suggest some guidelines regarding how we are to be while reading Holy Scripture or other spiritual writings if we want to foster the possibility that from conscious attention to the text we can come to a preconscious presence. We must try to facilitate rather than block or interfere with our spiritual creative potential. To facilitate this freedom, the following guidelines will be helpful.

Don't at that moment try to think and don't try not to think. Our greatest problem as Western people is that we are always immediately trying to figure things out rationally. We don't give intuition, imagination, life experience a chance to flow freely. We immediately make things into a problem.

On the other hand, we should not try too forcefully not to think. That attitude is not helpful in spontaneous spiritual reading either. It is again an ego attitude, willful and fixating.

We should try in a relaxed way to make ourselves comfortable and free from unnecessary bodily strain. Strained thinking is not just in the brain; it is incarnated in muscle strain in the body. For example, we may manifest excessive muscle strain that shows by the frowns on our forehead while reading, praying, or listening. When we are over-strained bodily, we cannot quietly dwell, meditate, or contemplate. When we are anxious, no free flowing of spontaneous thought and feeling takes place. So we must try in a relaxed way to make ourselves comfortable and free from excessive bodily strain. We should engage in progressive bodily relaxation.

When we are tense we cannot at once become untense. We can, however, gradually relax one muscle at a time. We can try to relax progressively. There is no chance for the preconscious presence to bring lively aspects to our minds if we don't first relax sufficiently. After a while we may become gradually relaxed. However, we must keep quietly and playfully in mind the spiritual text we have chosen to nourish our experiential life. The deeper our receptivity and relaxation, the emptier our mind in regard to other things unrelated to the text, the closer we are to the preconscious.

Summary

This chapter has dealt with the psychodynamics of spiritual presence. It started with an overview of the five dimensions of human presence as developed in our spiritual self-theory. This self-theory will be presented more fully in a later book. Highlighted were the general relations of these dimensions to one another and especially to spiritual presence.

After these general considerations, special attention was given to both the infraconscious and the preconscious dimensions of presence. We explained and illustrated the crucial role each of them plays in the incarnation of supraconscious spiritual experience in the totality of our human presence.

The relation of the activities of infra and preconscious to that of the regulatory ego consciousness was emphasized throughout. Where possible, means and ways were suggested to foster a creative spiritual presence by flexibly flowing with the propitious dynamics of the psyche.

This chapter has prepared us for the next one in which we shall discuss one important mode of supraconscious presence: the presence to one's own unique spiritual identity. The gradual discovery of this identity and our remaining loyal to this divine life call represent the most fundamental dynamic of a personal spiritual life.

VI

SPIRITUAL IDENTITY AND
MODES OF INCARNATION

I know myself as changing in mood, attitude, and outlook and yet as somehow mysteriously the same. My deepest desire is to be someone unique who lasts forever. A secret yearning for eternity wells up from the core of my being. I seek something lasting amidst the transitoriness of countless self-expressions.

What lasts is my spiritual or fundamental self. This core self is not of my own making; it is God's gift to me, not a gift that I have but the gift that I am. God first loved me into being as a new emergent self, unique on this earth. He lovingly continues to call me to that uniqueness He meant for me from eternity. I must answer this call to be myself by commitment and consecration, by a life that offers to God a wholehearted "yes."

This "yes" to the gift and burden of selfhood is at the root of my spiritual life. It must be incarnated in the concrete modes of life in which I live out my calling on a day to day basis. Some modes of incarnation become interwoven with my unique spiritual identity itself; they become lasting incarnations, essential if my life is to be lived in faithfulness to the Word who lovingly calls to me.

Other incarnational modes are passing. Through frequent use, they become familiar to me, making me feel at ease and secure. Yet in the ongoing history of my self-discovery, these ways may prove to be passing, not really as much a part of my life call as I thought they were. They have played a temporary role in the unfolding of my destiny; but at any moment the grace of self-discovery may gently ask me to relinquish them as only passing expressions of the spiritual identity with which God has endowed me.

Discovering My Unique Call

How does my unique call make itself known to me? Usually not by the sudden illuminations that may happen in the lives of specially graced people. An example is St. Paul. Thrown from his horse on his trip to Damascus, his life was given a new orientation. Another example is Mary of Nazareth, to whom an angel appeared lifting, so to speak, a tip of the veil hiding her unique identity before God. Even then it would take both St. Paul and Mary a lifetime to understand more fully what this first illumination would mean. I should not count on such a special revelation. For most of us the core meaning of life only bit by bit reveals itself in the act of living without any sudden orientation.

As I live in prayerful presence to what happens to me, in me, and around me, slowly a certain line may emerge. I see a certain direction; a hidden consistency makes itself known. The more this line clarifies itself, the more I become aware of which incarnational modes of presence are and which are not in harmony with the heart of my existence.

In the spirit center of my being, God keeps communicating to me in love what He wants me to be. He speaks also through the circumstances He allows in my life. I should remain in dialogue with this inner and outer voice of the Lord. I should try to find the thread that holds the events of my life together in this graced self-revelation of the unique me.

The discovery of the slender thread that weaves my life together happens in the adoring awareness of God's loving fidelity to His covenant with me. Even if I am disloyal to myself and unfaithful to Him, He remains faithful to me. Everything else in my life must be valued in keeping with this gradually emerging line of my life.

God is loyal to my spiritual identity that He created in love. Before I was, He loved me. In this love He made me come into being. On my side, I can accept or reject the gift of the unique me that came into existence without my asking for it or deserving it.

My ongoing loyalty to the gift-I-am causes me to incarnate this gift in certain ways of life. I am not forced to say yes to this gift. God's call does not compel a response. He waits with infinite gentleness and patience for my answer, an answer that encompasses my whole life and being.

Before I incarnate this spiritual identity in my daily life, I must also know that identity. Such self-understanding is not reached by introspection. Only a transcendent presence to myself in light of the Divine can reveal to me who I truly am. Enlightened by the Holy Spirit, I come in transcendent self-presence to see myself in my uniqueness. Strengthened by grace, I am able gradually to accept that self. Insofar as my unique self is revealed to me, I try to incarnate it obediently in daily life.

Spiritual identity, unlike vital and personal identity, cannot be found by means of a test or a clinical interview. The only test I have is the test of the underlying consistency of my life and its harmony with Church Doctrine and the wisdom of its recognized spiritual masters. When I increasingly discover who I am before God, my life becomes more consistent, more whole, more in tune with doctrine, traditional wisdom, and personal inspiration. I become increasingly able to realize what is the best option for me among the different life choices that confront me.

Choice and Commitment

Coming more in touch with myself, I become more sure regarding what is in tune with my hidden calling. Because this choice is the fruit of a spiritual knowledge gained in transcendent self-presence, I may not be able to defend it with arguments that sound convincing to the rational mind. It may be impossible for others to understand that a choice I made can be right for me. It is only in the long run that a whole chain of inspired decisions may make sense. They become meaningful in the total orientation that my emergent self begins to manifest. It is often only in hindsight that people discover the hidden consistency of many seemingly disparate choices made over a long period of time.

One condition for the ongoing discovery of my spiritual identity is the ability to distance myself from the circumstances in which I find myself or from the task in which I am actually involved. I must come to know what is the incarnation of the true me in this situation and what is due mainly to the peculiarities of the situation itself. I must grasp who I am spiritually in and beyond one or the other concrete life situation.

Such transcendent self-understanding helps me to see where my commitments should lie. Right commitments in turn deepen my self-knowledge. If I make a wrong commitment, at odds with my deepest self, the spontaneous unfolding of my spiritual life will be hindered. Anxiety, feelings of guilt, frustration, and repression are usually warning signs that I am failing to live up to what I am to be in the sight of God. Hopefully this awareness of mistaken identity comes to me in the period of preparation for a commitment, the period that precedes commitment proper. I can then change my option with the least harm done to myself and others.

Preparation for commitment is one way to discover by trial and error if this commitment is right for me. It is infinitely better to prepare myself for a commitment and discover that it is not my call than to flee into the no man's land of no commitment. Without reflection on all sides of a commitment—and trying out some of them insofar as it is morally and prudently advisable—I may never come to know what path of spiritual growth I am called to follow.

Choosing a spiritual path implies necessarily foregoing the possibilities of other paths. Incarnation means accepting my limits; it means affirming the reality of foregoing ways of life because I am called to another life style, of giving up talents never to be realized, places and persons never to be met. Without the experience and acceptance of my unique limitations, spiritual life is bound to remain formless, floating, ethereal. In other words, it will not be a real spiritual life. The true spiritual life in man is always an incarnated one, for man is essentially an incarnated spirit.

Lasting Congenial Modes of Incarnation

What distinguishes a lasting congenial incarnation of my unique self from what is either an uncongenial or only a temporary incarnation? Congenial incarnations mean that a concrete way of dedication that I choose proves to be congenial with my hidden life call. Uncongenial refers to any attempt to incarnate a value that is at odds with my spiritual identity.

God's creative call is revealed in my deepest self. In some way this call is my deepest self. It is not a call that I have but a call that I am. An Infinite Love tenderly called me forth out of nowhere and nothingness; an unspeakable Love emptied itself to redeem the identity that I lost sight of in sinfulness; an enlightening Love keeps calling me back to what I am.

My divine call or deepest self has, therefore, a lasting quality. Hence, my commitment to this call should be lasting too; it should participate in the permanency of my call itself. If I fail this Love by unfaithfulness to my commitment, I fail my deepest self and therewith my whole emergent self that flows from it.

Commitment becomes real through incarnation in my personal-vital life of the gift of spiritual identity that I am. Commitment thus has two poles, a divine identity pole and an incarnational pole. The pole which is my divine or spiritual identity is in essence unchangeable; it is permanent, the principle of the fidelity of my commitment. If there are apparent changes in this pole of my commitment, it is not because my identity has changed but because my knowledge of it has expanded and deepened during the history of the development of my spiritual life.

The other pole, which is the incarnation in my

spiritual identity in my concrete life, is changeable. This pole constitutes the principle of adaptation. Since I cannot enflesh my call at once, the incarnational pole of my spiritual life is ongoing; it is never achieved but forever achieving itself.

Necessarily any actual incarnation of my spiritual identity expresses only a part of this permanent call. The incarnational pole of spiritual life has to keep adapting itself to both the growing awareness of who I am called to be and to the awareness of the concrete unfolding of my daily life in the world. Without this fluid adaptation, I cannot be flexibly faithful to the loving call of the Divine that manifests itself in my innermost self and in my world. In other words, loyalty to my life call should be lasting but the personal-vital ways in which I incarnate this commitment are in some measure open to change.

Attuning Myself to My Divine Calling

To remain loyal to my spiritual identity when change is demanded, I must listen carefully in order to discover if I am still in tune with the Divine Spirit. Tuning in means an attuning of myself to the Divine, a becoming more at one with the Model of my uniqueness, the loving Logos in whom I am predestined from eternity and for eternity. This attuning happens in prayerful presence to the ebb and flow of daily experience; to doctrine, Scripture, and spiritual writings in the light of this experience; to common wisdom, reason, and reality. It is an ongoing process of bringing to awareness my hidden divine direction.

In this attuning I become aware of those incarnational modes of presence that are in tune with my calling. I realize that infidelity to them at any time would be an infidelity to my identity itself. A person like Mozart could find out that musical self-expression is so much a part of the incarnation of his life call that the refusal to express himself musically in any way at any time could be an infidelity to his identity.

By contrast, other modes of incarnation of my commitment will reveal themselves as less than necessary, as passing and incidental; others again will prove uncongenial with my spiritual identity and therefore harmful. Mozart could discover that a certain musical expression of himself in a select circle of Vienna was not a necessary but only a passing incarnation of his identity. He could also discover that busy socializing would be uncongenial with his life call and life mission.

Modes that are uncongenial should be dropped; the incidentally useful ones should be carefully examined as I try to discern if they are still effective or if they have become anachronisms that slow down the incarnation of my calling. The latter should fall out; they may then be replaced by new, more actually attuned modes of incarnation.

This spirit-enlightened continuous tuning in keeps my spiritual life on the right course. We could compare it to the steering of a car by an accomplished driver following a road he is used to. He adjusts the steering to the traffic without explicitly thinking about it as he did during his driver's training and may still do when caught in a tight spot or when trying to steer his car between two closely parked cars in a parking lot. Otherwise he tunes into the traffic implicitly.

The ongoing implicit tuning in that accompanies my daily spiritual unfolding becomes at times an explicit intensified event. These events occur in such moments as those of crises, suffering, sickness, anguish, and the threat of death. They can be lived as graced opportunities for a deeper discernment of which modes of incarnation are fundamental to my identity, which are peripheral, and which are not or no longer of service no matter how much I am at ease with them.

All modes of personal-vital presence are thus not equally essential to the incarnation of my unique spiritual life. This insight should not make me lose sight of the fact that commitment to my spiritual identity in Christ must be incarnated in some way in daily life. Otherwise my spiritual identity would lose its density; it would evaporate into the thin air of imagination and abstraction.

Life Call and Particular Commitments

Life call refers to the mystery of an all-embracing divine call; a call that covers the unique being of my whole life in all its aspects; a call that enables me to surpass as spirit self each finite temporal and concrete situation in which I find myself here and now; a call that articulates itself during my life in many specific calls.

The life call of Father Damien, for example, was articulated by the specific call to give himself, out of love for God, to abandoned and suffering people. This call kept articulating itself in all kinds of callings to service of the poor and downtrodden in Hawaii until it found its final specification in the call to dedicate himself to the lepers of Molokai.

My life call is thus not the same as other calls. It is

related to, but not identical with, the call to a career, trade, or profession in which, to a considerable extent, a person lives out his life call. For example, the professional call of John Kennedy to be a politician and statesman was in tune with, but not totally identical with, his life call. The presidency was a special profession in which he incarnated as well as he could his life call.

Neither is the life call identical with the call to the most basic situations in which people realize it, namely, the call to a definite lasting life form such as marriage, celibate life in the world, or religious life.

Life call is different too from the call to a changeable life style in which a person lives out either his spiritual identity or the basic life form or profession in which he realizes this identity. The life call is still related to those other calls, for it implies that a person in many cases may realize his unique calling to an extent in and through a fundamental life form and by means of one or more careers, trades, or professions that are in tune with his unique life call.

For example, it seems that the main articulation of the life call of Joan of Arc was to liberate her fatherland. She realized her call within the life style of being a prayerful, gentle, courageous person. She chose the basic life form of celibacy in the world. As a celibate in the world, she took on the task of court counselor and the profession of army commander. We can readily see how her life call is related to all these other articulations. She found out that, because of the person she was, she could live out her life call best in celibate freedom, in the situation of court counselor and army commander, in the life style of prayerfulness, courage, and gentleness.

Commitments in Tune with My Call

Commitment and consecration to my life call are not simply a question of constancy. "To keep going" in and by itself does not represent a full living of my commitment. Committed living is not merely a "bearing with"—a spartan "sticking it out." Such an attitude would paralyze my spiritual life.

Commitment and consecration mean being present to my task with my full personality. I must find myself again and again before God in examination of my life, in liturgy, prayer, recollection, spiritual reading. Out of that inspiration, I try to be uniquely present to what I am doing—to the car I drive, the cake I bake, the children I teach. If I see God in my task, I can be all there.

It is difficult to say what kinds of commitments are right for a specific person. It all depends on one's unique life call. During my lifetime, I incarnate my commitment to the life call in many particular commitments. What may be right for me may be wrong for my neighbor and vice versa. How do I know if my particular commitments are in tune with my call?

One criterion could be a certain consistency. If God has a unified plan for my life, it might be possible to discover some of this unity at least in retrospect. This consistency, however, is by no means an absolute criterion. God's secret plan for my life may entail so many changes and interruptions that my life looks splintered, split up, and chaotic from the human point of view.

Recall the life stories of displaced persons sent from prison camp to prison camp and after the war from country to country and job to job, losing en route members of their family. God nonetheless had a plan for them too. The mystery of the hidden consistency of the divine project in their lives may only be seen with the eyes of faith.

A sinner or neurotic person may show a remarkable consistency in the way in which he has built his life around an ambition that dominates him or around a neurotic life project. Therefore, the criterion of consistency cannot be final in and by itself; it has to be complemented by other criteria. The experience of prayer is one of these, the experience of inner peace another.

I can also ask myself if my concrete commitments foster or harm my physical and psychic health. Furthermore, I can consult others, asking them to help me to see better what I should do. And, of course, I must always ask myself if my options are in tune with Church Doctrine and with the wisdom of Christian tradition, Scripture, and spiritual masters as read by the Church.

If I am faithful to these signs, I may still make mistakes and fail but in the long run I may discover a certain continuous line in my life which will reveal to me the ways in which my commitments should be incarnated. Gradually my life becomes a total "yes" to God.

Concrete Incarnations of My Eternal Call

Spiritual life is thus not merely the discovery and growth of my spiritual identity; it implies the incarnation of that eternal call in all modes and acts of living. Spiritual life is the gradual spiritualization of the whole me.

Certain modes of incarnation of my life call in daily life are fundamental. This means that they provide the ground for a variety of other modes and acts. Each

fundamental mode of spiritualization orients the many
modes and acts it gives rise to. Let us first describe in
general these basic ways of being in the world that should
be spiritualized. After this description, we shall give special
attention to each one of these specific expressions of our
spiritual identity. Even this special treatment of each
fundamental mode of incarnation will be limited; it will
leave many questions open. The scope of this book
prevents us from dealing extensively with all such questions. A later book on our spiritual self-theory will deal at
large with many of these matters.

First of all, we should have clearly in mind the
fundamental modes of incarnation of our spiritual identity. Therefore, we should distinguish the following:

1.   Life call and life style, uncongenial and con-
      genial;
2.   Life form and vocational style;
3.   Profession and professional style.

Before describing these various modes in general, we
would like to illustrate them in two lives, namely, the life
of Thérèse of Lisieux and the life of President Lincoln.
One articulation of the life call of the Little Flower seems
to have been to live out and communicate to people the
little way of childlike love and surrender to God. The
congenial life style in which she expressed this life call was
a consistent totality of attitudes, acts, and attentions that
expressed continuously in small inner and outer acts loving
surrender to God in total trust, no matter the inner or
outer situation she found herself in. Prior to living her life
style in this way—a way that was congenial with her life
call—she lived it at least partly in an uncongenial manner.
This uncongenial life style entailed a somewhat childish
and emotional fixation on her family, especially on her

sister Pauline. This fixation led to a nervous breakdown when Pauline left for the convent and Thérèse had to face children and teachers in the school of the Benedictine Sisters, who did not extend to her the same warmth that Pauline had shown.

The life form in which Thérèse chose to live out her life call was the contemplative religious life in the Community of Carmel. The vocational style in which she lived out this call was a simple, inconspicuous, unsophisticated style of faithfulness to numerous small occasions offered by religious life in which she could express her love for God and mortify herself. Her vocational style was obviously different from the style in which Teresa of Avila lived out the same vocational life form.

In regard to profession or official task, Thérèse was appointed to a position of formation. Her professional style in fulfilling this function was simple and unassuming. She also brought this function in tune with her life call by using it to communicate to the novices the little way of childlike presence to God. She showed them how to be faithful to the small opportunities continuously presented by daily life to express and deepen one's love of God.

Let us now trace the modes of incarnation in the life of President Lincoln. His call seems to have been to live an exemplary life of effective concern for equality of justice among men. The congenial life style in which he began to incarnate this concern was that of thoughtful sensitivity to any discriminating injustice done to people. His congenial life style also implied a consistent and increasing ease of expressing indignation about such injustice. Then, too, he developed diplomatic ways of behavior to counteract such discrimination. The uncongenial aspect of his life style presented itself as an at times anxious ambitiousness, coupled with a feeling of insecurity that made him less than totally fair with his political opponents.

The life form Lincoln chose was marriage. The style in which he lived out this vocation to marriage was an attempt not to do injustice to his wife and children. He bent over backwards to humor his wife who was not the most easy woman to live with. At the same time he tried to prevent his life form of marriage from interfering with the incarnation of his life call within the political profession. The professions in which he tried to realize his striving for equal justice were those of lawyer, politician, statesman, and president. In all these professions, he grew in faithfulness to his life call. He came to stand more and more for justice for all.

The style in which he lived out his profession was different from that in which other presidents and statesmen had lived theirs. He was unusually considerate of people who felt discriminated against. He would spend time with a simple soldier who came to him with his complaints; he received into his home many downtrodden people who expressed the faith that he could help them.

Having illustrated these fundamental modes of incarnation in two different lives, we can now make some general reflections on them. We shall then deal with the same modes in more detail.

Fundamental Life Style

The first way in which we incarnate our drives and aspirations is in a fundamental life style. We try to be in the world in a certain way of reaction and response. This constellation of reactions and responses has a double aim.

One of its purposes is to adapt us to our environment so that we may survive and be as effective as possible in our daily interaction with people, events, and things. Another purpose is that of the expression of selfhood, the specific incarnation of who I am.

In the well integrated person these two purposes—situational effectiveness and self-expression—are increasingly in harmony. The harmonious person learns to incarnate himself in the world in a manner which, while being effective in some measure, does not betray what he basically is. His effective style is at the same time an expression of his deepest self.

When my life style is spiritualized, its main function becomes the full expression and effective incarnation in the world of my spiritual identity or life call. This orientation will gradually permeate and spiritualize all modes and acts that make up my basic style of moving, acting, responding, feeling, imagining, and perceiving. The life style is fundamental precisely in that it touches upon all modes of my inner and outer behavior. It is the primary vehicle of incarnation.

Life Form

The next mode of spiritualization is the life form I feel called to live. The three most fundamental life forms are the married life, the celibate life in priesthood or religious community, and the celibate life in the world. It is not difficult to see that the fundamental life form affects deeply my possibilities of living out my life call. My personal life is so interwoven with my life form that I cannot spiritualize myself if I don't see and live my life form as an expression of my life call. This life form could also be called vocational life form. In Catholic tradition, the word vocation is often used to indicate the calling to a life form.

Catholic tradition speaks, for example, of a vocation to the religious life or married life and is less inclined to speak about a vocation to a job. Of course, a job is a vocation too, but not in the same sense as one's life form is a vocation. We use the words "vocation" and "vocational" in the traditional Catholic sense. One reason for our usage is that we can speak then about the vocational style in which this life form can be lived out. We prefer to use the expression "vocational style" to distinguish it more clearly from fundamental life style.

Vocational and Professional Life Style

The life form can be lived out in a variety of vocational styles. Such styles are changeable and indeed do change in various cultures and cultural periods. My actual vocational style should ideally be an harmonious integration of my vocational style with my fundamental life style.

Another mode of spiritualization can be found in my profession, in the task in which I am involved often daily. Not all tasks have the same influence on my personality. In some cases, the task is really a life task because it is bound up with the person's make-up. A person like Mozart could probably not have been anything else but a composer without destroying himself. For some people teaching or writing is an occupation they do well, but they would be able to do other things as well. It would not harm the expression of their identity in the least if they would be involved in other occupations quite different from teaching or writing. Some people, however, *are* teachers and writers.

Finally, the profession or task in which my identity is expressed gives rise to a professional style. This style should be spiritualized in such a way that it becomes a vehicle of spiritual self-presence.

In the harmoniously spiritual person, we find an integration of fundamental, vocational, and professional styles. For example, a person like Thomas Aquinas seems to have expressed beautifully in his writing, teaching, and interacting with others the style of his spiritual identity and holiness, of his vocation as a priest and friar, and of his profession as a scholar and university professor. As a professor, his professional style lived in faithfulness to God's calling was different from that of a friar working as an assistant in a country parish. The latter, however, is faithful to his own professional style, to his own calling by the Eternal Logos. Both have in common certain aspects of the vocational style of being priests and friars. In regard to their fundamental life styles, they would be different again. For, as we have seen, the fundamental life style is the first and most unique expression of one's spiritual identity.

Another example of an integration of life styles if found in Dag Hammarskjöld's spiritual life. The spiritualization of Dag Hammarskjöld's personality implied a growing integration of a fundamental style of a celibate career life in the world, and a professional style of the accomplished statesman. We know from his diary *Markings*, and from communications of his friends, that toward the end of his life his spiritual self-expression had gained in unity. In his final days his whole style of statesmanship became an expression of his mystical union with the Lord and of his celibate life style as an expression of the same spiritual identity.

Following these general reflections on the various modes of incarnation, let us now look at each one of them in more detail.

Initial Fundamental Life Style as Uncongenial

The fundamental life style is relatively lasting; it is at the core of all other styles of the person. Because it is relatively lasting, it is also known as a person's character.

Initially, this life style is not in tune with the deepest spiritual identity of the person. It tends to be anxiety motivated, repressive, closed, self-deceptive, and defensive. It is dominated by pride and as yet incongruous with the divine call to unique selfhood; it is a style of unconscious anxious and defensive reactions to the environment. This defensive life style will never be totally eradicated; it tends to reappear under stress. Therefore, this initially formed life style has to be gradually transformed into a congenial style that is open to the call of my spiritual identity.

There is in us always a polarity between our initial uncongenial and our later congenial life style. One reason why this first life style is not tuned in thoughtfully to my spiritual identity is the simple fact that as a child I cannot as yet be thoughtful. Neither can I fall back like the animal on programmed instinctive reaction patterns. I am compelled to utilize instead a social reactive pattern, that is, an automatic set of social reactions, borrowed blindly from others, that forms the hard core of my emergent self, what we are calling our initial fundamental life style.

The initial style is not only defective as an expression of spiritual identity; it is also a mode of closure to the spirit. To understand this closure, we should realize that the spirit is dormant in the child, but not totally. Spirit is the human ability to be open to all that is, to the whole that transcends all incidental and isolated appearances of people, events, and things. A primitive opening up happens in the child, but this glimpse of the unknown evokes an initial experience of powerlessness and helplessness.

As the infant grows, he feels driven by the call of his uniqueness to leave the safe nook of parental protection. Once again the great unknown that looms beyond mother and father frightens him. In defense against this first taste of spiritual anxiety, the child begins to develop an initial life style or "character armor" that helps him to escape the call of the spirit.

This call evokes in him a feeling of lostness, impotence, and vulnerability. Hence the protective life style is built initially as a system of defenses against the implicit call of the spirit. Because the system is imperfect in the beginning, the repressed or refused anxiety keeps seeping through. It comes out in the dreams of children, in their terror of being alone in the vast darkness that seems to absorb them, in their need for hair-raising fairy tales, replete with witches and malicious animals. They need the concreteness of the horror story to focus their free floating anxiety on some object. To a degree, children can manage their fear of what is known concretely better than their spiritual anxiety about the unmanageable transcendent vastness to which the spirit opens them.

Anxiety of the Spirit

All children experience spiritual anxiety. Some of them are better able to cope with it than others. Those who cope better may not have experienced overly imposing or inconsistent parents whose unpredictable behavior made daily life even more threatening. Such children were never sure if they would receive loving acceptance, rejection, or indifference. Some children can cope better because they are less sensitive than other children. Others again are more successful in building up an effective defensive system; they have less cracks in their armor. Less spiritual anxiety is allowed to seep through. As a result they show less or no neurotic traits.

Some degree of defensive life style seems to be necessary in early childhood. The child cannot as yet cope spiritually with the vastness that transcends himself and all people, events, and things. He is not yet able to know about God, His divine love and generosity, about the saving redemption of Christ. Without this knowledge and experience, it is difficult to come to terms with the spiritual anxiety inspired by the opening up of the human spirit to the beyond. Without this armor to protect him, the child would be torn to pieces by his anxiety.

There are elements of experience and right reactions within this initial life style that can be integrated in a later spiritually open, flexible, and relaxed life style. The whole development of the spiritual life is in some measure a process of coping with this initial character armor.

Even religion can be understood and used as a defense against the anxiety of the spirit. Initially, the child does not know the spiritual meaning of religion. He is willing to use anything to overcome his feelings of impotence, loneliness, lostness, and vulnerability. Religion seems to provide magic means to shut out the anxiety evoked by spiritual awareness. Of course, the child does not consciously grasp the meaning of religion. Growing up, he simply takes on the externals of religion as practiced in the family. Without his being able to reflect upon it, these externals may be fitted unconsciously into his overall system of coping with anxiety.

Process of Purification

Growth in the spiritual life involves a lifelong purification of the defensive and magical ways in which we began to live religion as children. The whole spiritual life is a story of dying to the old style of life and being reborn with Christ to a new one in tune with our eternal calling.

In this process of spiritual growth I begin with an effort to purify myself from all the things that are not me, that are not my true and unique calling. According to the measure and depth of this purification process, I enter the way of illumination. My whole emergent self begins to be illumined by my spirit, which in turn is illumined by the Holy Spirit. Once I have been purified in my whole person and illumined by my unique identity in Christ, I may enter the way of union. My purified and illumined self begins to live a life style that is increasingly congenial with the divine call. My life is no longer a terrified flight from the transcendent unknown, from the overwhelming Presence that makes me aware of my vulnerability. Life now invites me to become at one with the divine plan of the universe, with the presence of the Divine Will in all that is, with the divine life of Father, Son and Spirit.

The deepest union with God demands the deepest understanding of and faithfulness to my eternal call. Such knowledge and loyalty calls for a final purification so deep that only God can effect it in the soul. God Himself must help me to experience how lost, lonely, and vulnerable I still am in spite of all the purification I have gone through. This ultimate purification by God can be a terrifying experience. The mystical writers compare it to a dark night. In these dark nights of the soul, the last remnants of the initial defensive life style are obliterated.

Living Creatively My Spiritual Identity

We have spoken mainly so far about the initiation of the defensive self-project in the child. This project receives a more pronounced development later in life. If I do not travel the redeeming path of the spiritual life, I remain unconsciously terrified by the immense beyond. My refused tending-of-the-spirit towards the whole and Holy gives rise to totalizing tendencies on the personal level of life. Without spirituality, I may easily become the victim of my own private idolatry, my own project of self-redemption, of release from repressed spiritual anxieties and guilt. The spiritless religion I began with as a child becomes like an opiate; it dulls and dampens any possibility for true religious experience.

Spiritless religion is often at the heart of the defensive self-project or life style. Religion becomes an elaborate magical and protective system of countless do's and don'ts. The most perfectionistic follower of a religion may be the farthest away from its spiritual meaning.

One of the central themes of the Gospel deals with the tension between law abiding religiousness, abused as a defensive measure, and religion as a vehicle of spiritual openness generating a flexible, graced, and spiritually congenial life style.

Spiritless Religion

Take, for example, the Gospel story about the tax collector and the Pharisee. The Pharisee went to the temple to pray as a man who had overcome all the anxiety and guilt every man is faced with when approaching the Eternal. His religion was the heart of his defense against his anxiety of spirit. He enumerates in his prayer the different facets of this defense: his fasting, his paying of tithes, his scrupulous following of every detail of the law. He was a man of religion, but not a man of the spirit.

The tax collector, however, a public sinner, was on the road towards the life of the spirit. He allowed the anxiety and guilt of the spirit to touch his awareness. At the same time this experience made him cry out for forgiveness, mercy, and redemption. His surrender to divine love and forgiveness enabled him to face the guilt and anxiety that always accompany entrance into the life of the spirit. The Lord concludes this story by telling us that only the man who allowed anxiety and guilt of the spirit to enter into his awareness and cried out for mercy went home justified.

This theme of the spiritless, defensive style of religion as distinct from the spiritualized, open style returns time after time in the Gospel. The spiritualization of religion is one of the main messages we find there. Christianity offers, among other things, the chance to awaken ourselves to the awareness of our initially spiritless and defensive religious life style and the invitation to a spiritualized style of true religious presence.

Each of us has elements in his character that are represented symbolically by the Pharisee, for each of us has at least some facets of a defensive, spiritless religious life style. We can all profit, therefore, from a spiritual master who helps us dig up the defensive elements we have repressed. This fact of our defensive make-up may also explain why people who want to enter religious life need a novitiate with a well prepared director or directress who can help them discern the unauthentic aspect of their fundamental religious life style so that they may move toward a more congenial expression.

Congenial Life Style

Congenial means literally compatible with what I have been born with. I have been born with a hidden spiritual orientation. To discover this orientation and to bring all of my life in tune with it is a lifelong task. The true incarnation of my spiritual identity is an opening into a congenial or congruent life style. This congenial style comes in some ways always after the initial, defensive life style has begun to be purified. Even when grace enables us to develop a congenial spiritual style of life, the initial style can take over again, especially when we are under stress. Therefore, we have to keep praying, "Lead us not into temptation."

The congenial life style is relatively stable. This style participates in the unfolding of the person in the light of his spiritual openness. Therefore, the congenial life style is marked also by a certain flexibility and obedient accommodation. Its adaptiveness to the intimations of the spirit does not mean that this style is totally fluent; it has a certain steadiness, so to speak, a flexible stability.

The congenial life style is not repressive or refusing as is the defensive. Instead of repression, it uses a process of suspension in regard to those things in life that are incompatible with one's life call. For example, a married man is not supposed to date other girls. If he is a spiritual man, he does not have to repress the awareness that it would be attractive to date other girls and that he feels tempted to do so. He does not repress, deny, or belittle such incompatible possibilities of life. Rather, in light of the spirit, he wisely suspends the living out of possibilities that are incompatible with the present incarnation of his life call. He puts these incompatible areas in parentheses, as it were. He realizes that they are not viable for him at this moment of his life.

The congenial life style is growth motivated; it prompts me to unfold myself more and more in full openness to the call of God. Obviously this action is different from that of the defensive life style, motivated as it was by the need to escape the anxiety evoked by a first opening of the spirit.

All of us are suffering in some way from a mysterious break between ourselves and the universe, ourselves and the Divine. Spiritual life is an attempt to overcome this split and, over a lifetime, to regain union with all that is, with the Divine. This union is difficult to attain, and impossible on my own efforts alone, as long as I continue to encapsulate myself in my own small universe as a defense against the terror evoked by awareness of the transcendent. The congenial life style helps me to ready myself for union with the Divine, a gift of Himself God may give me in His own good time.

A Call to Live Creatively a Stable Life Form

As we have seen, I remain faithful to my life call within a stable life form. Most of us, sooner or later, choose a basic situation—celibate life in community, married life, or celibate life in the world—in which to realize our unique life call. Spiritually speaking, we do not commit ourselves to a basic situation as such but within the situation to God.

For example, I may commit myself to God within the basic situation of married life. If my wife dies, I am still committed to God; hopefully I have grown toward intimacy with Him in and through my married life. By committing myself to God within such a basic situation, I promise Him that I will heed my unique calling within that situation, but I never commit myself to a situation as such.

My life call is, therefore, not identical with my life form; the latter is only one basic way in which my life call can be lived out and through which my spiritual identity is expressed.

Life call is usually expressed more fundamentally in a life form than in a career, trade, or profession. Life form is like a basic situation, a platform from which I operate. I may change the style in which I live the life form; I may change my career; but I usually remain in the same basic life situation. In my life call from all eternity is included the special life form I am called to, but the two are not identical.

My spiritual life may become stale if I believe that the call to a life form is identical with the fullness of my life call itself. I may feel that all I have to do is to be externally observant and make no attempt to personalize and spiritualize the living of my chosen vocation. I may feel I am a good religious, spouse, or celibate person in the world if I simply follow all the rules externally.

I can live my basic life situation like a robot, or I can live it creatively. I can learn to approach all matters connected with my basic life situation in light of the Spirit. Marriage, religious life, or celibate career in the world then turns into a spiritually creative married, religious, or celibate life. Any vocation in this life is ultimately a call to live creatively and uniquely my deepest spiritual identity since it encompasses and permeates all of these vocational callings.

Responding to My Life Call in Commitment to a Life Form

To find the life form that best expresses my unique spiritual identity, I may have to go through trials and errors. Before I commit myself to a basic and lasting life situation, I have to ask if this situation is really the best for the fulfillment of my eternal calling. Hence, the cultural custom of dating and of engagement before people decide to marry and the pre-entrance program, postulancy and novitiate before candidates take the vows is quite understandable. The same is true for the priesthood; a long seminary preparation, interspersed with moments of practice in settings in which priests function, helps the candidate to clarify for himself whether or not this kind of functioning is best for him.

The necessity of wise questioning can lead to a crisis of commitment. All commitment evokes the fear of committing a lifelong mistake. Because of this fear, I may get stuck in an excessively prolonged period of trial and error. However, the impulsive attempt to end the period of trial prematurely by a sudden willful decision is worse. Both excessive playing around and impulsive decision making may imply unfaithfulness to my unique life call.

Flight from Decision for a Life Form

Another danger implied in the fearful flight from decision is the regression to earlier stages in life. I begin to play the child role again. In adolescence, some anxious young people never begin to make up their own mind in regard to personally opting for a lasting life form. Instead they regress and become like children again. For example, they blindly imitate movie heroes or members of their gang as children imitate their parents. Their decision regarding a life form, say that of marriage with this or that type of girl, is more dictated by what seems to be "in" at the moment than by an insight into what would be best for them personally and uniquely.

Another way out of a definite commitment is escape in drugs and other distractions from the decision to be made, such as popular movements, social enthusiasm, charismatic fascination, faceless crowds, collectivities, or following the rule without thought of inner life. There are all kinds of escapes that make the initial finding of my unique inner self before God difficult, if not impossible.

Fear of the Unknown

A great danger is the temptation to refuse to make a choice out of fear. All of us fear the unknown, the "non-being" involved in committing oneself to the unknown future in priesthood, marriage, or celibate life in the world. Because commitment always entails a jumping into non-being, it evokes anxiety. We all tend to worry about the unforeseeable.

The danger is not so much that we fear, but that we make fear of the unknown—implied in lasting life decisions—the center of our lives. Many make fear of the unknown in any life decision central and so make no decision. They stay perpetual adolescents. However, choosing fear as the center of my life also implies that I have made a decision, indeed the worst possible one, the decision not to become a real person by means of commitment.

Even a person who does not marry or opt for the celibate religious life should not allow himself simply to drift into a celibate career life in the world. He must overcome his fear and eventually make a decision. Sooner or later he should opt for this celibate life form on basis of mature reflection on his life call, his personal situation, and the pleasant and unpleasant aspects the future of this life form—like every other—may have in store.

A person, for example, may devote his whole life to science. That devotion entails a certain life form. He may not marry because he would not have sufficient time to devote to his family. So he makes a decision; he sees his unique spiritual self as called by God to dedicate his life to science within the single life form. He may fear loneliness in his old age. Yet, he, as all of us, must overcome anxieties and take risks to come to full humanization.

Vocational Style

The life form is lived in a flexible vocational style. This changeable vocational style, however, should remain in tune with the life form and with the congenial life style at the heart of the emergent self of the spiritual person. It is important to keep in mind the distinction between vocational form and vocational style. Sometimes the words life style and life form are used interchangeably. This may lead to confusion. The vocational style in which we live our life form may change, but the basic form of life itself cannot change without ceasing to be that form. Marriage can be more open in style, but it has to maintain the same basic form—ideally a lifetime commitment of two persons to one another and to their children. The same is true of religious life. There are certain essentials to this form, but different styles in which these essentials can be lived out.

Task Calling

Each life is, so to speak, a promise, for in each life the Sacred has planted certain possibilities to do certain things well. Some are called to sweep floors, others to teach, still others to be musicians, scholars, mothers. Each contributes somehow to the culture. I never know totally how I am called to contribute. I only gradually discover my calling and what I can do best. My life is thus a promise that I can uniquely participate in some dimension of mankind's Divine Call to unfold itself before God.

My call, in other words, is a call within a call. From all eternity the Divine Word willed our little planet within this universe. The same Eternal God, in and through the Divine Word, calls persons to be more than blind nature, he calls them to unfold mankind and world in creative ways beyond the givenness of nature. We call this unfolding "culture."

Culture can refer to putting diapers on crying babies; it can mean inventing agricultural methods, cleaning, cooking, making music. The simplest activity, beyond mere given nature, is culture; culture is meant to be a participation in the great call of the Divine, beckoning mankind out of and beyond mere given nature.

Within this all encompassing Divine Call, each of us is called to contribute something and to grow by our contribution, whether we serve as cook, dishwasher, teacher, formation director, or whatever. We are called to do something in the totality of the divine calling forth of mankind and world. In this sense we can say we are uniquely called within a call.

In the ideal case, I would realize my unique calling to an extent in and through one or more careers, trades, or professions that are in tune with my spiritual identity. My task is not the only opportunity in which I can realize my life call, but, if possible, my choice of task should take into account my life call. The latter far transcends and encompasses any task. I should thus not be downhearted if life compels me to be involved in an enterprise not to my taste.

Faithfulness to the Life Call

Some people enter married, religious, or the celibate life in the world and have not yet grown sufficiently in the spirit to bear with the fact that they may be unable to find a task that perfectly suits them. They become despondent, frustrated, and begin to live lives of quiet desperation.

Usually celibate people are more able to do the work they like, even if it involves less income, for they are not responsible for a family of their own. Many married people have to make a living in jobs they do not like or deserve, from the viewpoint of their talents. They have to feed and educate their children and maintain a family home. A decently paying occupation is necessary for the fulfillment of these family duties even if the task does not fit their justified ambitions and unique potentialities. They should realize that faithfulness to the life call implies for them first of all faithfulness to their marriage and their children.

The call to marriage and its many complex obligations may be more basic for a specific person than the call to a special task or career. In the case of a job they do not like, they should remember that they incarnate their life call and spiritual identity not only in their work but also in their total dedication to wife or husband and children. They can still be faithful to their life call in their task by trying to make the best of their occupation in spite of the reluctance they feel for this work, mindful that this occupation too is an articulation of God's will for them in this concrete inescapable life situation. They can understand the task, moreover, as also a means to fulfill their more basic call to family life.

Many tasks are in tune with our abilities and basic calling and still we may not like them. We may not always find interesting what we can do well, even the countless tasks in which we can realize to some extent our personality. We must realize it is not so important whether we like an occupation; we should be grateful already when the task is not totally at odds with our spiritual, personal, and vital make-up.

All our life, after we have found in some measure our spiritual identity, we have to keep renewing and deepening our loyalty to the call. There is always the danger that we will get lost in our activities—in school, babies, science, career, spouse, family. We can get so involved that we forget that all activity should be an inspirited realization of our spiritual call.

Professional Style

Just as the fundamental life form can be lived in many styles, so too certain tasks give rise to a special style. Especially the professions tend to evoke a certain style in their practitioners. Judges have a style of life that differs from that of mechanics. Farmers act and behave differently than university professors. Undertakers differ from bartenders. Yet not all judges, farmers, professors, undertakers, and bartenders behave exactly in the same way as their colleagues. Various professional styles seem to be possible within one and the same profession. I should choose the professional style most in tune with my fundamental and vocational style as lived in the light of my life call and unique identity.

The more my spiritual life becomes incarnated and integrated the more I will reach a unity of life style that expresses personally, vocationally, and professionally the person I have been called to be from eternity.

VII

INTROSPECTION AND
TRANSCENDENT SELF-PRESENCE

In the former chapter on the discovery and incarnation of one's spiritual identity, it was mentioned that this could not happen by mere introspection but primarily by transcendent self-presence. In this chapter we will highlight the role of transcendent self-presence in the spiritual life.

Two Forms of Reflection

While developing a theory of man's spiritual unfolding, I discovered the importance of a right balance between two forms of reflection, one being introspective, the other transcendent.

Let us say I suddenly lost a dear person; a husband, wife, parent, friend passed away. I feel not only immensely sad but guilty. I feel ashamed about the times I could have been more pleasant for the deceased but was not. I reproach myself for visits I neglected, letters I did not write, kind words that were never spoken. I keep asking myself why I did not do what could have been done easily, why I failed this dear person so badly during his life. I try to recall all of the lost opportunities in which I could have been of help and I was not. I ask myself over and over again how I could have been so negligent. I feel compelled to explore my past. Was it perhaps the same when I was a younger person? Does my lack of interest in others go back to things that happened at home when I was a little child? Am I as thoughtless with my other friends who are still alive? How can I as fast as possible remedy my lack of concern, my absorption in myself? I begin frantically to analyze every detail of my dealings with others.

This whole process could be described as one of introspective reflection, of looking anxiously into myself, of being present to myself in an aggressive attempt to figure everything out, to dig up the roots of my failure, to trace it back to the past, to analyze piecemeal my thoughts, feelings, deeds, and expressions.

I can also be present to myself, my guilt and failure in a different way. Yes, my friend passed away. I feel guilt and shame about the many times I failed him. I put myself totally before the Divine Majesty with my sadness, guilt, shame, and failure. My main attention is not directed towards my feelings but toward the Divine Presence. I adore His Holy Will that took my friend. Prayerfully I renew my faith that His love lets all things work out for the best. My failure may have helped my friend to become aware of the limitations of friendship in this passing world. I humble myself before God who grants me the purifying awareness of how sinful and self-centered I really am. My inner humiliation, accepted in peaceful surrender, creates more room in me to be filled with the Eternal Presence. I renew my faith in His redemptive love. With a contrite heart, I profess to Him my guilt, put myself in His hands, experience His constant mercy. I rekindle my hope that He will make everything right in the end, that He will give my friend in eternity what I could never give him during his life. I grow in a new love for God and man, feeling more at home than ever with a suffering and redeemed humanity whose guilt, failure, and need for salvation I compassionately share. Relaxed and peaceful, I allow now—against the background of eternal mercy—my failures of past and present to emerge in my awareness. In light of His compassionate love, I ponder quietly possible ways to gradually improve my life insofar as it pleases Him to give me the grace to better my predicament. This second gentle way of self-presence, I call transcendent reflection.

Introspective reflection tends to be analytical and aggressive; transcendent reflection tends to be integrated and gentle. In introspective reflection, we isolate the "reflected upon," such as guilt and shame, from the larger backdrop of reality. We not only cut the "reflected upon" off from the larger whole to which it pertains; we also cut it up in its inner wholeness. In our first example, we did not put our failure in the perspective of God's all encompassing providence and forgiveness; we engaged in a fragmenting analysis of every aspect of our feeling and failure.

Introspective reflection implies a focusing process in which the background is either blurred or lost. Both inwardly and outwardly, it is divided. It purposely loses sight of the totality and goes at its object aggressively. How aggressively we tried in our first example to force insight by digging up all we could recall of the past. This aggressiveness of thought is beneficial in that it helps to make us more strict and precise. While this approach is excellent for our necessary analytical pursuits, it is destructive for any kind of transcendent reflection that underlies our awareness of spiritual at-oneness. In our first example, we were isolated in our guilt and shame about the negligence of our friend during his life; we felt cut off from God and man.

What I term transcendent reflection is the opposite of

introspective. In it, we may reflect upon ourselves, others, and nature to become one with a Divine Source, mysteriously united in an Eternal Origin. We reflect meditatively upon the whole of creation, its enormity and simplicity, out of which we all emerge. In our second example, we never left the all pervading presence of the merciful God, His loving and all encompassing Providence and His unfolding creation; the ultimate meaning of our shame, guilt, and failure was related to this Divine Origin from whom we all emerge.

This reflection is not divisive but unitive. It is transcendent. It makes whole; it attunes us to a mysterious totality that already is; it is a healing reflection. Far from being dissective and aggressive, it is meditative and gentle, a gentle preservation of all things as given and as tenderly held in the splendor of a Divine Presence. It is a source of spiritual living. Whenever we reflect upon ourselves, upon our own inner life meditatively, I call such reflection transcendent self-presence.

It might be helpful to note here that every person is engaged in some kind of spontaneous reflection. It is a natural thing for us to keep some kind of mental journal about the things we are experiencing. To be human is to live somewhat reflectively, either introspectively and analytically or meditatively and unitively, or by means of both.

Our culture sets great store by utility, efficiency, success. It fosters aggressive analytical reflection which helps build science, technique, and efficient organization. Because we are so efficiency minded, we even examine ourselves in an aggressive analytical way when we engage in introspection. But one cannot rest in this predilection for the analytical. It is only one side of the story.

Exclusive introspection affects badly not only our spiritual but also our psychological and bodily health. Mere introspection without let up makes us lose touch with reality; it leads to self-centered isolation; it enslaves us to self-preoccupation and to the anxious urge to reach at once an unrealistic ideal of self-perfection.

Because transcendent self-presence is a condition for the emergence of the life of the spirit, it is presupposed by any authentic way of spirituality; it is therefore one of the essential topics to be reflected upon in fundamental spirituality.

Transcendent self-presence is called transcendent because it enables us to transcend, that is, to go beyond, the practical and sentimental meanings things may have for us in terms of our own private needs, ambitions, drives, and expectations. Transcendent self-presence pushes us beyond the limited here and now meanings of our own particular problems, childhood traumas, sensitivities, faults, and projects. In and beyond all of these, it integrates our lives contextually, that is, it helps us live in the context of the whole of reality, of which we are part, and with its divine all-pervading source. We begin to see ourselves in the loving and redeeming perspective of Divine Presence.

In transcendent self-presence, we do not center on ourselves as isolated persons facing the task of overcoming isolated problems and projects; neither do we tighten our hearts to scrutinize our own feelings or take stock of our progress. In both cases we lose the fruit of transcendent self-presence. We become disquieted instead of deepening ourselves in an atmosphere of equanimity. We may end up with a self-centered emotional piety instead of ending up in Him, the Eternal Truth of our lives.

Transcendent self-presence sees us not as isolated but as sustained and centered in the light of Divine Presence. A gentle avoidance of any return to ourselves as outside the Divine Light is an essential condition for transcendent self-presence.

Each kind of reflective presence to ourselves—introspective or transcendent—has its own purpose, time, and place. Our vision of ourselves as interwoven with the whole of reality should be primary, the introspective view secondary. Both views remain always necessary; one cannot take the place of the other.

Historical Development of Introspectionism

Prolonged study has led me to the insight that the art and discipline of spiritual self-presence has been neglected increasingly in our Western culture. An overemphasis on introspective attitudes has seriously hindered the spiritual growth of Western man. This did not augur well either for his psychosomatic welfare or his daily efficiency.

Traces of the art of transcendent self-presence can be found in ancient philosophies, in the Bible, the Church Fathers, early monastic writers, later spiritual masters, as well as in the pre-Christian spiritualities of the Far East. Studying these traces in light of my thought on the two types of reflection, I felt only recently able to articulate more explicitly this aspect of my theory.

Transcendent self-presence is not a concentration on ourselves or anything in ourselves as isolated from the rest of reality. It makes us look upon ourselves in a less strained way, seeing ourselves and all the things that touch us against the broader horizon of the mystery of a Presence that embraces all of reality. Transcendent self-presence goes beyond a "What-is-in-it-for-me" attitude; "How-can-I-use-it; What-can-I-do-with-it." In a contextual dwelling on our experience, we bind all the meanings of our life, its victories and failures, with the providential pattern of the universe, with the experienced or believed order of things of which we feel ourselves a part. We see ourselves as illumined by the light of the Divine, as interwoven with the mysterious rhythms of cosmos and world, of culture and history, as bathed in a Divine Presence that permeates all and is the loving origin of each one of us and our daily world. By the same token, we begin to experience the ordinary everyday grind as co-originating constantly with us within the successive life situations we have been called to cope with graciously.

At a certain period in the history of Western man, somewhere between the 15th and 17th centuries, the interest in spirituality was gradually replaced by other preoccupations. Many people, of course, kept longing after the spiritual life, but society as a whole lost touch with spirituality as a vital concern. The rise of the Renaissance, with the growing emphasis on science and technology, made the knowledge and perfection of this world the focus of attention. The medieval view of reality collapsed. A humanistic view took over. The living awareness of the sacred dimension of reality was lost. Man no longer experienced his interwovenness with his fellow men, with nature, history, and the cosmos as constantly originating from the Divine Presence. His self-in-isolation, facing a competitive society, became the nucleus of his personal concern. This heightened fascination with his own world, and his ego at the center of it, led him to concentrate excessively on what happened in his isolated interiority. He became obsessed with the need for ethical and psychological self-realization. He became more enthralled with self-perfection than with intimacy with the Sacred. For many, this development meant the neglect of an experiential spiritual life, no matter how well they actualized themselves ethically or psychologically as members of different churches or humanistic organizations.

Toward the end of the 19th Century, the scientific world view extended itself to man himself. Psychology, psychiatry, anthropology, and sociology began to study man in isolation from the eternal presence that transfigures the cosmos. To be sure these human sciences gave us a wealth of insights that could eventually be integrated in a deeper and richer, but also more practical and realistic, spiritual image of man.

In line with man's already changing vision of himself, the psychological disciplines began to perfect methods of introspection. They stimulated man even more to look reflectively at what was happening within himself, without relating these inner events to the horizon of meaning beyond himself. He began to look at people, events, and things primarily to assess how they might affect his private fate. Their deepest meaning within the whole of things began to escape him. The introspective methods thus mushroomed in many forms. They could be used by the person alone or under the guidance or stimulation of an analyst, therapist, counselor, or sensitivity group.

A climate of introspectionism and therapism pervaded the culture. All sorts of experts—psychological, psychiatric, sociological, anthropological—began to take the place of the great spiritual masters of the past. Under this new guidance many people became inclined to center their lives around a well organized, world-centered interiority. Unwittingly, people tried to fill the vacuum left by the disappearance of the art of transcendent reflection in the light of a loving faith. Introspective self-presence substituted for transcendent self-presence.

I don't contend, of course, that introspection is useless; it can be highly advantageous, a definite gain in the arsenal of human means for growth. I believe that our loss is only that people find it no longer necessary to integrate introspective self-presence into a primary and deeper transcendent self-presence.

Effects of the Decline of Spirituality in the West

The decline of the practical knowledge and wisdom of spirituality led various experts in religion to borrow blindly introspective and therapeutic methods from the prestigious sciences of man. Some of these experts had already lost living touch with the treasures of spiritual wisdom in their own tradition. They were unable to recast these new man-centered insights in the light of an all embracing spiritual vision. These insights remained foreign and therefore harmful bodies within the body of traditional spiritual wisdom and knowledge.

As a result of the neglect of the spirit-dimension, life in the West became precariously onesided. If people live long enough onesidedly, it will show up in their minds and bodies; it will affect their mental and physical health. This is what happened, especially in the last decennia. People experience themselves increasingly as lonely fighters for self-actualization in a hostile world they feel no longer embedded in; they become overly anxious to beat the fast pace of time, to outdo competitors; they live and work in a hurry; they become filled with hidden hostilities towards those who threaten to outshine them. They miss the wider vision of the spirit to save them from this growing self-preoccupation. This anxious struggle also badly affects their bodies by steadfastly releasing glandular overdoses of chemicals in the bloodstream. This excess harms arteries, brain, heart, and other vital organs. It is one factor among many that contributes to heart attacks, strokes, ulcers, and digestive disorders. Cultures that neglect the unfolding of the spiritual dimension of man are prone to such diseases.

The increasing physical and nervous deterioration of Western mankind, partly as a result of onesided ego living, may prove a blessing in disguise. When other panaceas fail to stem the tide of such illnesses of body and mind, people will be forced to look again for the lost experience of interwoveness with the wider horizon of mystery; for at-oneness with what is beyond the visible and tangible, the experimentally verifiable; for that region of existence where excessive competition, envy, and time urgency become senseless.

We are on the verge of a rebirth of the awareness of the human need for transcendent self-presence. Unfortunately, many people begin to feel this need but are far from ready for a sound and true transcendent vision of themselves within the whole of things. As a result, many become victimized by the occult, by exotic fads, by weird mysticism, witchcraft, astrology, eastern cults. Others, however, may be fortunate enough to find true spiritual masters who will open up for them forgotten pathways to the life of the spirit. They may receive, as a gift, the art of transcendent self-presence that is a condition for spiritual unfolding. They may be liberated from a mere introspective attitude that for so long has dominated their lives.

One of the major drawbacks of the introspective attitude is the alienation of man from the context, horizon, and wholeness of the whole and Holy as it reveals itself in simple everydayness. Spiritual self-presence tends toward connectedness with daily things and situations and with the Holy hidden at their core.

Introspective reflection makes our own self and its urgency for instant self-realization central, embroiling us in a futile battle against time and against real or imagined competitors for success and survival. All things—our meetings with others, our work and charities, our religious and apostolic endeavors—may be measured in terms of self-perfection, of a matching or outdoing of the efforts of other strivers after social or apostolic success. Isolated self-actualization becomes the measure of all things. For countless Christians, too, the Christian life becomes narrowed down to a project of theological sophistication and moral self-perfection.

Of course, we should take our own needs and abilities into account; but they should not be the only and ultimate measure of our thoughts, feelings, and actions. Persons and things encountered in daily life must not be assessed only in terms of our own self-perfection and of the fulfillment of our proud missionary "do-gooder" image. How they may foster or hamper our personal growth ought not to be our main concern. In that case we tend to make our ego, its projects, its eagerness to "do, have, and show" the quasi-divine center of our world. We cut this self-perfecting ego off from the real world where the Divine is the center from whom and to whom the true meaning of all things flows. We no longer see people, events, and things in their own God given richness and density; they become mere occasions for self enhancing missionarianism, envious comparison, painful competition, frustration, and the tyranny of time tables that make us feel important. We think we are thinking about others and our task, but we are really thinking about ourselves alone. /

Transcendent Self-Presence and the Life of Spiritualization

In transcendent self-presence, we are present to ourselves as showing up in the light of God and as interacting with people, events, and things as they also show up in His light. We experience ourselves as unique manifestations of the will of the Father, equally immanent in all that happens around us. Our essential questions are no longer, "What is in it for us?; how are we benefitting ethically, psychologically, emotionally?; how do people and things affect our needs and the hypersensitivity of our lightly bruised ego's?; how do we find fulfillment?" Rather our questions are, "What is the appeal of the Spirit expressed in the demands of everyday?; how do these demands manifest a deeper underlying reality?" /

Rather than beginning with the isolated self out of touch with its daily surroundings and the horizon of the sacred, we try to surmise what the situation asks of us as the incarnation of God's mysterious call. We begin to uncover our hidden transcendent self, willed from eternity; its discovery and growth is meant to be silently interwoven with the mundaneness of our daily duties and their numerous demands on us. Then the life of spiritualization can truly begin. /

Of course, we must take into account among all the other signs of God's will for us the divine signposts that show up in our own personal make-up, background, temperament, talents, and deficiencies. The transcendent dimension of the spiritual man's self-presence sees this make-up as a sign post of the Divine, whereas the introspective dimension of his self-presence examines the concrete details of the temperament, talents, and deficiencies God allowed to develop in him. Moderate introspection is necessary. We say "moderate," for "taking into account among other things" is quite different from making our introspective self-preoccupation the measure of all things. The introspective dimension of self-presence is in this case wisely subordinated to the transcendent dimension of self-presence.

The transcendent approach to life happens also to be healthier; it leads to less isolation, aggravation, anxiety, despair, to less futile anger, worries, and fights against people and situations that cannot be changed anyway. At the same time it grants steadfast readiness to labor for the liberation of humanity where and when possible within the limits of our personality, even if, in this battle for the Kingdom, our egos may be bruised or our lives destroyed. Spiritual self-presence envisions a self that transcends when necessary the limits of life and ego fulfillment.

The transcendent approach is healthier also because it does not allow us to wall ourselves up within our inner worlds nor to evade our ordinary shared everydayness where demands have to be met, things done, promises kept.

The point I have been trying to make so far is that there is a danger that "therapism" and "introspectionism" will take over in our lives because their influence is so widespread and uncritically applauded in our culture. They tend to weaken our ability to cope. When excessively indulged in, they can make us wishy-washy, overly sensitive and preoccupied with our own feelings. We lose the strength to be wholly present where we are, sharing the ordinary everyday grind, ready to get our hands dirty in the muddle of life as it manifests itself since the fall of man.

Further Dangers of Introspectionsim

Another of my findings is that when a person is always looking at himself merely introspectively he cannot help but become mesmerized by all the limiting dimensions of his person, life, and situation. I have come to the conclusion that the person who sees himself in isolation must necessarily see himself as a depressing collection of countless limitations: limitations in appearance, health, background, knowledge, temperament, virtue, intelligence, emotional range and intensity, chances and opportunities. No matter how gifted a person, he is bound sooner or later to collide with the prison walls of his limited existence. He can only go beyond them by accepting them.

Wholehearted acceptance becomes possible only when these limits are seen in the light of God's plan for him—for his limited but unique participation in the history of salvation and culture. Outside this perspective a person may feel as if he has just been dumped into this confusing world like a grain of sand tossed up and down by unpredictable winds. No wonder the person without spiritual life can feel so schizoid, lonely, and alienated, disgusted with life and the meaninglessness of it all.

It is better to start with a transcendent presence to oneself as a unique meaningful part of the pattern of the Divine Will in the universe. Then it is possible to cope more serenely with the numerous limiting aspects of one's life without being flung into despair or succumbing to a frightening "crisis of the limits" when one grows older and experiences his limits more vividly. Too many people who begin to get in touch with themselves—in isolation from the larger horizon of the Divine—end up as overly competitive, excessively guilty, anxious, and depressed, filled with self-depreciation.

Transcendent self-awareness is an integrative awareness of one's whole life blending harmoniously with the life of faith. It enables the person to dwell prayerfully on himself as deeply loved and cared for by God within the situation in which He wants him to be and to grow for his own good and the good of others. This compassionate look on his rooted, sustained, and divinely loved self does not lead to strain and self-preoccupation, as does the look of introspection at a lonely self lost in an indifferent universe and loaded with guilt that does not find Divine Redemption.

I discovered also during my research that the introspective attitude inclines the person to overrate his childhood history. Introspection implies retrospection within his closed off inner world. Not in tune with the Divine Source from which all things flow forth the person tends to see his childhood as the ultimate source of who he is at present. Blinded by insight that is exclusively psychological, he may not be present to a transcendent mystery that saved and carried him in and through that childhood history and in spite of that history. Transcendent self-presence, however, enables him to accept the painful limitations of his youth even if they gave rise to life long hang-ups, imperfections, and neurotic tendencies. They are accepted in faith as challenges to be met and as such allowed by a Divine Love who will ultimately transform the person here or in the life hereafter, if only he tries gently to make the best of the past in the present. Transcendent reflection makes him look in reverence at

Divine Providence speaking to him in and through the childhood God allowed to happen to him. Transcendent dwelling does not allow him to see his past in isolation from God's caring.

Another danger of a merely introspective and retrospective vision is its possible abuse as an excuse for lack of self-control. The cover-up of such a person may be that his mother did not love him; the clergy were too rigid; he was so spoiled by his father that he is now unable to exercise self-control.

To be sure, one of the means of making the best of the past may be a period of counseling or therapy. God may have meant that help for some of us during our life time in this period of history. He never meant that such psychological techniques should be extolled as our ultimate salvation. Neither psychology nor psychotherapy should be totalized as the only and ultimate road to liberating intimacy with the Divine.

Two Kinds of Willing

In developing this aspect of my theory of spiritual personality, I was gradually able to formulate a distinction between two kinds of willing and freedom. I began to differentiate a primary transcendent willing or receptive volition from a secondary or ego-willing. The latter I called in some of my writings executive or managing willing. I then related introspective self-presence to executive willing and transcendent self-presence to spiritual receptive willing. Again both kinds of willing are necessary in the fully functioning person. People are inclined, however, to engage in managing willing when receptive willing is called for.

For example, I can will to write a poem. I can go to a quiet place, put pen and paper before me, try to distance myself from other occupations and distractions and to dwell on the theme of the poem I want to write; but I cannot will in the same way the poem itself nor the inspirations, feelings, and images that accompany it. The harder I try, the more the inspiration seems to recede.

Managing willing involves all the preparatory steps just described and, following the inspiration, all the subsequent "executive steps," such as writing the poem, correcting, typing, checking, and retyping the inspired words. In between these executive actions, there must come a moment in which spiritual receptive willing takes over.

Likewise, I can organize time and place for prayer and spiritual reading, but I cannot will myself to be inspired by the Divine or uplifted by spiritual reading. In other words, there are many things in life we cannot force or will in a managing way, among these joy, love, and religious experience.

The introspective person may find that he tends to live more on the level of executive willing. He is a willful person who plans his life without dialogue with the Divine Will; he neglects to develop a more receptive attitude, open to manifestations of God's will in everyday life situations. It was this kind of willing that got us into what I have called a capitalistic type of spirituality of post-Renaissance times when people tried to buy salvation by piling up stocks of good works and indulgences. Managing willing is often needed, but it should be enlightened by receptive willing, by my obedient willing of the Will of God.

Transcendent Self-Presence and Community

A person, caught by his ego-will and unenlightened by spiritual vision, might appear to surrender his individualistic stance when he binds himself together with other "ego-willers" into a group or organization. In reality he may not change a bit; he only joins a larger ego corporation. He swells the power of shared willfulness; he expands his own self-preoccupation with the self-preoccupation of the group. Such a group can neither see reality in its own right nor the individual members of the group as they objectively and uniquely are allowed to be by God. The introspective community—alternatively enthused or bemused—sees only its own present mood or need; everything else is measured by its momentary moodiness.

True community living on the level of the spirit is marked by the primacy of transcendent self-presence. It transcends the temptations to totalize any missionary or social enthusiasm of the community or any pressure group within its midst. It tries to be open in dialogue to the manifestation of the divine uniqueness in the many concrete life situations to be faced by unique members of the community.

Introspective members cannot relate to others in the community, especially those who differ from them in outlook on the personal or vital levels. Lacking in transcendent self-presence, they may not be experientially aware of their oneness in Christ, the eternal Word, in whom all are contained as little words. Therefore, they cannot be present to the transcendent self of the community which goes beyond all surface differences.

Because we are all different, we are called to be opponents in many issues. Our deeper at-oneness rests, however, on the transcendent vision that God allows each of us to be helpful in his own way. Our insights may differ from those of others, but somehow God uses all things in His ultimate project for this earth and its history.

Occasionally, a certain agreement on the practical level is necessary for our effectiveness as a group. What we have to watch out for are enthusiastic agreements of a more idealistic nature. They may represent nothing more than a vital reaction to our own collective moods to which we are sensitive due to our shared introspective attitudes.

Ego-willing and introspectionism belong to the same life style, that of willfulness. A community built on the combination of ego-willing and moodiness is bound to flounder. True community is a gift to be received not forced; it is received only by those who try to live together in a transcendent vision of themselves and the community as a whole.

Practice of Spiritual Reading Related to Transcendent Self-Presence

One of the facilitating conditions for a spiritual life is the practice of spiritual reading. Spiritual reading is a reading that helps us to discover our true self in the light of God's self-communication in and through His word in Scripture, in the Church, in spiritual writers. Because its main aim is transcendent self-discovery, everything depends on our mode of self-presence during this reading. A person who approaches his spiritual reading for the sake of information only, for exegetical, literary knowledge, or for affirmation of his own moods, prejudices, and sentiments will be unable to grow to an understanding of what God is asking of him through these words. If he takes up the same texts in a spirit of transcendent self-presence, he will experience them as sources of wisdom that reach far beyond the interests of his own anxious ego. He will make these sources the measure of his life instead of making his own project of life their measure. The transcendent person lives his life against a much wider horizon. He does not reduce its message to his own solipsistic need. He allows Holy Scripture and the words of spiritual masters to be what they are and to speak to his deeper spirit-self. His transcendent dialogue with the richness of these spiritual writings saves him from his own narrowness.

The person who lives in transcendent self-presence is not only in genuine dialogue with the message of Scripture and spiritual writers; he keeps also in dialogue with the rest of reality, with his own inclinations, with his actual words and deeds in daily life, with his fellow men, their experiences and expressions.

Fantasy Life of the Introspective Person

Introspective self-presence, on the other hand, makes the link with daily reality tenuous; it entails the danger of one's living a grandiose fantasy life. Unable to see the transcendent beauty and truth of the treadmill of daily life, the world becomes boring, dead, dull. He tries to escape its uneventful routines by living a fantasy life fed by unchecked desires, flamboyant ambitions, needs, and drives. He begins to hunger after the extraordinary, the not-everyday, the exciting, the novel, the grandiose, the impressive, the latest, the newest. This fantasy world of the introspectionist is often marked by illusionary projects and make-believe accomplishments. He may feel that others misunderstand him; they are against him because they refuse to feed into his deluded self-appreciation. He secretly may say to himself, "If only they knew the great guy who lives among them!"

Each of us can get out of touch with the fact that he is quite an ordinary person, not called to set the world afire. Of course, each of us, whether he lives in transcendent or introspective self-presence, has a fantasy life. The fantasy life of the introspective person is rarely in tune with his common surroundings whereas that of a person who is spiritually present to self as interwoven with his concrete world, originating in the Divine, is nourished steadily by the deeper meanings he discovers in rather pedestrian circumstances.

The spiritually present person is intuitively open to the extraordinary richness hidden in the concrete people, events, and things he meets while living a prosaic day to day life. He begins to realize how ordinary everydayness is spiritualized and divinized in a special way by the Incarnation of the Divine Word, who became man in the pedestrian situation of a life lived for the most part as an unnoticed worker in Nazareth. He wants to participate in the hidden life of Jesus by finding and adoring the deeper divine meanings of his own simple daily life. He is less tempted to ambitious or anxious fantasies about himself and his future than the introspective person.

Spiritual life is trustworthy to the degree that it is faithful to the everydayness of the common life, lived as the manifestation of deeper mystery, by a person who keeps in touch with all of its ordinariness and inconspicuous routines. Fewer neuroses will flourish in him. He will be task-oriented, a person who gets things done, less subject to addictions, overdependency, rationalizations, compensations, and wish fulfilling fantasies. Transcendent self-presence will make him aware of the fact that his deepest self is already God oriented and loved and redeemed by Him. This faith is really healthier than having only an analytic awareness of his faults, sins, and limits.

The life of the spirit should keep in touch with everyday inconspicuous existence. Whatever takes the person unnecessarily out of the ordinary daily life in Christ is suspect. It isolates him and tends to make him closed, proud or depressed, the victim of willful spurts of self-centered imagination.

The deeper we go into the study of the impact of an exclusive introspective attitude on our religious outlook, the more we discover its deforming influence. Introspection, as we have seen, may give rise to a preoccupation with our isolated interiority. It tends to give us the impression that the Divine Presence manifests itself only within our closed-off inner life. We become less aware of the God who is the Beyond in the midst of our daily life. He is somehow in all people, events, places.

A mere introspective self-presence thus tends to isolate us from the Divine Presence in everydayness. Transcendent self-presence, on the other hand, puts us in touch with our culture, with the whole tradition out of which we emerge, with the cultural period God has called us to live in. If we cut ourselves off from this ground, our isolated self begins necessarily to project a kind of ideal world in no way "contaminated" by our real past or present. We are like astronauts floating above the world in airtight capsules. If and when we return to our limited tradition and cultural period, we may have a reentry problem. We feel dismayed by the difference between our dreamworld and the earthiness of the tradition and cultural period with which our lives are intertwined. We may react with distrust to anything our tradition and culture has to offer. Instead of benefitting from the limited best our background and present epoch have to give us, we throw out the whole bag, so to speak. We end up becoming uprooted men who cannot find a path to joyful and vigorous participation in the tasks of humanity. We begin to "live only in our heads;" we take that to be the whole of reality.

Rhythm of Mindfulness and Forgetfulness

If we suffer from this problem, we must broaden our mindfulness to include a more intuitive transcendent presence to the deeper meaning of our vital, emotional, and spiritual life. We may then become tuned in once again to the whole of our spontaneous life in the midst of the real world.

Such wholeness will affect not only our self-presence but also our self-presentation to others. We don't give people the impression that our words are "out there" while we are some place else. We are really *in* our words and gestures. They sense that we are not parroting what "they" think, say, or write. Others cannot escape the impression that we have personalized what we express not only intellectually and critically—which, of course, is necessary—but also we've appropriated it with our whole being in light of our experience of lived transcendent self-presence to the Divine.

This is not to say that we should always live in total mindfulness, vigilance, and reflection. Mindfulness is most beneficial when balanced by a kind of forgetfulness. We need to establish in our lives a rhythm of mindfulness and forgetfulness in a healthy sense. We need periods of quiet in which we can be reflectively mindful of the deeper meaning of our life, but we also need to live our lives in a spontaneous way, forgetful of our reflections, reimmersing ourselves in the natural flow of daily life. There should be dialogue between reflection and the rest of life but never in such a way that vigilance and thoughtfulness take over totally and destroy our spontaneity. Without this healing forgetfulness, we would become alienated from the manifestation of God's will in the sacrament of everydayness. Reimmersion in daily life is also a homecoming, a being about the things of our Father.

Gentle Reflection

By now it should be clear why the way of gentle reflection can be distinguished from the aggressive way; it is the way of stillness and repose. Its aim is to come to a union of the deepest self with the Divine Presence.

Transcendent self-presence awakens us from illusion. In our fallen condition we take mirages for truth. We are ego-centered when we should be God-centered. We have lost inner wholeness, a loss that obscures the splendor of the Divine Presence in our life and world. This loss leaves us victims of a multitude of illusions that distort our perception of people, events, and things. Enchanted by projects, ambitions, possessions, we become blind to God, who is our Center. We live in illusion.

Gentle reflection implies a certain detachment from daily involvement. This distance helps us to discern the illusionary ways in which we relate to God, self, and others. We begin to awaken from illusions. We experience the Divine Presence as the true center of our life. We awaken to the true nature of reality, both created and uncreated, seeing things from within God as it were. We no longer view men and other creatures as self-contained entities external to God, to one another, to ourselves. Within the Spirit of God, all created things exist in intimate togetherness with one another. Gentle reflection is thus a means man uses on the way to a greater state of wholeness and to an increase in sanctity and participation in the divine nature.

One of the most beautiful themes of gentle reflection is that of the resplendent divine indwelling in the depths of our true self. At certain moments, God may halt the movement of meditative reflection and make us feel the mysterious flame of the Divine Presence ever glowing within. God draws us irresistibly into the divine mysteries He Himself reveals in the silent depths of the core of our being. What we learned from faithful gentle reflection becomes now one simple lived experience. Any spiritual good we do, think, feel, or possess does not originate in the isolated self; it is dependent on the grace of God at the root of our deepest self; it originates in Him.

During transcendent self-presence such pauses of wordless presence may grow in frequency, intensity, duration. This experience may be so overwhelming that it grows difficult at times to engage in any reflection. Transcendent self-presence by means of reflection should be set aside at the moments God grants us the grace of a deeper mode of presence—a presence that goes beyond any limited word, image, or reflection and keeps us silent before the mystery of the Eternal Word.

VIII

SPIRITUALITY AND INITIATION

The specialty of the director or directress of personal spiritual initiation can be illustrated best by looking at the program of a novitiate. In the West the novitiate—being mainly directed towards spiritual initiation—offers the best paradigm also for less intense and less concentrated programs of initiation, such as part time programs for diocesan clergy and the laity.

In the novitiate the master of spiritual initiation is in charge of the formation program and must demand from the teachers under him that they, if possible, relate classes, conferences, seminars, readings, and spiritual direction to the spiritual growth of the candidate. This obligation of faithfulness to his unique specialty is confirmed by *Renovationis Causam* in which it is stressed that no formal courses in theology are to be taught in the novitiate.

Personal spiritual initiation should be rooted, of course, in basic Catholic doctrine. For this reason the master of novices must make sure that only those persons enter the novitiate who have acquired in the pre-entrance program or if necessary in the postulancy a sufficient grasp of basic Catholic teachings.

The whole novitiate program must be through and through Christ-oriented, Church-oriented, and Scripture-oriented. However, the approach to Christ, Church, and Scripture in this special year is not primarily, formally, and explicitly philosophical, systematic-theological, or exegetical but spiritual, in the sense of the great spiritual masters. They refer again and again to Church Doctrine, to Christ, to Holy Scripture while never making any of these doctrines the exclusive object of prolonged intellectual analysis and formal theological elaboration. They constantly refer to these sources insofar as they can draw on them to enlighten their initiates on the concrete living of the spiritual life.

Church Doctrine is the foundation on which the whole program should be built and the point of reference for classes and seminars. Inspired by the example of the great spiritual masters of the Catholic tradition, the program of the novitiate makes Holy Scripture—especially as read by the Church in its liturgy—a source of spiritual thought and inspiration.

Initiation and Transcendence

The master of initiation thus has as his responsibility to introduce his postulants, novices, juniors, or seminarians into a spiritual transcendence as distinguished from a philosophical, theological, or pastoral transcendence. We shall center our discussion of spiritual transcendence on the initiation of the novice into this dimension of spiritual life. The same principles apply with the necessary adaptations to other periods of formation and to the practical initiation into the spiritual life of diocesan clergy and seminarians, laymen and women.

As we have explained in our book on *The Vowed Life*, a religious must be above all a witness for the transcendent dimension of life. This dimension must affect his whole life, his thoughts and feelings, his mind and heart, his times of rest, his times of action. Only Christ can take him up in this dimension of transcendence that permeated and dominated His own life here on earth. He alone can make the religious deeply aware of the transcendent meaning revealed to us in His words. The only thing He asks of him is that he make himself humbly ready for this gift. Then He will let him share in His presence to the omnipotent and ever loving Father.

The time of initiation into the spiritual life is a favorable time for the religious to become ready to receive the grace of spiritual transcendence. The central period of this time of initiation is the canonical year of the novitiate. A wrong understanding of the meaning of transcendence at this time may lead to a mistaken notion of the transcendent meaning of religious life as a whole. Moreover, what we will say about the transcendent meaning of the novitiate can be applied as well to the spiritual dimension of other periods of formation, and especially to the time of ongoing formation during which the religious must be shown how to keep the transcendent dimension in the center of his life. It applies also—with the necessary adaptations—to the spiritual initiation of diocesan clergy and laity.

The Historical Setting for Transcendence

In the last decades we have seen increasing emphasis on the problem of rapid social change. Some people stressed that the priest and Christian religious today should be taught mainly how to be of relevance to this fast changing society. This justifiable ideal of social relevance was at times over emphasized in some initiation programs. As a result, these programs lost depth and balance. The horizontal dimension of life was accentuated at the expense of the vertical, transcendent one. Occasionally, initiation into a living spirituality was twice subordinated: once to the practicalities of formal theological training and once to the preparation for social apostolate.

Training in formal theological discourse and in social practice should not be the purpose of the novitiate, as the Vatican documents make clear. Central should be a worshipful initiation into the two great transcendent mysteries of the faith: Trinity and Incarnation. These mysteries have to be worshipfully celebrated and reverently related to the living of a fundamental or foundational Catholic spirituality rooted in the Doctrine of the Church. Then, in light of this spirituality, the novice can reflect on his own spiritual life, on his growth towards fulfillment in Christ, and on the deepest meaning of human history in which, as a religious, he is called to participate after his initiation.

The priest, the religious, and the Christian lay person should live in the faith that history too has a transcendent and not merely a secular dimension. He is called to witness by his very life for this transcendence. His Catholic tradition teaches him that the salvation of man can never be achieved within secular history. He must symbolize in his life the answer to the deepest need of man, the need to be rooted in the Divine Transcendent, who came to redeem the world. Only in Christ can the Christian work joyfully in freedom and dignity within the house of history.

The essence of religious life is thus to be a witness for the transcendent dimension of life and history. The priest or religious, who has given up certain human freedoms and pleasures, tells us by his very life that there is more to human existence than what the eye meets or the ear hears. He reminds people that this world is not the ultimate home of humanity.

Initiation into Spiritual Transcendence

Initiation into religious life must make central the mystery of transcendence. The tension in formation at this time is not between personal sanctification and social relevance. Nor is it a tension between the contemplative and participative expressions of the priest life and the religious life. It is a tension between the divine transcendent meaning of both the personal and social life of the priest and the religious, on the one hand, and the secular humanist meaning of this personal and social life, on the other.

The novitiate offers an ideal time and place to help the initiate to ground himself, his whole being, in the divine transcendent dimension. It is definitely not a time to be overly preoccupied with intellectual discussions of possible changes in theologies, in Church structures, or in the structure of the diocese or the religious community. Continual heated discussions about possible theological and structural changes may interfere with the special meaning of this one canonical year in the life of a religious. Such daily argumentation may prevent the young initiate from opening up to the Lord in a spiritual way, a way that goes beyond mere intellectual pursuit.

Transcendence means going beyond. When we speak about going beyond this secular humanistic life toward a personal God, we speak about spiritual transcendence.

Spiritual transcendence is a prayerful presence in faith. Prayerful presence implies a living, faithful contact with the transcendent meaning of reality. This reality may be a text of Holy Scripture, the words of a spiritual master, a part of the liturgy, a beautiful sunset, a fellow human being. For example, I am participating in the liturgy of the Holy Mass. I look in reverence and recollection at the liturgical action of the pouring of wine and water into the chalice. God may give me at this moment the grace to participate with my whole being in the prayer of the Church said by the priest:

> By the mystery of this water and wine
> May we come to share in the Divinity of Christ
> Who humbled Himself to share in our humanity.

Let us say further that I am a novice. God has seen my many daily attempts at recollection, silence, and solitude; my attempt to dwell in meditation and spiritual reading on His holy words. He has seen my humble openness to the director of novices. With great love He has seen also how my community spares no time and cost to have one of its best members prepared during many years of study, prayer, and course work for what St. Thomas calls "Ars artium regimen animarum," which means that the art of arts is the direction of souls. This moment of liturgical action has been chosen by Him to respond to all that preparation of a generous prayerful community, of a devoted well-prepared director of novices, of a humble recollected novice who tries daily to live a life of loving faith. He gives me the grace of an undisturbed presence in faith to the transcendent meaning of these words of the

Church to the sacred dimension of this liturgical action of the priest.

What happens to the novice in this moment of full presence in faith? He forgets momentarily about himself and his little world. He is, as it were, taken up in a deeper reality that goes beyond him, that literally transcends and absorbs him. At such moments he does not feel separated from Christ praying in and through His Church. Neither is the Church experienced as something outside of himself to be studied, analyzed, criticized as an object of sociological study. He is wholly at one with the praying Church in Christ.

Outside of this full presence in faith, the novice may relate to God and His Chruch, to his community, and to the world in many different sensate and intellectual ways. As a person with five good senses, he is aware of the material dimension of reality, in this case, of the visual and audible action and words of the priest. He is also a person of intelligence. Perhaps he was a college student before he entered the novitiate. He took a lively interest in innovative theologies. His intelligence opened him to the intelligible dimension of the Church, of his religious community and the world. He is capable, therefore, of making the action and words of the priest intelligible in a theological way. Full spiritual presence in faith, however, gives a knowledge that complements the knowledge of the material and intelligible dimensions of reality. Prayerful presence in faith makes him at one in a special way with the transcendent dimension of reality.

The sensate, the intellectual, and the spiritually transcendent dimensions of presence are thus three dimensions of one and the same primary power, that of knowing the truth. Prayerful presence happens primarily on the third level, the level of spiritual transcendence. This prayerful presence is what fosters a spiritual outlook and life style in the young initiate. This life style in turn facilitates his deeper prayerful presence at special moments.

Knowledge of the Transcendent

The novitiate—as other programs of initiation—is a year of discovery, the discovery of the transcendent dimension of a life lived in faith. The novitiate as a whole, therefore, must first of all facilitate the practice of a living faith. It must create conditions that may be used by God to grant the initiate at certain moments a sense of His Divine Presence. The novitiate should foster a climate of quiet conducive to the beginning of a loving and abiding presence to the Divine in faith, a climate that may be used by God in His own good time for the inner enlightening of the novice.

There are various types of knowledge of the Transcendent. The novitiate concentrates mainly on one kind, without denying the validity and importance of the others.

A first kind of knowledge of the Divine Transcendent is the philosophical. It can grant us a natural intellectual transcendence. Philosophy of God helps us transcend from the knowledge of creatures by causality to their Creator, who is the source of all that is. This knowledge is highly valued in Catholic tradition. It is by no means the highest possibility of transcendence for man. It is surely not the knowledge the novitiate should specialize in.

The second kind of transcendent knowledge is built on Divine Revelation as it comes to man in the Doctrine of the Church. It is the knowledge of faith. This knowledge, while exercised by our human faculties, transcends these faculties insofar as they are aided by a light infused by God Himself called *lumen fidei*, the light of faith. This knowledge of faith is certainly necessary for the initiate. One of the purposes of the pre-entrance period and the period of postulancy is to provide the prospective novice with the conditions conducive to a balanced knowledge of the basic Doctrine of the Church, a knowledge that will orient and facilitate his life of faith. A person can deepen and clarify this basic knowledge of the faith in two further ways that do not exclude but complement one another.

One way is that of systematic theology. It is the way of sophisticated intellectual explanation, exploration, elaboration, and possibly innovation of Church Doctrine. It is a way of intellectual transcendence like philosophy. The transcendence of theology, however, is far greater than that of philosophy because it is not a transcendence by means of natural reason alone, but a transcendence by means of natural reason enlightened by faith. This way of formal theology is suspended for the novice by the instruction *Renovationis Causam.* For this style of intellectual theological transcendence—no matter how important before and after the novitate—is not the appropriate style of transcendence for a person to be initiated in a life of intimacy with God.

The other way of deepening the faith is that of spirituality. Spirituality is fostered by special conditions in one's life in the hope that God may grant at certain moments a spiritual knowledge directly of Himself. This living knowledge of God is the highest form of transcendence we can reach here on earth. It transcends even the limitations of words and concepts to which philosophical and theological transcendence are bound by their nature. Compared to the transcendence of this kind of knowledge, the intellectual knowledge about God yielded by formal philosophical and theological knowledge may seem like straw. St. Thomas himself is believed to have used the metaphor of straw to indicate what his formal theological knowledge looked like in light of this most transcendent knowledge of love rooted in living faith. St. Thomas' metaphor does not mean that theological knowledge is like straw in and by itself, but only that it *seems like straw in comparison to* the transcendent knowledge God may give at times when we, with His grace, persevere in a life of faith and love.

To be sure, all three kinds of knowledge—the philosophical, theological, and spiritual—are valid, mutually complementary, and deeply enriching. When actually lived by the same person, they cannot be separated but only distinguished from one another. Each in its own way reveals to us the same transcendent divine object. They do not contradict each other; they complement and sustain one another. Ideally, they all should play a role in our lives; but at different occasions, at different periods of life, one of the three kinds of transcendent knowing should be especially fostered. Each kind of knowing has its own type of expert, respectively the philosopher, the theologian, the spiritual master.

The novitiate, in light of *Renovationis Causam,* should especially foster a modest beginning of the most transcendent kind of knowledge: spiritual knowledge.

The spiritual knowing fostered in the novices by spiritual direction, rules, environment, courses, conferences, readings, prayers, and exercises leads to moments of loving penetration of these mysteries of faith that are formulated in the spiritual Doctrine of the Church and of its acknowledged spiritual masters.

Many novices today have already finished college or at least junior college. Some of them may have been exposed to a variety of philosophies and theologies but not to the spiritual masters. Such theologies may have been tentative, daring, filled with conflicting abstract and complex views delighting and preoccupying their busy searching intellect. The initiate should not reject the true knowledge he may have received. It is simply that he has to come experientially closer to the same God whom he knew from afar by philosophical and theological reason. He is not invited to deny any truth he learned by means of philosophical or theological discourse. He is invited only to approach in living love and faith the same God he knows about already intellectually from his studies and readings in college or in the pre-entrance program, the same God about whom he may gather much more intellectual knowledge later, when he has finished his novitiate. In short, the spiritual life in which he is to be initiated is a life of transcendent knowledge by love, rooted in a living faith.

This does not mean that a novice should not be instructed, for example, in discursive meditation. He most surely should. The point is that the discourse in discursive meditation has a different purpose, style, and meaning than discourse in the formal study of philosophy and systematic theology.

Discourse and the Life of Dwelling in Faith

To understand the purpose of discourse in discursive meditation, let us take as an example a meditation on the birth of Christ. The birth of Christ is for our meditative presence not a truth to be demonstrated or reasoned out. In meditation we are present to a living Person, not primarily to an intellectual truth. Discourse means in this case that we consider prayerfully various aspects of this mystery of the Incarnation, a consideration that may give rise to our living, adoring, and loving presence to this Person. Such considerations, if graced by God, may move our will to love and surrender, to union with the new born Christ.

In systematic theological discourse, this birth of Christ is studied as an intellectual truth. The student asks himself how he can understand the Incarnation intellectually insofar as this is possible. He asks, for instance, if the God-man has all the human capacities. Does He have soul and will? Is He subject to all the laws of human development?

In other words, in discursive meditation, we want to become a lived presence to, a loving being with Christ. In systematic theological discourse, we want to come to a deeper intellectual understanding of the truth which is the Incarnation. In theological discourse, our attitude is primarily one of mentally mastering, of grasping intellectually. In discursive meditation our attitude is one of becoming ready to be grasped as a whole person, to be taken hold of, by Christ in a relation of mutual love.

Discursive meditation may lead sooner or later to a moment of prayerful presence in which all discourse falls silent. Discourse in prayer may become a temporary means that burns itself out. The function of discourse in systematic theology is an essential lasting part of theology. Systematic theologies want to expand, deepen, and enrich themselves also *as universes of discourse.*

The initiate in the life of the spirit should not be sorry but grateful for the moment when his discursive thought is somehow hindered and made superfluous, for he may then find himself filled with a silent longing for God. Discursive meditation is a preparation for the loving action of God in the person so that a life of love and prayerful dwelling in faith may begin to develop. Yet this beginning life of prayerful presence is not something any spiritual director or novice by himself can evoke at will. It is a gift of God; it is the work of grace. In other words, God does the main work in the novitiate. The work of the initiate is to leave behind him for one small year his preoccupation with formal philosophical, scientific, or theological study. Even this cannot be done without the help of grace, especially if the novice happens to be attached to his studies. The work of the initiate is simply to dispose himself, to be more and more receptive to God's work within him. In the active life of study or social work before the novitiate, the natural abilities of the novice play a great role. In this work of daily transformation of his own inner life much more is done by God. Jesus must become the chief worker while the main attitude of the initiate becomes one of expectancy and reverent cooperation.

Temporary abstinence from the pursuit of formal theological knowledge increases his receptivity for the living kind of knowledge God may grant him during a more mediative abiding with the truth of faith.

Formal theological knowledge of God, no matter how necessary for many reasons, is inadequate and imperfect. Formal theological knowledge in and by itself is not sufficient for a life in which the living flame of divine love burns brightly. St. Thomas, following Augustine and

Boetius, teaches that God transcends any form that intelligence can conceive. In *The Ascent of Mount Carmel,* St. John of the Cross maintains: "Faith causes darkness and a void of understanding in the intellect" [Book II, Chapter 6, Paragraph 2] "For though faith brings certitude to the intellect, it does not produce clarity, but only darkness" [Ibid.] "Everything the intellect can understand. . .is most unlike and disproportionate to God" [Book II, Chapter 8, Paragraph 5]

True, the novice who is a beginner cannot do away with all concepts and images as the great spiritual masters did, but the beginning of the way of the Spirit can be fostered when he is at least willing to abstain for one small year from a preoccupation with the increase of concepts and images through the pursuit of studies in formal theology.

To sum up our reflections thus far: in the novitiate the stress is upon a knowledge of God by love. God can be known by a loving presence to Him and His Revelation in a more transcendent way that He can be known intellectually. The one year delay in formal theological study is not more than a preparation for a loving presence to God that goes beyond theological knowledge of Him without denying or diminishing the worth and necessity of a theological knowledge of God to be concentrated upon at other times and places. The temporary suspension of formal theological studies is to allow the flame of love to burn brightly. This suspension contributes to inner silence which is even more necessary than outer silence, if this year is to become a resolute beginning of unique transcendence. It is a year in which the initiate begins to know God more by love than by intellectual reasoning. And knowledge by love is superior to knowledge by intellect, as

St. Thomas explains. The will, he says, is superior to the intellect by reason of its end. According to St. Thomas, conceptual knowledge brings God down, as it were, to our level; it imposes upon Him the concepts we take from the surrounding world. Love, on the contrary, goes out to its object: it goes to the essence of God Himself, as He is in Himself. Love may reach God in this life, but not intellectual knowing alone.

In light of this knowledge gained by love, the theological knowledge of God may seem like ignorance. In *The Spiritual Canticle*, St. John of the Cross writes: "It seems to the soul that its former knowledge, and even the knowledge of the whole world, is pure ignorance by comparison with that knowledge." [Stanza XVII, Paragraph 11] No person, no matter how learned in theology, truly knows God unless he also loves Him. Yet, this grace may only be granted after a long time of longing for God while growing in poverty of spirit. The novitiate is a first initiation in this way. Therefore, the initiate is invited to put aside for one year the pursuit of theological knowledge so that he may have a taste of the wisdom of God. Strictly speaking, of course, love as love cannot know. The knowledge of love means simply that the depth of love and longing guides the intellect. As a result, the mind of the lover is filled with a wisdom that does not come from without through the senses but from within from an abundance of love.

St. Thomas tells us that love unites us with God. He explains that in love we become at one with God in spirit. This enables us, he says, to understand things divine with an intuitive accuracy. He continues that it is love that really penetrates into things divine and obtains a knowledge the discursive intellect can never discover.

A Time of Purification and Integration

It is the life of faith and charity that should be fostered in the initiate.

Living faith is already informed by charity and illumined by the gifts of charity; it is a loving, enlightened, and effective faith that animates, moves, and inspires the life of the believer. Of course, this living faith will have to keep growing all of his life. It may be easier to begin to grow in that direction if the initiate has set himself free from other ways of knowing and striving for at least one year in the beginning of his religious life.

To begin to live this life of loving faith, to allow it to spiritualize one's whole being, the novice or any other initiate needs purification and integration. No divine transcendence is possible without the work of purification that has to be initiated and sustained by grace. St. Thomas points out that man suffers from a loss of right order. This disorder of man is the result of original sin. He writes: "As a result of original justice, reason had perfect control over the lower parts of the soul, while reason itself was perfected by God and was subject to Him. Now this same original justice was lost through the sin of our first parents, as already stated; so that all the powers of the soul are left, as it were, destitute of their proper order, whereby they are naturally directed to virtue; which destitution is called a wounding of nature." [Ia IIae, q. 85, a 3] For this reason initiation into a life of spiritual transcendence implies that the novitiate should offer spiritual direction, courses, and structures that will help the novice to start the life long task of inner unification. He must gain a first insight into the elements in his life that make him scattered, dispersed, and disharmonious as a result of original and personal sin.

He must be helped, moreover, to begin the great work of directing his faculties and experiences to God. This restoration of order in his life has been made possible only by the grace won through the suffering and death of Christ. Therefore, the Sacrament of Penance, in which Christ's redemption is applied to his sinful life, has a special place in the novitiate. It purifies the novice from sin and guilt of which he becomes more and more aware in this year of divine self-transcendence. Confession alone, however, does not take away the underlying disruptive tendencies that make him ambitious, jealous, envious, arrogant, self-centered, dishonest, sensuous, over-sensitive, resentful, lazy, greedy for praise and attention. In service of divine transcendence, he must learn to look at himself so that he may become aware of what are the sources in his life of his mistakes and failures.

In regard to this look at himself, he must be aware of contemporary influences that may prevent him from entering the road of Christian transcendence. The novice may become the victim of a kind of introspective reflection that leads to self-centered isolation. What he needs is a transcendent reflection that helps him to see himself in the loving and redeeming perspective of Divine Presence. One is reminded here of the differences between introspective and transcendent self-presence discussed in Chapter VII of this book.

Contemporary Obstacles to Transcendence

It may be clear by now that the transcendence of the graced spiritual life can be distinguished from a philosophical and theological transcendence. It may also be clear that the novitiate is a year of transintellectual transcendence of the person in living faith and love.

A novice who has grasped experientially the distinction between theological transcendence and the transcendence of graced spiritual life may still be hindered on his way to this latter transcendence by influences outside the novitiate that affected him before he entered. Each cultural period yields its own special obstacles to spiritual transcendence. Such obstacles may come from cultural movements, fads, and views that happen to be ripe in the cultural period in which the novice is living. Presently there is a great interest among young people in transintellectual knowledge and experience, in a kind of natural transcendence that goes beyond philosophical and scientific knowledge. This is due partly to a certain boredom with the technical and activistic outlook of society. It is nourished by Eastern religions such as Zen Buddhism, Sufism, the Hare Krishna movement, the movement for Transcendental Meditation, the emergence of new spiritual orders outside of Catholicism, such as the Holy Order of Man. It is fostered also by the striving after religious experience by means of drugs such as LSD or mescaline. Certain psychologists, too, feed into this widespread interest in transconceptual experience. They observed that transconceptual thought may help with the solution of repressed problems and in the unification of the person. A certain scientific evidence is accumulating that natural transcendence can have this effect. Especially the bio-feedback experiments have done much to give credibility to the process of transconceptual thought and its beneficial effects. Among students, a spin-off from all these movements is a growing interest in various exercises that may foster this kind of transcendence.

Present day novices may come from colleges where such interests were prevalent. They may have been exposed to courses, seminars, and readings in this area. They may have experimented with this kind of transcendence themselves. It should be clear by now, however, that the psychological state of self-transcendence is only of secondary importance for the spiritual person. The paramount question in Christian self-transcendence is if this transcendence is initiated, achieved, and permeated by the transcendent gift of divine grace. A candidate for the novitiate may be excessively interested in psychological techniques of transcendence. Before he is allowed to enter the novitiate or postulancy, he should be helped to see the superior role of grace in Catholic spiritual transcendence.

Here we can see the importance of a pre-entrance program which prepares the candidate for postulancy and novitiate when he is still living and working in the world. Spiritual direction in the pre-entrance period should make him aware that the motive for transcendence must be divine love for God. He should realize that supernatural faith and love can be operative also in a mind filled with concepts and discursive reasoning, but that no technique can bring the mind to God as He reveals Himself to the soul by grace.

The whole initiative in the divine transcendent life of the spirit comes from God. God usually works, however, in tune with the laws that operate in the human psyche and spirit. Therefore, we may find certain similarities between phenomena of human and divine transcendence even when God gives man a supernatural gift that goes beyond his natural capacities. The supervised, personally-adapted spiritual reading program, that forms, along with regular spiritual direction, the core of the pre-entrance program,

can be of help in fostering this awareness of the difference
between human and divine transcendence.

Implementing Transcendent Reflection

To help the novice on this transcendent path of self
understanding, of the "restoration of order in disorder"
that St. Thomas speaks about [Ia IIae, q. 85, a 3], of this
loving faith and presence, daily courses and conferences
are necessary. The novice is not the first one who
attempted to enter this way. Countless people before him
have followed this path in the history of mankind. Many
of them became outstanding spiritual masters and writers.
A number of them are acknowledged by the Church as
representatives of her Doctrine. The novice should be
introduced to certain aspects of the wisdom of these
masters. He should be instructed in the life of prayer, in
spiritual exercises, in a spiritual approach to Holy Scripture, the Mass, the Sacraments. The field is practically
limitless; the sources to choose from are so abundant that
even a life time of study could not exhaust them. Perhaps
some directors or directresses of novices were not familar
with these sources. This could have been one of the
reasons behind their surprise about *Renovationis Causam's*
wise insistence that no formal courses in theology should
be taught. Without these courses taught by themselves or
theology professors, unprepared directors or directresses
might not know how to fill up the time of the novitiate.
The enormous field of classical and contemporary spiritual
writings and studies was a closed book to them. Perhaps
they received the wrong preparation. They may have been
prepared to be professors in systematic theology who were

then asked to initiate novices spiritually in a kind of transcendence different from the intellectual.

Renovationis Causam forbids formal courses in theology in the novitiate, but what about informal theology? Should theology not be mixed informally with the courses and conferences to be offered in the novitiate? Our guideline to answer this question should be again the purpose of the novitiate. It is to be an initiation into a life of divine intimacy that presupposes a temporal stilling of the curiosity and agitation of the intellect.

Spiritual life should be rooted in fundamental Catholic doctrine. This doctrine can be called theology too. However, it may be misleading today to call theology indiscriminately the Doctrine of the Church; for there are many theological views that are not yet Church Doctrine and may never become so. To call Church Doctrine theology without further distinction may be misleading, for it may give the impression that both Church Doctrine and any new theology have the same value and dignity. New theologies are emerging all the time; there are process, personalistic, cosmic, ecumencial, death of God, political, and situational theologies, to name only a few.

Some of these new theories seem to contradict one another; others are complex and abstract. To mix their tentative statements informally with conferences and courses on the spiritual life in the novitiate would not serve the simplicity and quiet of spirit that is essential for this year of spiritual transcendence in faith. The year of initiation in the life of divine intimacy is not the year for even informal discussions about transfiguration or trans-substantiation, infallibility or indefectibility. The novice should be initiated in a Fundamental Catholic Spirituality, a spirituality rooted in the Doctrine of the Church, based on the teachings, traditions, and directives of the Catholic Church and its Magisterium. The teachings of the Catholic Church are more than mere theology. Over and above theology, they have been raised to the dignity of common Catholic doctrine. Fundamental spirituality as communicated in the novitiate should refer informally to these teachings of the Church when the spirituality taught naturally evokes such reference.

In accordance with *Renovationis Causam*, the novitiate should not offer formal courses in systematic theology for all the reasons we have expounded. Moreover, the initiate, if necessary, should have been instructed in basic Church Doctrine before he entered the novitiate during his pre-entrance program or postulancy.

It is true that many priests and religious may have profited greatly for their spiritual life from the reading of new theological visions. While these new teachings may be most inspirational, they may not be fundamental Church Doctrine. Only time will tell if they will become part of everyday Church teaching. In the meantime, as long as they are not disapproved of by the Magisterium, they can be a source of enlightenment and inspiration. We ask only would it be wise to root the first spiritual initiation of novices in tentative theologies? Would it not be wiser to root that first initiation in the teachings of the Church, indicating how the acknowledged masters of Catholic spirituality *informally* refer to those teachings? The fundamental Doctrine of the Church about the spiritual life should be a hidden axis around which the whole program of the novitiate turns day by day—a hidden axis, referred to constantly but informally, while initiating novices into the life of the spirit.

The stress on Church Doctrine does not mean that

the making of new theologies is not of importance. What exploratory theologians try to do is necessary for many reasons. Let me mention only a few.

The fullness of Catholic life in the world is not only a question of fundamental spirituality, of personal intimate union with God in Christ. This intimacy may later urge some religious, after their novitiate, to gain deeper intellectual insight into the attempts of theologians to tie traditional teachings in with the findings of science and thought today, to discover answers to contemporary problems and needs, to help humanity devise a system of ethics that can benefit its present condition. In service of the apostolate, a religious, after the novitiate, may be allowed to participate intellectually in the dialogue between doctrine and the social cultural trends of thought that dominate the modern world. This realm of study is beyond that of fundamental spirituality. It is beyond the sacred art and science of personal intimacy with God in Christ, which is the prerogative of the master of spiritual initiation and the central interest of the novice in his canonical year. This realm of new theological adaptation is not the core of the spiritual life, though for some religious after the novitiate it can be a genuine apostolic expression of this core and foster consequently a deepening of their spiritual life.

Theologies, of course, may contain an inspiration to the spiritual life, but as long as they are tentative doctrines they should not be considered the ultimate and exclusive foundation of the spiritual life. Some of the tentative views of the innovative theologian may be adopted sooner or later by the Church in her daily teaching. Then these views are no longer mere theology or tentative doctrine; they have been raised to the dignity and certainty of Church Doctrine. From that moment on, they may be referred to *informally* during the courses and conferences in the novitiate, provided they are relevant to the life of intimacy with the Lord. The wise director or directress does not refer unnecessarily to doctrines that are still tentative, for building on a tentative doctrine means building on a foundation that later may appear to be a false foundation. Moreover, such references could lead to unnecessary confusion and complexity during a year that must prevent superfluous intellectual complications. Such intricacies detract from the quiet of mind that prepares for the transintellectual knowledge of faith and love described by St. Thomas and St. John. Moreover, no matter how scholarly, inspiring, convincing, and attractive such tentative doctrines may be, they do not yet participate in the divine certainty which is the privilege of the Magisterium only. There is more Church Doctrine about the spiritual life than can be absorbed in one year of novitiate. Why not root one's first initiation in that doctrine?

God wants the novice first of all to keep caring for his intimacy with Him, not to get lost in the indiscriminate reading of numerous new theologies, but to deepen himself in the simple fundamental teachings of the Church about grace; about union with the Holy Trinity in Christ; about the meaning of the sacraments and the Holy Mass for his spiritual life; about the meaning of the Church itself for his inner growth in faith and love; about the prayer of the Church in its liturgy. All of this should be offered to him first of all in the context of the teachings of the spiritual masters, for they have already made this fundamental Church Doctrine the starting point of a spiritual doctrine that inspires and enlightens the initiate about the intimate living of the message of the Revelation in such a way that it unites him with God.

The novice should be, therefore, a Christ-oriented, a Church-oriented, a Scripture-oriented person in a spiritual sense. He should dwell on the mysteries of the faith humbly in a spirit of prayer. He should not spend this year of spiritual transcendence in endless arguments about various possible intellectual explanations of these mysteries. Prayer is not an exercise in apologetics. He should be a person of deep Christian faith. He should let the truth of the Church seep in, becoming increasingly aware that he can never become intimate with God by his own learning or power. Only grace can give him a spiritual life. He must come to believe deeply that God will grant him this undeserved gift, if he keeps prayerfully dwelling on what the Church teaches about the fundamentals of the spiritual life and what her spiritual masters express practically and inspirationally. Then in God's own good time, he may receive the divine gift of intimacy that no human study or inventiveness by itself alone can force or compel.

Program of Initiation

What we have said thus far about initiation should be embedded, of course, in a definite program. We could define a novitiate program as a balanced, self-consistent order of facilitating practices and incarnational occasions that foster the emergent spiritual life of the initiates.

"Balanced" means that each practice of the order of daily life should complement all others. All practices, lived in harmony and balance, should facilitate the spiritual life of the novice without harming the wholesome development of healthy needs and aspirations. There must be time for the novice to be alone in nature or in the quiet of his private room, time to be with the community in a relaxed way, time for bodily exercise, for practical duties, for recreation, prayer and meditation, for spiritual reading and reflection, for the keeping of a spiritual diary, for the aesthetic dimension. All of these practices should be lived in a style that facilitates initiation into a well integrated spiritual life. Therefore, we may also call the ideal program "self-consistent," indicating the harmony that should exist among the different practices, all supporting one another in light of the overall aim of the canonical year. This program is an "order" insofar as the whole system of practices is regulated in a certain schematic way. The purpose of this order is to avoid arbitrariness, to provide a structure which creates an atmosphere of certainty and consistency. This atmosphere, in turn, promotes inner peace and recollection and helps to overcome agitation and restlessness. It is understandably difficult to live such an order if one has not been introduced to its meaning and practice during the pre-entrance program and postulancy. Without this preparation, the canonical year itself may be nothing more than a pre-entrance program or postulancy.

Some order of facilitating practices is necessary. Since the initiate, like all men, is an incarnated spirit, it is never enough for him to concentrate only meditatively on the essentials of the spiritual life. He must be faced with practical occasions and situations in which he can incarnate this life.

Such practices should be facilitating. They do not cause the spiritual life; they merely facilitate its initiation. It is only grace that causes the spiritual unfolding of the novice. The director must ask himself from time to time if the existing structures, conditions, rules, and regulations are still facilitating this initiation. Do they still foster the relaxed recollection, the inner stillness and transcendent presence to one's life that make possible, with God's grace, the emergence of a spiritual life? The director should strive to devise practices which are facilitating not only for the group but also for the average person within that group. This requirement is based on the insight that spiritual life is ultimately a life of the individual person. The life of the community can support this personal spirituality but not substitute for it. For that reason, there should be sufficient room in the novitiate program for private prayer, reflection, and study, for solitude in nature and in the privacy of one's room. One can see, therefore, the advisability of having the novitiate in the country and of having it built with rooms that are sufficiently soundproof to diminish the distractions from inside and outside the house.

Such practices, as lived by all, foster in each novice the right dedication. When novices pray together or participate in the Holy Mass, their devout presence together is an inspiration for each one of them, offering a kind of mutual edification.

Another expression in our description that may sound unusual is "incarnational occasions." We have seen already that human spiritual life needs to incarnate itself in daily reality to be a real spiritual life. The balanced order of novitiate practices should be experienced as a series of concrete occasions to express one's fidelity, adoration, love, and humility in concrete actions or observances. Later in this chapter, we will explain how important the concept of "occasion" is for the prevention of a mentality of blind repetition, which could feed into the hidden neurotic tendencies of the initiates.

Such facilitating practices and incarnational occasions foster the spiritual life extrinsically and intrinsically: extrinsically in the sense that these practices offer themselves first of all as external occasions for inner growth; intrinsically in that the initiate must personalize and interiorize the deeper meaning of such practices.

An important occasion for growth in any program of initiation should be the presence of the director. The best possible program may have little effect without his inspiring and animating presence. The poorest program can be effective if the director is a person of true spiritual presence and inspiration. He must be present as a person who himself is on the way toward God, who tries to live a prayerful life, who is present to the Presence of the Divine. This quality of presence holds true for spiritual directors of any program of initiation.

The Wrong Way of Living Rules and Regulations

The structures and practices we are speaking of can be lived in many ways. If an initiate becomes tense because of structures, it is often not the fault of the structures themselves but of the way in which he tries to live them. He should learn to live the daily rule, so to speak, as an orchestration of his life before God. He must grow in the art of living the rule personally, graciously, aesthetically, prayerfully, **harmoniously**, leisurely. He should see each practice of the novitiate program as a different instrument to be played by him in a relaxed way and to be harmonized in the orchestra of his self-unfolding spiritual life.

Rules and regulations of the novitiate can be lived in a spirit of repetitive training. In that case, their blind repetition shades easily over into an automatic manisfestation of the neurotic tendencies that are in each of us. Spiritual exercises done in a spiritless repetitious way may reinforce the hidden neurotic process.

The core of any neurotic process is blind automatic repetition. Neurosis basically means that a person in a situation does not answer to the situation as an enlightened, flexible, free person but in an automatic way. He repeats automatically a reaction of the past whether or not the reaction is appropriate in this case. For example, if in childhood the situation was such that a person felt he could survive only by withdrawal, now, no matter the situation, he may automatically repeat this withdrawal reaction. Directors of initiates must be careful, therefore, in using any blind training techniques, for such training may reinforce tendencies to automatic repetition. It may take away personal response.

Training demands a blind reaction to key words. If the person already has neurotic tendencies, training may play into these or deepen them. Some neurotic persons may like training for this reason. Repetitive drill in regard to spiritual reading, for example, may foster more bad spiritual reading habits than good ones. Some may have been trained merely in how to do spiritual reading functionally; they were drilled to read for fifteen minutes, being sure to read the whole time to "get it in." Some people love this automatic repetition. If someone tells them exactly what to do they feel relieved. They are fearful of reflection or of relating the text of spiritual reading to their personal lives.

Mere functional repetition, without growth in insight and personal presence, is self-defeating. It does damage to the spiritual personality by hampering the spontaneous, intuitive, that is, preconscious and supraconscious, functions. Spiritual understanding cannot be learned by an ego-repetitive type of training because of its different nature and orientation; it is free, creative, and open, while such training is blind, stereotyped, and narrow.

Does this mean there is no place for repetition? There is a place for it as long as we do not see it as the way to spiritual growth and understanding. Rules and regulations should organize a repetition of regular "occasions" for spiritual dwelling and understanding. Thus, for example, it may be useful to have a regular time for spiritual reading and meditation.

We must carefully understand the expression "occasion for spiritual dwelling and understanding." An occasion would be a time provided for meditation, spiritual reading, or the like. If these occasions are to lead to spiritual growth, the initiates must do other things inwardly, such as calming down, pacifying their minds, placing themselves before the Divine Majesty. Even then spiritual understanding does not necessarily happen. It is necessary, however, to have such occasions. Symbolically they create room in the day to focus more directly on one's spiritual growth. What will happen during these occasions is not something one can be sure of or decide ahead of time. Special occasions for spiritual growth through meditative dwelling are not the same as spiritual growth itself.

Most people need such occasions. For example, students need lectures and other occasions of learning. No normal teacher expects them at all times to absorb what he tells them, but it does help to have classes as occasions for learning.

There is thus nothing wrong with the repetition of occasions, provided it is clear that the fruitfulness of such occasions is dependent on inner attitudes. Some religious people faithfully went to the chapel and sat through the time of meditation but did not really meditate. They had not been helped to meditate personally. Instead they were just drilled to fill the outline of occasions: be on time in the chapel, spend the required time for the exercises, and so on. Occasions were not really used by them as means to foster spiritual development.

Spiritual Repetition

We must distinguish this repetition of right occasions from a different kind of repetition in the core of the spiritual life. People may experience repeatedly a loving presence to God, perhaps during the "occasion" of meditation, liturgy, spiritual reading. This repetition is different from automatic repetition on the ego level.

On the spiritual level, a repeated presence to God steadily deepens this presence; while it seems the same, it is all the time changing, not in focus but in depth. The same happens in human love. A person can repeat "I love you" many times to his beloved; this repetition done in a loving way is not automatic but an expression of an ever-deepening attitude or experience. The same can be said of my repeating to God, "I adore You."

Freeing Repetition on Lower Levels of Life

There is also a desirable automatic repetition on the lower levels of life that frees the person for spiritual presence. Such repetition should be fostered not for its own sake but for the freedom it grants.

For example, we all have a way of getting up, dressing, going to work. We do all of these customary things automatically, without thinking about them, thereby keeping our mind free for other more important things. Automatic functions on the lower levels of existence liberate us from a preoccupation with trivia. When we say "lower levels," we mean things like dressing, like the common politeness of everyday interaction with those we do not know intimately, how we use tools; the basic movements of the body in dance, sports, driving a car. Such automatic repetition is out of place when we must do things that really count in life. So-called blind repetition in work techniques, however, can set us free for the deeper creative orientation of work.

Spiritual reading, for instance, cannot take place except in personal presence to the text. This presence would be difficult, if not impossible, if the acts of holding the book, of reading words and letters, would not have become automatic acts demanding of us no explicit attention. Compare what happens when we read in a foreign language we have not yet mastered; it is difficult to be spiritually present to a text we are painfully trying to translate.

Ego-repetitive techniques that purport to effect in and by themselves personal growth give the wrong impression. Over-estimation of the transforming power of regulations alone may have been the mistake made in certain novitiates and seminaries during the past century. Occasionally directors may have given the impression that if one followed all the rules functionally he would be a saint. This is not true. External rules ought to be used as occasions for inner growth; they do not guarantee this growth in and by themselves.

Initiation and Education to Self-Knowledge

Initiation, without a steady education to self-knowledge, can never lead to spiritual wisdom and maturity. We must know what is moving us. Do we behave in a certain manner because we are compulsive, over-anxious, hysterical, perfectionistic? The director must educate his initiates to self-understanding before God, a process which, like initiation, is never complete; it can always go deeper.

The director must render conflicting feelings and their consequences less fixed and rigid by bringing them within the realm of conscious selection, direction, and control. Spiritual direction, particular examen, journal keeping, spiritual reading, and discussion can be of help here.

The director has to help the initiates to grow in a relaxed kind of self-control. Enlightened self-control helps to neutralize the infraconscious conflicts, affects, and defenses that give rise to rigidity. Spiritual directors often taught self-control but the wrong kind, that is, control of only the surface symptoms of inner conflicts, affects, and defenses. Self-control was not sufficiently directed at the sources of such secondary symptoms.

Perhaps a person early in life had a traumatic experience with authority that was subsequently repressed in the infraconsciousness. A conflict developed. As a result the person has become either over compliant or over rebellious. Instead of helping him discover the underlying source, the tendency in a director may have been just to focus on the symptoms.

Advice was given such as "Try to be kind and humble when you meet a superior. Don't look so angry when you are asked to do something." "Control your impolite language when speaking to somebody above you." The initiate feels himself in a bind; the inner surge to react excessively to authority is still there; he still has the same inclinations. Following these admonitions, however, he controls only the external expression of his rebelliousness by an act of will. If he does not get to the source of his negative behavior, there will be more conflicts and bigger problems after the time of initiation. Initiates need a self-control rooted in knowing and working through the inner sources of their problems.

Another example of a person who suffers from hidden conflict is seen in someone who is lazy and excessively slow. This person develops pains and illness whenever a job is mentioned. The answer to his problem is not simply to tell him to get to work. Rather the director has to help him find out why he feels that way. Perhaps he fosters in himself the wrong imaginations. What fantasies dominate his mind? Why? Maybe his mother treated him like a precious piece of china.

The director, in short, has to treat the inner cause not merely seek an external solution. Otherwise the inner source of the wrong attitude will remain. Only its symptoms are suppressed, with a tremendous expenditure of energy. This daily waste of energy to keep the lid on problems like those of anger, aggression, and resentment is harmful to the health and effectiveness of the person. Moreover, the problems do not go away. After initiation they will come out, when, for example, the person is in the classroom teaching. Then his repressed feelings endanger the emotional life of his students. This problem is especially crucial for participative religious. Because of their future key positions in parish, hospital, and school, their unsolved inner conflicts can become a threat to the emotional health of the population.

Here are some additional examples of such conflicts and where they can lead. Some initiates always procrastinate and don't know why. From early in life, they were inclined to dawdle, to waste time by idling. Compulsive dawdling can be a subtle expression of an inner struggle with authority. Perhaps the initiate's mother—or her substitute—may have been excessively authoritarian. She may have tried to hurry the child up—in eating, dressing, toilet training, walking. The child seeks a way to get back at this powerful adult. He begins to dawdle about eating, excreting, washing, dressing and undressing. Once this resistance has become part of his infraconscious reaction pattern, it emerges constantly and monotonously as one way to get at authority; it stays with him for a lifetime—at play, in chores, in studies. If he does not gain insight into these tendencies, no freedom from them is possible. Such paralyzing tendencies may persist during and after the novitiate. Indeed, some of these patterns may persist to plague the life work of the religious.

The director in this case—instead of going to the heart of the matter—may merely exhort the dawdling novice, out of love for God, to use all his will power to hurry up. The well meaning initiate may throw himself anxiously into undisciplined, chaotic, and hurried activity. His overactivity is again stereotyped; it has the same blind, repetitive quality as his dawdling. This neurotic reaction will only be reinforced if the director praises the novice for trying so heroically to cope with his procrastination.

We do not speak here about a serious clinical neurosis that could not be dealt with in spiritual direction. The person ought then to be referred to a therapeutic counselor. We have in mind only the more or less common neurotic tendencies found in many persons that can be handled by a well prepared spiritual director.

If a director notices that a novice does something wrongly and tells him so, the novice might be inclined merely to switch behavior on the surface. He may want to please or impress the director, or feel relief from the guilt feelings he induces.

Another person may seek relief from inner pressure not in procrastination but in compulsive rushing. This person, because of unconscious needs, conflicts, and anxieties, does not dare to tarry. He finds himself running from one half-finished task to the next.

A third one may battle an inner terror of losing himself in dependency on authority. He tries to diminish his fear of dependency by automatic defiance. No matter what the director suggests, teaches, or proposes, such a person will defiantly find fault with it.

Automatic compliance is another defense against inner fears. Rigid and excessive submissiveness is typical of the person who cannot read, reflect, or act creatively; he merely does functionally what he is told; he only complies. We can find religious who have done extraordinarily well in school, college, and during formation years, but they have done so on basis of a neurotic submissiveness. When the person reaches middle age, this submissiveness may explode under the pressure of unresolved, underlying problems.

Others cannot see or hear what is clearly said or written. Blockage may occur at moments when a conference, advice, or passage in a book threatens to make them aware of repressed conflicts.

Many suffer from unsolved sibling rivalries. A person may have experienced in his family a competitive rivalry with his brothers and sisters. This rivalry is easily reawakened in the novitiate, especially if there are just a few novices. Unconsciously, the person falls back on this family scheme of the past; a rivalry arises, the source of which is unknown to him. It may express itself in one of two ways. He may feel overstimulated to look and do well in the novitiate. He must prove to himself, his director, and his peers that he is better than the others. Or he suffers from over inhibition. In this case his fear to show up badly in this compulsive competition gives rise to discouragement, inferiority feelings, false humility, deep insecurity, and withdrawal from any relaxed and reasonable pursuit of excellence.

If the director finds it advantageous to discuss with the novices the possibility of such conflicts, he should do so in a way that would not evoke excessive and anxious introspection. First of all, he may wisely present such problems in a general way discussing them with the group as a whole or placing them in the content of a conference or lecture. In his discussion he should portray these tendencies as normal, as something we all have to cope with to some degree though not to the extent of their becoming a serious neurotic deviation. He should help them to look at such tendencies from the viewpoint of spirituality and not merely from that of psychology and psychiatry. He should show that God allows such problems in us since the fall of man and that we should bear with them as our part in the suffering of Christ. He should help them to see against a wider spiritual horizon the human defenses that may happen to different people in various ways and degrees. He should also stress that there is no neurotic tendency that is not partly influenced by the culture. Thus an achievement culture such as ours often leads to sibling rivalry. This insight too puts the problem in a wider perspective.

If the person comes for individual consultation about one of these problems, the director should be sure to put it against a wider spiritual and cultural horizon to prevent the person from engaging in more introspection than necessary.

To help the initiates personalize such general insights, he can illustrate them with stories and examples. This personalization of insights comes almost spontaneously, except in severe neurotic cases. The latter are not usually found among the novices; they should have been treated before admission to the novitiate. He must bring out his point several times from various angles in the hope that the novice will be able to see what it means for him.

The insight of the initiate will never be perfect and finished. As he grows older he will see more; life stimulates insight. The director, on his side, tries to foster a degree of self-knowledge sufficient to free the novice from passive submission to the tyranny of ancient and submerged patterns in his personality. The initiate must realize in turn that he is allowed to feel things and to become aware of what is behind them.

Blind disciplinary techniques are only seemingly successful. They may give the novice merely an anxious feeling that he must control something while reading, reflecting, and interacting with the community. They fail, however, to make clear what exactly is to be controlled inside the novice so that he may be more open to the Divine in a peaceful way. He risks the danger of misdirected willfulness if he does not know what is to be controlled. To find the latter, a process of self-discovery is necessary.

The initiate should avoid the opposite exaggeration of complete freedom, of acting out all feelings, of letting go without limit. Unreserved acting out does not bring self-understanding and self-mastery in and by itself. Blind letting go can distort and block insights into the causes of inhibitions. For example, a directress should not suggest to a sister who is shy that she should suddenly display an excessive outgoingness. For one thing her shyness may be normal for her. Even if the novice is really inhibited and anxious, the directress should not force an external change on her. A forced letting go without insight is not the solution for her shyness.

Unwise techniques like these can block the preconscious opening up of the initiate by intensifying the activity of inhibiting neurotic forces. For example, if a novice directress shows an excessive authoritarian attitude, it can block the relaxed opening up of the novice. Such an attitude may reactivate infraconscious reaction patterns of a rebellious or over compliant nature in novices who have had unpleasant experiences with authoritarian persons. On the other hand, if the novice directress is too sweet, motherly, and kind, there can also be a blocking of self-discovery, for she may reactivate attitudes the novice had as an infant toward her mother.

Certain techniques can overstimulate the novice by playing on marked neurotic obsessions and compulsions. For example, some who enter may come from an anxious overstrict Catholic milieu and suffer excessive pseudo-guilt feelings combined with a moralistic achievement drive. A novice director may stress repeatedly: "This is a year of decision; every hour counts; you will have to account to God for how you spend every minute of this year." In that case, those who are inclined to excessive guilt feelings may overreact.

Unrealistic idealization and the fostering of excessive guilt may be harmful. An unrealistic expectation of community does not speak of community in its fundamental sense but of the myth of community as "sweet togetherness." This dream gives rise to floaty feelings and unreal hopes. Worse still, it can also give rise to guilt complexes and paranoid feelings. If persons living in such an idealized community are supposed to be open all of the time to everyone about every feeling, then the person can feel excessively guilty about not being open enough or paranoid about the dire consequences of what he has revealed or thinks he has revealed to others.

The Director of Initiation

Our discussion of the nature of spiritual initiation in the religious community, of the initiation program, and the various ways of living it, made us aware of the crucial role of the director of initiation. It raises questions about his position, his selection, his preparation.

The master of religious life stands at the heart of the consecrated life. He is called by the Lord to inspire and safeguard the continuous rebirth and abiding presence of his community *as religious*.

This person at the center of religious life has been designated in the West as novice master, director or directress of postulants, novices, juniors, or as director of a seminary of religious. Historically his position is central and primary. The consecrated life in East and West emerged when celibate men or women gathered around a wise and experienced master of interior life to be taught and formed in the ways of the spirit. Living contact with the master of spirituality was thus a first means of religious development and inspiration.

The expansion and increasing institutionalization of religious life had the effect of lessening the central position of the master of religious living. This tendency was strengthened as religious communities in the West became responsible for extensive cultural and social services. The demand for professionals was pressing. Time, energy, and attention had to be expanded to select and prepare religious in such specialized fields as nursing, social service, and education. Selection of efficient, task-oriented superiors became paramount. The core person of religious life, the master of spirituality, became less central. Less time and effort was given to the choice and preparation of this crucial person who would have the responsibility of communicating the religious life form itself to initiates entering these communities.

Consequences of Deficient Preparation

The consequences of diminishing what should be a primary concern could be devastating. Unformed spiritual directors may substitute for the cultivation of interiority a training in outer style and manner no longer rooted in true self-unfolding. Well prepared directors, on the other hand, would be able to unveil the motivations guiding this mode of living and to evolve in the initiate means of appropriating personally and renewing creatively some of the habits, customs, and devotions revered by generations. The not fully prepared master of the inner life may exert a onesided influence. Instead of unfolding patiently with each candidate unique modes of presence to God, he may unwittingly confine spiritual life to mere conformity with customs and devotions and thus fail to set in motion the dynamics of turning one's whole being toward the Lord.

As long as religious life escaped questioning, the consequences of such deficiencies did not appear so clearly. Now that this questioning is almost universal, many are unable to experience anew the spiritual meaning of their consecrated life, which may not have been communicated to them in a living way during the years of their formation.

Some may have found on their own, or in contact with a spiritual guide, the road toward self-integration in presence to the Lord. Others, however, may leave, confused, embittered, and sometimes distorted by a split between peripheral devotions, impersonal patterns of living, and their hidden need for personal spiritual unfolding, which such behavior and piety alone cannot accomplish. Others again may attempt to turn religious life into something it is not, for instance, a mere service association. Still others may develop personality disturbances, for they were not able to find and integrate themselves under wise and sensitive guidance in the vital years of initiation.

Responsibility of the Master of Interiority

The broken line of spirituality developed over the centuries by outstanding masters in the light of the basic doctrines, traditions, and directives of the Church must be taken up again and enriched by present insights. It is the responsibility of every religious, and especially of those in formation, to make this tradition viable and effective for the men and women who come to religious life from contemporary culture.

The specific responsibility of the master of interiority in regard to these initiates is vastly different from that of the professor in systematic theology, the psychologist, sociologist, therapist, or analyst.

Because of practical pressures, one may estimate more highly the training of religious for technical, educational, and scientific degrees which could bring status, influence, and remuneration to the community. When this tendency prevails, it may lead to an underestimation of the need to allot sufficient time for the preparation of a master of interiority.

However, most significant for the survival of religious life *as religious* is to assure that new members receive an initial formation that instills in them as future priests, educators, nurses, and social workers the living awareness that they are not mere professionals in their respective fields; they are called to witness implicitly, and explicitly if appropriate, how their form of participation in the culture can be lived and integrated within a living faith and spirituality.

For the average religious, the success or failure of his religious presence in the culture depends almost wholly on the spiritual initiation received at the crucial beginning of his consecrated life. When this meaning is lost or never well-established, is it any wonder that he may ask himself why he should live his professional task in the world within the frame of this consecration?

Time Needed for Preparation of Director

Three years seem a minimum for a fundamental initiation of the future director into the knowledge, experience, sensitivity, wisdom, and art of guidance and communication necessary for effective personal and spiritual formation.

It would be impossible, and therefore irresponsible, to try within less time to achieve the inner transformation the spiritual director himself is in need of; to acquaint him with the spiritual doctrine of the Church, with classic and contemporary masters of spirituality; to teach him the viable contributions of the human sciences; to train him in the art and dynamics of formation, guidance, and counseling; to acquaint him with the ways of prayer, its obstacles and possibilities; to make him understand and evaluate the manifold contemporary cultural and social influences, confusions, and prejudices his future initiates will have to clarify in themselves and to cope with under his guidance; to train him in pertinent research in spirituality; to help him develop the difficult art of expressing himself clearly, concisely, convincingly, and attractively in his lectures and conferences; to teach him theoretically and practically how to deal with personality problems and dynamics and how to structure initiation programs in tune with the directives of the Church; to make him a master in spotting and evaluating symptoms of psychopathology that may interfere with the religious unfolding of the initiate.

Transition from Student to Director

Even after these few years, it is desirable that the future director first serve as an assistant to others already well formed and experienced. This delay in assumption of full responsibility will give him the opportunity to evaluate duties and problems typical of his community and of the house of formation to which he is assigned.

Moreover, not being burdened immediately with administrative details will enable him to reflect on the wisdom and experience assimilated in the minimum of three years of preparation. This reflection serves his translation of newly gained knowledge into lectures and conferences that adapt these insights clearly and attractively to the level of understanding, the mood and language of the candidates he has to reach. Gradual transition from student to director of formation is feasible if the community concerned regularly has persons in preparation. The newly prepared spiritual director may then find a predecessor already formed and functioning for a certain time as a master of religious life. Assisting him will enable the future director to profit from the experience of the present person in charge.

Choice of the Director of Initiation

Religious life is in a crisis. Yet this life may go on; it all depends on the depth and strength of spirit the formation personnel can foster in those who enter the community. New members will not stay merely because of the work the community is responsible for. They can do similar work—perhaps even better—as secular priests or missionaries, lay teachers, nurses or social workers.

Moreover, those who enter the novitiate program may already have a job, skill, career, education, and apostolate.

They would be foolish to enter religious life only to carry on what they were already doing. They come for more.

What they want is a wisdom, a way, a style of spirituality. A wisdom that will help them to live a richer life, that will give new meaning to what they are already doing for others. A way to come in touch with God in themselves, in others, in their work, more in touch with Him than they could be on their own. A style that shields and fosters their growth in the spirit during their daily task, more so than was possible before they entered religious life.

To sum it up, those who enter want the first thing religious life has been made for: deeper spiritual living. Only God can ultimately give them this, though He usually chooses the master of spiritual life as a channel for this gift. Without masters of the life of the spirit, what can a religious community offer? What is its use? Why should it go on? These are the questions aspirants may be asking.

Inspiring the Young to a Spiritual Life

The continuation of religious life may thus depend on one thing: that the superiors concerned choose the best religious they can find and allow them to be formed as spiritual directors, no matter the cost and the time.

Recent studies show that chapters of renewal have suspended many rules. This trend may go on, in which case the continuation of religious life more than ever will hinge on the personal life of each religious. However, it is no easy task to inspire the young to live a spiritual life, to lead them to inner rules now that many of the outer rules are no longer in effect.

Many novices have a college education. They have studied the human sciences. Their teachers may have taught them a way of life that impressed them deeply. A spiritual director must help them to purge their knowledge about the art of personal living, to perfect it in light of the wisdom of the Church and the great spiritual writings to which he introduces them in a contemporary way. If the formation director were to leave their college information about the art of living untouched, it might haunt them for a lifetime and prevent the spiritual life from ever taking hold in them.

How can a person help novices in this way without sufficient study and preparation? To be an effective spiritual director in a time of few external rules, it is no longer enough to be a devout and strict religious who knows and keeps these rules. More is required.

Therefore, the person chosen to prepare himself for spiritual leadership should be better than average intellectually. He must be able to keep up research in spirituality. He must be sharp enough to see through himself and through the people he guides. Otherwise they will manipulate him by playing on his own pet ideas, worries, needs, desires, and ambitions, of which he himself may be unaware.

This person should be of better intellect than the average college or graduate student, though not necessarily brilliant. A person who is brilliant may be fond of his own cleverness; he may miss the humility and the unassuming behavior of which a master of the spiritual life should be a striking example. He may be unwilling and unable to speak simply and clearly to young religious less gifted than he. Nor may he want to live the somewhat hidden life of a director of formation. He may be so fond of abstract ideas and their logical arrangement that he has lost touch with his own emotional and spiritual experience. Then he cannot be in touch with the same experience in others. A brilliant person may be so smug about his book-knowledge that he has become deaf and blind for life-knowledge. He simply cannot hear what is said when people discuss the wisdom that comes from personal life and experience. Before hearing and digesting their words, he is already reducing what they say to neat little abstractions which fit into some system of concepts he has read or thought about. If, however, a brilliant religious also has what it takes to be a deeply humble and wise master of spirituality, so much the better.

The director should not be too young and not too old. If he is too young, he may not have found himself. He may feel insecure, in need of being liked, praised, and admired. Unsure and ambitious, he may want to show off how clever and independent he is. He may not be able to listen humbly to those who have to guide and teach him when he prepares himself for his responsibilities. Full of himself and his problems, he may not leave much room for God's grace, which is the main transforming force in his life. A too young person easily misses the docility and receptivity, the quiet of a mature prayerful mind that would help him to dwell on the spiritual wisdom of the Church and of past and present spiritual masters.

Lacking experience in life as it really is—not as he imagines it to be—he may not be settled firmly in religious life. Faced with the problems of initiates, he may discover how unsettled, floating, and imaginary his own religious life really is. This crisis may take too much time and energy to allow him to give himself wholly to the task of spiritual formation and study. He simply is not ready for it. The essence of religious life may elude him; he may be overcome by immature enthusiasm, by an idealism or social utopianism not grounded in day to day reality.

The person selected should not be too old either. He must do a lot of research in spirituality. He must learn a whole new method of study and how to discipline himself daily if he wants to become helpful. Many readings are required. His mind must still be keen enough to unravel difficult texts, his memory sharp enough to recall a variety of facts and theories. For an older person, it may not be easy to master the art of counseling and spiritual direction. To learn this art well, he must face his own needs, faults, motives; he may have to change his views. For a person settled in his ways, this change can be difficult to take.

Ideally, the person chosen should have suffered the hardships of the everyday common life of those who are no longer in formation or study but concretely at work. He should have proved to those in charge that he can give himself quietly to his daily duty, plodding away no matter the commotion around him. He should be able to keep his balance, his peace and common sense, his in-touchness with everyday reality, his sense of humor.

Level-headed and down to earth, he should be free from exaltation, from wild spurts of fantasy, from a bent toward the exotic, the novel, the impressive, the grandiose, and the uncommon. Neither should he be plagued by a violent enthusiasm for purely personal views that could harm the growth of the young people he has to guide were he to force his ideas on them.

This person should have an interest in study and research in the area of spiritual life; a sensitivity for people coupled with the ability to see through their schemes, pretentions, and self-deceptions; a capacity for speaking to a group in a way that makes things clear to them and at the same time genuinely inspires them.

Strong Enough to Stand Alone

The master of religious life should be able to stand on his own two feet. Personal and spiritual growth in solitude is a delicate venture. The discovery of self, the absence of distractions, the quiet and silence that heighten sensitivity—all this makes novices vulnerable and impressionable. No outsider knows—as the spiritual director does—where each novice is at a certain moment. An outsider can do untold harm when he "butts in" unwisely. The novice master must be strong enough to keep him out, even if he is disliked for doing this.

He must also be strong enough to ward off religious who want to bend the formation program in the direction of their pet projects. Well meaning, hard working religious, who happen to be engaged in some special kind of activity like nursing, social work, education, foreign missions, may be enormously enthusiastic about their work. All of these endeavors can be excellent, but none of them in and by itself is the essence of religious life. The novitiate must before all else be an occasion for growth in the essence of this life. Training for a special kind of work comes later. The spiritual director should thus be strong enough not to give in when some religious try to transform his novitiate into a practical training center for the kind of work they happen to be doing.

The novice master must also be strong enough to stand alone at times. He is the shepherd of the spiritual meaning and wisdom of his community. He keeps these spiritual treasures alive and up to date by his prayerful research and study. His community, like all communities, is one of fallen men. Its members may forget the religious meaning of the incidental work they are doing. Blinded by their enthusiasm, they may make a special work in itself the exclusive purpose and meaning of their life.

At such moments, when his community may be on the verge of spiritual decay, the director of religious life must be strong enough to stand alone. He must make clear to his novices that a community cannot survive as a *religious* community if its heart and essence is lost, if it becomes a service association instead of a life association.

Problem of Immaturity

Immaturity in a spiritual director would not necessarily be straightened out by his direction of others. On the contrary, his function may deeply harm him, for he may live his role only on the level of his own immaturity, weakness, self-deception, and ambition. He will find weapons and defenses in the ideas he learns and then use them to show off a wisdom, maturity, and spirituality he does not really possess. He may become adept in the manipulation of people around him; he may learn the right words to say, the right manners to display. He knows how to sound and look like the wise man he really is not.

What is more serious, how can one tell if his quirks are merely signs of immaturity or a lasting part of his personality? If the latter were to prove true—and the risk is always there—it would be a grave injustice to the community to trust its future to him. We must stress again that it is the master of spirituality who will make or break

religious community life. The religious entering the community may only become as wise and balanced as their
spiritual directors are. Indeed, the master of spirituality
will have more responsibility for the survival of the
community than any general or provincial superior, any
chapter or counsel. Since the loosening of central authority and rules, the power and strength of religious life have
been transferred from the outer to the inner life of each
religious. The one who has the key to that life has also the
key to the future of the religious community to which he
belongs. History has handed this key back to the spiritual
directors and animators.

Surely it is difficult to find the right person. It is a
momentous decision to make; all others pale beside it, but
it is infintely wiser to pray and search for the right person
than to risk a wrong decision and therewith the future of
religious life in one's community.

FUNDAMENTAL SPIRITUALITY AND
SPIRITUAL DIRECTION

Leaders of various denominations are concerned about the growing number of faithful who feel restless, tense, and strained as a result of their inability to integrate their spiritual life with contemporary culture, art, and science. A similar concern can be noticed among those civil authorities who are responsible for the mental health of the population. They increasingly realize that the percentage of the population adhering to religious tenets is high. Any effort by civil authorities to raise the mental health of the population as a whole is doomed to failure as long as they cannot secure the cooperation of religious denominations. These denominations must be able to counsel their faithful in ways of making spirituality an integral part of their life and their life an integral part of spirituality. With such spiritual direction behind them the faithful are less likely to experience the tenets of their faith in a schizoid way that splits them off from contemporary life, from society, and from their neighbors who do not cherish the same spiritual convictions.

Lack of integration and loss of peace are manifest in many believers, among them those who have dedicated their lives to religion, such as rabbis, ministers, priests, theologians, chaplains, nuns, brothers, and seminarians. Similar tensions appear in societies formed by them, such as congregations and parishes, schools and organizations, religious orders and associations. Such communities are wondering just how communal life based on spiritual tenets can be lived in tune with modern insight and experience.

The principles of spirituality themselves are not so much at stake as is their insertion in present life experience without betrayal of the truth, either in spiritual formulations or in contemporary knowledge. The psychological and social-cultural impotence of the believer to harmonize life and spirituality may arouse the apprehension that something is wrong with principles of spirituality themselves, that they are alien to life. Once this suspicion is born, it is nourished by the daily experience of the painful consequences of this lack of synthesis; it finds, moreover, ready confirmation in the sayings and writings of those who dismiss spirituality and are prone to identify the deficient psycho-social incarnation of spirituality with spirituality itself. This malignant growth of mistrust may result in a silent lapsing away from the faith or in the loss of a religious vocation. Such failure could have been prevented if a timely spiritual director of these groups and individuals had healed the split between the truth of the life of the spirit and the human wisdom of living a meaningful existence.

Breakdown of Spiritual Direction

We may ask ourselves why our generation is faced with a crisis of integration of a magnitude seemingly unknown to former generations. Because it was always beneficial to counsel believers on the harmonization of daily living and spiritual life, religions in the East and West developed systems of spiritual guidance. Today in the

West, however, this development has more or less broken down. When we read letters and biographies of the centuries in which spiritual masters lived, such as Meister Eckhart, Suso, Tauler, Teresa of Avila, John of the Cross, Ignatius or even later Olier, Bérulle, and Libermann, we realize at once that spiritual direction, at least among religious, priests, and devout laity, was common in the past while it seems at present almost non-existent.

We suspect that both phenomena, the contemporary split between life and spirituality and the breakdown of spiritual direction, are interrelated. Our hypothesis is that spiritual direction was abundantly available in other centuries partly because it was a less perplexing enterprise than it is in this period of history. In medieval times religion was other-worldly in orientation. The cultural world, moreover, was less differentiated and distracting than contemporary society teeming with new discoveries, insights, and techniques. Primitive medicine, science, feudal hierarchy, simple technique, and limited organization were easily harmonized with a religious presence to reality. A spiritual director familiar with the life of prayer and contemplation could guide the soul in its ascendance to God. The contemporary believer, however, is born into a culture that reveals the world as task and challenge. By osmosis and encounter, he assimilates the passionate involvement of his contemporaries in the development of the earth and its riches. The problem that looms heaviest in his life of faith is that of an authentic permeation of his religious and worldly life with his presence to God and man.

Another aspect that made spiritual direction less complex in a former era is that of man's spontaneous dependence on guidance that went with a lack of education. While in medieval times a small intellectual elite reached sublime heights, the vast majority of the population even in convents and monasteries could not read or write. Consequently, a majority of people asking spiritual direction were not touched by the confusing variety of thoughts and views that we glean from newspapers and magazines, movies, radio, and T.V. At present, a religious counselor would rarely meet a soul devoid of any of the insights communicated by the human sciences. Moreover, this steady stream of information is constantly changing as the dynamic sciences of man confront us with ever new discoveries.

In other words, a spiritual director feels compelled to keep up with the actual changing impact of the human sciences on the culture of people under his care. He must be trained not only in the art of integration but also in the art of making explicit what moves mankind today in its self-appreciation and in its appreciation of a meaningful existence.

We have already touched at least indirectly on another dimension of contemporary spiritual direction that distinguishes it from spiritual direction in the past, namely, the dimension of the scientific self-knowledge of man which was almost non-existent in medieval times. We witness a tremendous development of the human sciences. Men, women, boys, and girls asking religious guidance participate spontaneously in this scientific orientation without full awareness of its structure and its subtle, continual permeation of their culture. Indeed, the life of these directees transforms itself steadily under the influence of new insights in these fields.

To be sure, the enlightenment of any one of these areas is by itself too limited to alter their life significantly. However, many innovations in the realm of cultural and scientific specialization do carry implications for the wisdom of living. These implications transcend their fields of origin and filter down into the pre-reflective realm of preconsciousness where they collide and fuse, erode former convictions, and insert a new awareness that leads to the birth of a new vision of man.

This lived vision is contagious. It is silently communicated in movement and gesture, in dress and comportment; it permeates steadily the expressions of the mass media of communication. Our directees may live such a new image in attitude and action before they know it rationally. Sooner or later, however, the need for integration of this emerging image of man with their spiritual life will compel them to reflect on it and to render it explicit so that they may know what propels them so powerfully. They will feel forced to scrutinize it critically and to utilize it as a principle of renewal in everyday life in such a way that they do not betray the faith to which they are committed.

The spiritual director must try to foster in his directees a reflective presence to the contemporary view of man, for this awareness may set them on the road towards authentic spiritual integration. The director, therefore, should be a master in the art of raising to the level of reflective thought the pre-reflective view of man that influences preconsciously the lives of his directees. Effective spiritual direction today demands active participation of the groups and individuals directed, a participation which helps them to find their own unique way in this harmonization of spirituality and life. This participation may have been less necessary for spiritual advisement given in a feudal era when groups and individuals were not as yet so much focused on their individual differentiation and not faced with highly specialized assignments and situations in a complex society. As a result, they felt less compelled to develop their own specific project of spiritual integration in tune with the psychology of their special task and social position; they more or less mirrored the style of spiritual integration typical of the homogeneous group to which they belonged.

One main problem of spiritual direction today is the wholesome harmonization of the spiritual, personal-social, and vital dimensions of life. A sound spiritual life should not set a person or community apart from the world. Rather, an authentic spiritual inspiration will involve them with others in the world, each one in accordance with his own individual make-up and unique eternal calling.

Attempted Solutions of the Crisis of Spiritual Direction

Responsible leaders are beginning to realize more and more that the spiritual director and teacher needs a new type of preparation for his task and that it is desirable that some gifted men and women be made free for such special preparation. Initially, the difficulty arose from trying to choose from one of the already existing programs. These programs basically prepared people for an assignment in society fundamentally different from the task the spiritual director and teacher is supposed to fulfill. To be sure, the teachers of such programs were quite willing to add a few courses in which they would kindly mention that the main insights of their field could also be applied to spiritual direction and teaching. This sympathetic concession, however, was not the answer.

The first discipline asked to supply preparation for

the spiritual director was theology, especially in its dogmatic, educational, and catechetical dimension. It soon became clear, however, that the orientation of systematic theology answered a different kind of need, namely, the need of teaching clearly and convincingly the content and meaning of the religious tenets of the denomination concerned. The person formed this way was quite capable of teaching the systematic theology of his church and of advising the members of his denomination on the application of these teachings to their lives in a general way. But he was not ready to grapple with the problem of how to integrate the spiritual dimension of personal life with the other dimensions coming to light through increased knowledge of the human sciences.

Experiencing the insufficiency of this preparation, responsible leaders in religion began to look in the opposite direction. They vaguely realized that the social sciences carried a message that could be relevant for the spiritual director and teacher. This was the beginning of a period in which churches and denominations allowed an increasing number of students to specialize in psychology, psychotherapy, therapeutic counseling, sociology, and psychiatry. They expected that the crisis of spiritual direction would be solved if only a sufficient number of clergymen would be trained as professional therapists, psychologists, psychiatrists, and sociologists. Disillusion was unavoidable when the stream of graduates of these departments returned to seminaries, convents, colleges, congregations, and parishes. Somehow they did not fulfill the high expectations. It seemed that the specialization of their training made them effective for certain specialized assignments but found them at a loss in the larger task of spiritual direction and teaching. To be sure, they were excellent in clinical counseling, in the administration of tests, and in executing research projects which clarified some relevant details of the measurable aspects of life. But almost no one was able to direct himself penetratingly and effectively to the individual problems of the integration of spiritual life with insights of the human sciences.

As might be expected, the denominations, communities, and schools concerned were acutely disappointed when they invited the average clergyman thus trained to address himself to the group as a whole about one of the issues of spiritual integration facing them. Their failure was not surprising for spiritual direction transcends psychotherapy in scope, aims, and foundations. While the professional psychotherapist may feel satisfied when he has helped his client to find his way back to human encounter and reality, the spiritual director has to go beyond this stage. It is his task to assist the person who is already wholesomely alive or who has been restored to meaningful existence by psychotherapy. This person is still faced with the life-long challenge of integrating within his personality his openness to God, his faithfulness to heaven and earth. The simple fact that he is healthy and again in touch with reality and with his fellow man is not enough to accomplish this aim. On the other hand, unable to find this integration, he may be in danger of losing both his spiritual life and his peace of mind.

As we have said, even the most intensive study of psychiatry or psychotherapy cannot teach us how to integrate concretely these two dimensions of human existence. It is the well initiated specialist in spiritual direction and teaching who can effectively assist the faithful in this adventure.

Another disconcerting result of intensive training in

psychotherapy in certain quarters was the neglect of spiritual direction and teaching for the sake of psychotherapeutic preoccupation with a small minority of disturbed members of the parish, congregation, school, or religious community. I remember a conversation with a member of the state department concerning a grant for counseling training for clergy. This representative was justifiably concerned about possible pernicious consequences of grants for such purposes. He told me that he and his constituents were disturbed by reports from certain churches complaining that some of the clergy trained under such grants had turned into daily counselors of a select minority and had no time left to study creatively the issues of the integration of life and spirituality faced by their congregation.

These and similar observations do not mean, of course, that no clergyman or nun should specialize in the scientific methods of psychology, sociology, and psychotherapy. Their knowledge will be helpful in the detailed exploration of certain scientifically researchable aspects of human society; they may also be of assistance to the disturbed faithful who are not yet ready for spiritual direction and teaching. We want to stress only that mere training in psychology, psychiatry, sociology, or psychotherapy does not offer the definitive solution for the problem of integrational spiritual direction. We do not deny that certain attitudes and methods developed by psychiatrists and psychotherapists can be of relevance for the art of spiritual direction. In fact, a certain amount of psychiatric and psychological knowledge may be necessary for the spiritual director in order for him to spot those people who need psychiatric or psychotherapeutic treatment before they are able to profit fully from spiritual direction.

We conclude that the solution for the problem of the breakdown of spiritual direction at this moment of history can be found neither in systematic theology alone nor in a mere psychological, sociological, or psychotherapeutic sophistication. We are faced with a totally new situation. A new field of study and preparation is needed which adequately prepares talented and balanced people to help modern man integrate his spiritual dimension with the manifold other dimensions of his world-involved personality. In light of this insight, we can now describe what the preparation for spiritual direction should be.

The spiritual director is called to assist groups and individuals in finding the most effective means of integrating their spiritual life with the social and personal implications of contemporary life. What is the proper preparation for such a task? First of all, the future director should become acquainted not only with the main contributions of the human sciences, but also with contemporary art and literature as a means of understanding the contemporary predicament. He should, moreover, be familiar with the main insights, attitudes, and methods of psychotherapy, insofar as they can be made relevant for spiritual direction. Finally, he should be trained in the ways of effectively communicating his insights to the group he is called to direct by means of publication or conference. Most important of all is the development of his attitude and ability to do pertinent research. This will enable him to keep in tune with the developments of his culture and society, of the human sciences, and of the spirituality of his denomination.

While the medieval situation was one of limited change, the contemporary and future situation of mankind seems to be one of explosive alteration. Man's new attitude of aggressive openness towards reality and towards the mystery of his own life is at the root of an ever-accelerating movement of enlightenment. The spiritual director of tomorrow will be worthwhile to the degree that he can keep abreast of this dynamic development and to the degree that he can integrate its results within a fundamental spirituality.

Spiritual Direction and Research Orientation

What is concretely implied in an integrative research attitude which is germane to spiritual direction? The spiritual director of tomorrow should be able to explore intelligently and effectively the available literature, publications, lectures, conferences, or discussions about the life of the spirit insofar as they are related to the specific topic on which he is invited to direct society, community, or individuals. He should be able to explore art and literature insofar as they express and symbolize the human predicament relevant to the issue on which he has to lecture or advise. The same is true for his study of philosophical anthropology in regard to the problem concerned.

The typical research orientation of the spiritual director implies also the development of an attitude and an ability that we may call "dialectical-integrative." The unfolding of this capacity in the student makes it possible for him to integrate within a coherent well-balanced spiritual vision the variety of insights gained from his research in the human sciences, philosophical anthropologies, and cultural-artistic expressions. This dialectical-integrative quality enables him to wisely integrate these insights with the fundamental spirituality of his denomination or with the special demands of the spiritual calling of those believers whom he is counseling, whether in his writings, conferences, or consultations. Finally, he should be able to humanly harmonize this knowledge with a sensitive response to the psychological needs of those with whom he has to share this integrated knowledge. In other words, he must be able to make it relevant to their specific life situation, which, in turn, is influenced by a variety of factors, such as age, social-cultural condition, cultural background, vocation, education, and occupation.

Spiritual Direction and Therapeutic Counseling

The future spiritual director and teacher should develop within himself those sound attitudes that are at the root of an effective counseling relationship. We discussed already the misguided attempt to substitute therapeutic counseling for spiritual direction. Here we want to stress that the spiritual director should be trained in the utilization of certain fundamental attitudes of psychotherapists without necessarily becoming a psychotherapist himself.

We should realize that the original purpose of psychotherapy is to assist disturbed individuals who have lost contact with the world and their fellow man and who want to regain their hold on reality and their trust in man. It is impossible to counsel people effectively in the integration of life and spirituality as long as they are out of touch with life and people. These lonely men and women should return to humanity before spiritual direction can really take effect in their tortured existence. In order to nurse a person back to reality and to a trustful interaction with his fellow man, one does not have to be trained in spiritual direction; neither does one need the elaborate knowledge of a comprehensive fundamental spirituality. A psychotherapist without religion could fulfill this function well by manifesting an authentic understanding and acceptance of the person and an ability to help him see how and where he unconsciously fosters the unhealthy attitudes which interfere with his openness to reality and to others. Once the patient is restored to that basic trust which is the primary condition for a meaningful integration of his life, he can successfully cooperate with the spiritual director whether he meets him as a part of an audience or in a personal one-to-one encounter.

Psychotherapy, however, is a time-consuming enterprise obliging the therapist to spend many hours, sometimes years, with a small number of disturbed individuals whom he tries to keep in touch with reality. Eventually, he hopes they will reach a level of trust and security which will enable them to begin the positive growth and integration of their personality in the spiritual dimension as well. It is clear that the spiritual director would betray both his calling and his specialized study and preparation if he only concentrates his time and energy on nursing back to reality a small group of parishioners or religious. By doing so, he would be lost to the majority of the Christian community who expect from him enlightenment on the possibility of harmonizing life and spirituality in their specific situation.

Unfortunately, spiritual directors in the past were not always aware of the special predicament of these directees who were suffering from the disturbances, alienations, and estrangements we have just described. They were inclined to counsel these people in exactly the same way as they counseled the healthy members; even worse they might reproach them for being strange and oversensitive, unresponsive and even resistant to a spiritual direction from which others seemed to profit so well. This attitude was not only unjust to these sufferers but compounded their difficulties and those of their communities or families. The subsequent discovery of psychotherapeutic methods and attitudes beneficial for people who could not be reached by spiritual direction led to an exaltation of psychotherapy.

We see in the history of spiritual direction a surprising swing from one extreme to the other. While spiritual direction was characterized in the past by an absence of therapeutic understanding, now it became in certain instances dominated onesidely by the psychotherapeutic orientation. Enthusiastic about the new methods, a few religious leaders went so far as to send people for training in only therapeutic counseling and to appoint them afterwards in responsible positions as seminary directors, directors and directresses of novices and juniors, chaplains of schools, and religious counselors of lay organizations. The results were not always as effective as predicted. All some of them could do was to nurse back to reality those alienated novices, seminarians, and devout laity who needed therapeutic care. When this feat was accomplished, those in their care began to express a need for advanced spiritual direction and instruction; the therapists were caught barehanded, for many were not prepared to answer their clients' questions. For all their scientific knowledge, they had not yet developed the research attitude and ability to find the integrative response to the concrete problem of life and spirituality facing these communities, lay associations, and families.

Another manifestation of the same problem is that of

group psychotherapy. In this case, the treatment of the individual who feels disturbed or out of contact is replaced by the therapeutic treatment of a whole group of individuals similarly afflicted. Most important in such treatment is the permissive climate which allows each individual at his own pace to relate to others in the group and to express openly feelings which he has repressed or suppressed because of deeply rooted anxieties and suspicions. Such groups tend to develop an unusual sensitivity toward the feelings of their members and a willingness to deal with these feelings cautiously and kindly. This atmosphere is of the utmost importance in a group of insecure people dealing with each other's raw sensitivities. However, when a spiritual director trained in this therapeutic attitude starts to apply the methods of group therapy to his congregation, parish, seminary, novitiate, religious community, or lay association, the result may be more debilitating than invigorating. If one deals with the majority of relatively healthy people, as if they were liable to crack up under any remark that may hurt their sensitivity, one makes them oversensitive in matters in which they were perhaps strong before and had a high level of endurance and tolerance. As a rule, we weaken man when we demand less from him than he is able to give. The substitution of spiritual direction by group therapy in religious communities has led in several cases to a weakening of the moral fiber of the community.

After these words of caution, it may be safe once again to indicate why the future spiritual director can benefit from some familiarity with therapeutic counseling. Psychotherapists developing effective modes of contact with their patients were able during this process to discover certain conditions of human encounter which are beneficial in any type of counseling, including spiritual direction. By exposing the student to some practice and theory of this specific experience, he will be able to discover for himself certain basic attitudes that can make him more effective as a spiritual director without his becoming a full-fledged psychotherapist. Most significantly, critical reflection on psychotherapy will enable him once and for all to experience the limitations of psychotherapeutic counseling in view of the aims of spiritual direction.

The student needs this insight in order to be able to break through the myth of the all-powerfulness of psychotherapy which carries with it the glamour bestowed upon it by movies, T.V., and other mass media. As long as the spiritual director has not conquered the desire to be the all-powerful and magical therapist, he is relatively useless for his task, for he will be inclined to resort to mere psychotherapy instead of rising to the demands of spiritual direction.

Another advantage of this temporary involvement in psychotherapy is a growing awareness of the concrete manifestation of serious disturbances in people who need this kind of care. This experience, combined with a study of psychopathology, will prepare the spiritual director for one of the most important aspects of his task: the distinction between the majority of people for whom he has to care as a spiritual director, and the small number whom he should advise to go into psychotherapy before they can expect to fully profit from spiritual direction. That is why a program in fundamental spirituality should not only train people in dialectic-integrative research in this field, but also give them some critical insights in psychopathology and in psychotherapeutic counseling. The main concern in this area should be to make clear to spiritual directors why and how they can benefit from and yet transcend psychotherapeutic counseling in order to become more effective spiritual directors. We may add that the study of psychotherapy may make the student realize that he himself has a problem of relating to people and reality. In this case, he may be able to overcome his incapacity by going for counseling himself.

X

THE STUDY OF THE HUMAN
DIMENSION OF CATHOLIC SPIRITUALITY

To fully master the field of Fundamental Catholic Spirituality, one should gain insight into the dynamics of human spirituality. Such a study of the pre-revealed dimension of Catholic spirituality should be preparatory to and supportive of the study of Catholic spirituality.

Systematic theology utilizes the metaphysical insights of the philosophers. In like manner, a spirituality rooted in Divine Revelation can profit from the psychological, biological, and physical insights of scientists and from the spiritual and practical insights of scholars in various human disciplines.

This chapter will be devoted to a discussion of the pre-revealed human aspect of Catholic spiritual life. Our interest will center on such topics as the meaning of this dimension; the sources of its study in the arts and sciences and in philosophical studies of the spirit; the integration of the outcome of all such studies by means of a theoretical framework and methodology. We intend also to consider at the end of this chapter ways in which students within the courses and seminars of Fundamental Catholic Spirituality can be introduced to the study of the human dimension of spiritual life.

This proposed integration of the study of the revealed and pre-revealed aspects of Catholic spiritual life is meant to be a dialectic tool to stimulate thought about possible references to the pre-revealed dimension of spirituality, references that are to be included in courses and seminars taught in a program of Fundamental Catholic Spirituality. This integration could be compared to the manner in which students in systematic Catholic theology are introduced to the study of relevant philosophical and psychological concepts.

Image of Man as a Spiritual Being

Underlying all forms of religious teaching, direction, guidance and counseling is an implicit or explicit image of man as a spiritual being. This image influences theological, spiritual, ascetical, mystical, catechetical, and pastoral theories as well as doctrines and practices of all religious denominations. It is an image of the naturally spiritual man that suggests to us what the spiritual nature of man and mankind is; the dynamics of its development; its influence on the other dimensions of human personality and society; and the conditions for its wholesome growth.

Our conscious or pre-reflective image of the spiritual man is partly philosophical, partly experiential. In the past, this pre-reflective image was usually a mixture composed of certain tenets of traditional philosophy and personal life-experience. Today, however, this traditional image of spiritual existence is complemented by the impressive development of the sciences of man, specifically those which deal with man as human. For example, such sciences as psychology, psychiatry, human history, cultural anthropology, and sociology have enlarged considerably our empirical and experimental understanding of man and society. Confrontation of our pre-reflective image of the spiritual man with the insights gained from these sciences can give rise to a new image of spiritual life in tune with the insights of the human sciences.

We cannot answer the problems of contemporary spiritual living as long as we are implicitly guided by a view of spiritual life that is antiquated and no longer in touch with the evolution of human knowledge. We need rather a theory of man and the human community in its spiritual dimensions which integrates consistently the findings and insights of the human sciences with traditional views, so that we may derive from both a better understanding of the spiritual person. Such a theory of man as a spiritual being, among other things, should make explicit its assumptions and its implicit relatedness to philosophical thought, without betraying its primary character as being a comprehensive theory rooted in experience and relevant to the practice of spiritual development. This reflection on our image of spiritual man should be not only a concern for this moment of the human evolution, in which we experience the beginnings of an integration of traditional views and modern scientific insight, but also an ongoing endeavor.

The human sciences which emerged in the last century are here to stay and steadily expand. Therefore, dialogue between our image of the person as a spiritual being and the ever new discoveries of the human sciences should be an ongoing endeavor; otherwise, the image of spiritual man underlying our Fundamental Catholic Spirituality will be at odds with the human personality as we know it.

Objectives and Methods of the Study of the Human Dimension of Catholic Spiritual Life

Having realized the need for this integrative study within a program of Fundamental Catholic Spirituality, let us try to determine the objectives and methods of this study, a study that actually constitutes a sub-field of Fundamental Catholic Spirituality.

When we ask ourselves what is the objective of the study of the human dimension of Catholic spiritual life, we may say that it is to study the naturally spiritual man and his community, as disclosed by the human arts and sciences.

Secondly, we can ask ourselves how, or in what light, do we study this spiritual man as revealed by the social and human sciences? To begin with, we study the disclosures of these sciences in light of the human experience of spiritual life. This implies that we make the experience of the human dimension of Catholic spiritual life explicit in a scientific, phenomenological way so that we may be able to initiate a dialogue between this explicitated experience and the findings of the human sciences. Out of this dialogue new insights will emerge, which in turn will illumine our view of the naturally spiritual man who is graced in the Catholic spiritual life.

What we need, then, are theoretical-integrative concepts which can help us to establish a comprehensive theory; this theory in turn can help us integrate the insights and findings of the arts and sciences into a comprehensive view of the naturally spiritual man and his community.

Many human sciences uncover or create theoretical concepts that are quite useful for the integration of various insights and findings in regard to the spiritual personality and its development. A comprehensive theory of the spiritual person, however, presupposes the integration not only of these findings but also of their interrelationships with one another and with human nature as spiritual. Such an overall integration is feasible only on the basis of synthesizing theoretical concepts concerning the spiritual nature of the human person, concepts which are sufficiently comprehensive to connect all these findings without distortion either of their original contribution or of the spiritual nature of man. In order to determine what binds these phenomena to one another and to man's spiritual nature, we need the contribution of a philosophical spiritual anthropology, which tries to describe man's spiritual existence, and in so doing, presents us with concepts that are comprehensive. Because these concepts are comprehensive, they will be capable of integrating our studied phenoma of spiritual life with the findings and insights of the human arts and sciences. The knowledge thus synthesized in the study of the human dimension of Catholic spirituality can, in turn, be integrated in the central synthesis of the knowledge of Fundamental Catholic Spirituality.

Integrational-Foundational Concepts in Spirituality

In the study of the human dimension of Catholic spiritual life, we may use such philosophical concepts as "integrational concepts." These concepts may be described as follows. They are concepts that refer to postulated structures that can explain in a unifying way phenomena observed in personal and shared experiences or observed by the human sciences. Integrational concepts should prove to be useful for the meaningful integration of the greatest number and variety of such observed spiritual phenomena and their relationships. Examples of such integrational concepts can be found in other chapters of this book where we deal with concepts such as human and divinely illuminated supraconscious, infraconscious, preconscious, and conscious; spiritual self, personal self, vital self, and so on.

For a comprehensive theory of the human dimension of Catholic spiritual life, we need besides these integrational-foundational concepts many more subordinated concepts. Such subordinated concepts serve to connect with the integrational-foundational concepts the spiritual phenomena uncovered by analysis of the experience of self and others and the study of the human sciences. The integrational-foundational concepts themselves are either borrowed from philosophical anthropology and from the basic theories of the human sciences or established by Fundamental Catholic Spirituality itself.

An example of such subordinate concepts can be found in Chapter VII where we speak about introspective self-presence and transcendent self-presence. These concepts present a unified explanation of two different series of phenomena relevant to an understanding of the spiritual life. Yet they are subordinated concepts insofar as they connect these two integrated series of phenomena with the integrational-foundational concepts of presence, self-presence, supraconscious and conscious presence.

Let us now look briefly at the role such subordinated concepts play in regard to the contribution of the arts and sciences to the science of spirituality.

The various arts and sciences and their subdivisions may deal indirectly with isolated profiles of spiritual life.

Such aspects of the human dimension of Catholic spiritual life, or aspects which can be made relevant to the latter, are abstracted from the spiritual life as a whole. They are objectified by the sciences for methodological reasons of research. The full meaning of these isolated or facilitating features of spiritual life can be grasped only when they are reintegrated in our knowledge of the whole of man's spiritual life. It is precisely the objective of the study of the human dimension of Catholic spirituality to accomplish this provisional reintegration of all knowledge potentially pertinent to Catholic spirituality.

The provisional comprehensive view of spirituality—thus reached on the pre-revealed level of knowledge—has to be critically reviewed again in light of the central knowledge of Fundamental Catholic Spirituality. This critical review of the pre-revealed synthesis of spirituality prepares the way for a final integration of all revealed and pre-revealed knowledge about the spiritual life in the encompassing synthesis of Fundamental Catholic Spirituality.

The foundational concepts of the spiritual life point precisely to those unique dynamic structures which constitute man as the spiritual being he is by his very nature. Such spiritual dynamics can pervade all profiles, features, and processes of man's life. Therefore, they can present us with the synthesizing ideas we need if we are to create order in the otherwise unmanageable diversity of the countless phenomena we observe in the process of spiritualization. Only such synthesizing concepts will be able to connect in unifying explanations whole series of seemingly disparate data and insights that are relevant to a full understanding of man's spiritual unfolding. Such concepts are necessary if we are to come to an orderly understanding of the human dimension of Catholic spiritual life as a natural basis of the supernatural dimension of the same spiritual life.

The Role of the Study of Experience in the Study of the Spiritual Life

It may be useful to return now, for a moment, to the first principle of study we mentioned, namely, the principle that we should study the disclosures of the human arts and sciences about man and society in light of our experience of the manifestations of the spiritual life. It may be clear now that this demand is a necessity not only for a critical study of the theories and findings of the human sciences, but also for the evaluation of the concepts offered by various philosophical anthropologies. What we want to aim for is an understanding of the spiritual life as it really is. Consequently, our theory of spiritual life should be based on our experience or perception of spiritual life as manifested in reality, not on mere wishful thinking, subjective imagination, or theoretical prejudices about spiritual life.

In other words, a fundamental human spirituality has to be purified of all distorting images, wishes, and prejudices that are not in harmony with our fundamental experience of the spiritual dimension as it is lived in daily life. Therefore, the first task of the student of fundamental human spirituality is to study—in the light of his own and others' experiences—the perspectives, ideas, concepts, and theories made available to him by the various philosophical anthropologies, arts, and human sciences. He will ask himself what really is experienced in these concepts, judgments, theories, or reports, as opposed to only hypothetical explanatory concepts implicit in the judgments and recordings of so-called facts or data. His theory of the spiritual life should be based on the experience of this life by himself or others, though he may be aided by insights and findings of the arts and sciences in order to become better aware of certain areas of experience about which he would not otherwise have been able to think.

He may discover that a concept, theory, or report is mistaken or contaminated by prejudice, in which case it should be corrected or rejected. Intersubjectively validated experience alone can be the base of a trustworthy fundamental theory of the natural spiritual life and can never be replaced by theories, hypotheses, models, unverified philosophies, or any other views that are not verifiable in human experience.

The student of fundamental human spirituality will build his theory, therefore, on comprehensive concepts, but these concepts themselves should be rooted in the firm ground of reality-experience and not in mere theory. For the same reason, the student building on a comprehensive theory of fundamental human spirituality will borrow from philosophical anthropology only those concepts that are rooted in experience and verifiable there also. Any further development of those comprehensive concepts should be an explicitation of what is implicit in the experience expressed by these concepts.

As we have seen earlier, the integration of the contributions of the human sciences to an understanding of man's spiritual life presupposes also a study of that which, in the formulations of the human sciences, is based on real experience as distinguished from unverified models, hypotheses, and implicit philosophies. Only then is a dialogue possible between the experience of man's spiritual life as a totality, expressed in foundational concepts, and the experience of isolated profiles of spiritual life, found by a phenomenological purification of the formulations of the human sciences.

The methods necessary for rooting our theory in experience are the methods of natural observation and phenomenological explicitation of the results of this observation. Natural observation and description of the observed present us with phenomena of spiritual life and behavior in their first appearances. The phenomenological method then leads us to the inner structures of these phenomena and liberates our perception of this structure from personal and cultural prejudice which may still remain unchecked and undetected in natural observation, description, or experiment alone.

We have seen that comprehensive concepts used in the study of the human dimension of Catholic spirituality should be rooted in experience. This requirement implies that the student should not restrict himself, for example, merely to the study of the basic tenets of an updated Thomistic philosophy of spirit and the spiritual life. This Thomistic study may be his first and most important source, but, next to this Thomistic philosophy of the spiritual life and in the light of it, he should critically evaluate some of the spiritually relevant studies of those philosophical anthropologies that attempt to root themselves in a critical phenomenology of human experience. Such philosophies may present him with some concepts that can be critically related to the concepts discovered in the study of the experiential aspects of the human dimension of Catholic spiritual life.

The study of the human dimension of Catholic spiritual life has thus as its objective the formation of an integrative theory of spiritual life from the viewpoint of human experience and of the human sciences—an integrative theory rooted in a philosophical spiritual anthropology that is supported by updated Thomistic views of the life of the spirit and sustained and nourished by some of the insights into the spiritual life gained by phenomenological philosophies. The final objective of this study is to offer integrated material to the central enterprise of Fundamental Catholic Spirituality, which is to synthesize and offer—as guidance for the praxis of the spiritual life—all relevant revealed and pre-revealed knowledge about spiritual living.

Program of Studies in the Human Dimension of Fundamental Catholic Spirituality

Every student of Fundamental Catholic Spirituality should be introduced to the study of all essential dimensions of this field. One of the basic dimensions of this field is that of the human dimension of Catholic spirituality. St. Thomas has taught us that grace does not destroy nature but complements and perfects it. Hence, we note the crucial importance of the study of this natural dimension. Without it, the student of this field would have a hard time trying to understand the human dynamics utilized by grace as it spiritualizes the person. It is difficult, if not impossible, to understand the pathways of grace if one is unaware of what precisely is graced. Just as the student in systematic theology is lost without some introduction into the philosophical thinking utilized by theology, so too a student in spirituality would be lost without an introduction into the study of the human dimension of Catholic spirituality. This study is the ground floor presupposed by all further studies of Catholic spirituality. In like manner the study of philosophy is the ground floor on which all further studies in systematic theology are based.

We are now able to propose possible introductory courses into the human dimension of Catholic spirituality, courses that should be integrated within a program of Fundamental Catholic Spirituality. This proposal will be based on our discussions in the foregoing pages regarding the nature and place of the study of this basic dimension of Catholic spiritual life.

First of all, the student of Catholic spirituality needs to be exposed within the context of courses on Catholic spirituality to some basic Thomistic and phenomenological views regarding the human dimension of spirituality. Ideally, such exposure could take place not necessarily in separated special courses but, if possible, in the context of courses on Fundamental Catholic Spirituality itself and of research in this field. Such an integrated presentation may help the student see the unity of the prerevealed and revealed aspects of the spiritual life.

The same integrated presentation would be important for a second series of courses into other aspects of the human dimension of Catholic spirituality. These would acquaint him with scientific theories of personality and especially of the spiritual dimension of the human personality. A third series of courses would be related to the various human sciences and their subdivisions, insofar as their present findings and insights can be made relevant for an understanding of man and society as spiritual. A fourth type of course would give attention to the arts. What can sculpture, architecture, dance, music, literature tell us about the spiritual life of man.

It is not my aim to discuss each of these areas at this

time, though I would like to make a few remarks about the contribution of literature to spirituality. Men who write books such as Silone's *Bread and Wine* and Kazantzakis' *Report to Greco* are deeply intuitive authors. In describing their personal or fictional characters, they grant us a profound insight into how man lives. They are not merely observers in a psychological sense. Neither are they mere philosophers. They are men of experience. They describe experientially the ways in which people can live their lives.

The literary writer, unlike the student of spirituality, is not concerned with the systematic development of the science of concrete spiritual living. He does not share our interest in the presuppositions, subjects, and methodology of such a science and the integration of as many data and insights from the sciences as possible insofar as they are relevant to the praxis of living. Yet a wise reading of the writer's work grants us a felt understanding of human life and its relation to a true or false spiritual outlook.

Novelists deal mainly with the experiential not with the normative aspect of life. They don't tell us how to live spiritually but portray strikingly what people go through when they strive after their version of success and happiness. They may draw upon psychological insights, experiences, and observations but always within a sensitive insight that offers a practical intuition into human life and action.

The novelist is not a psychologist but a moralist in the widest sense. The word moralist may conjure up for us a stern person who wags his finger telling us how to be good. *Mores,* however, means *ways*; the novelist describes ways in which people live, good or bad, edifying or disconcerting. Indeed, we may venture to say that the psychology of many a novelist often goes far deeper than the psychology of clinic and laboratory, for the novelist is gifted with preconscious knowledge about the practical living of people that no mere science can give.

Such authors as Dostoyevsky and Solzhenitsyn have deep insight. Their approach puts them in the fellowship of those who study a theoretical-practical science about human life. Their books may be far from pious, but because they are interested in concrete living, which is always related directly or indirectly to a true or falsified spiritual outlook, they may be helpful to the student of spirituality.

A last group of introductions within the context of courses and seminars on Catholic spirituality should be of a directly practical nature. We are thinking here about references to certain aspects of the human dimension of Catholic spirituality that the student has to come to terms with in himself. Here again this study should not be done in a course or seminar totally separated from considerations of the revealed and graced aspects of the Catholic spiritual life. If separated, it could give rise to a split in the student's life. The concrete lived Catholic spiritual life forms an indissoluble unity in the person who lives it; the human and graced aspects should, therefore, be shown in their mutual interpenetration.

The student needs also some initiation into the art and discipline of spiritual direction. Spiritual direction touches necessarily on certain aspects of the human dimension of the Catholic spiritual life and the way of guiding it. We affirm the necessity of referring to certain insights and findings provided by counseling and psychotherapy, provided that such insights and findings are related to the traditional and contemporary wisdom of Catholic spiritual direction developed in light of Scripture, doctrine, and the teaching of recognized spiritual masters of the Church.

Finally, it would be necessary to offer guidelines for research in the human dimension of Fundamental Catholic Spirituality. A thesis on a topic of interest to Fundamental Catholic Spirituality cannot bypass this dimension. In other words, we would advise that a thesis on any topic of Fundamental Catholic Spirituality should have a foundational division dealing with the human dimension of the topic concerned. Only after this division should the student deal with the revealed and graced dimensions of his topic, keeping these later divisions in dialogue with the first division. We will return to this kind of research in the following final chapter of this book.

Characteristics of Research in the Human Dimension of Catholic Spirituality

Research in this sub-field of Catholic spirituality, and the foundational dimension of the thesis that results, should be characterized—as are the later divisions of the thesis—by its being relevant, comprehensive, experiential, theoretical, foundational, and communicative. When we say *relevant* we mean to emphasize that this division of the thesis and the manner in which it is handled, should be directly related to the development of spiritual life in our time. The student of fundamental spirituality is thus prevented from losing himself in abstractions that take him away from lived reality.

This human dimension of his thesis should be *comprehensive* in that it draws on the insights and findings of all the arts and sciences insofar as they illumine the practical aspect of spiritual life chosen for study.

The *experiential* aspect demanded of the thesis as a whole means that the student shows that this dimension of his study can be related to life experience. He demonstrates this relevance by using illustrations and examples from real life and by a psychological phenomenology of experiences relevant to his subject matter.

The characteristic expressed by the term *theoretical* indicates that this basic part of his research is not the detailed, empirical approach typical of the human sciences. His should be a theoretical research and, more precisely a comprehensive-theoretical research, meaning that the student, through use of the dialectical method, tries to synthesize all relevant insights and findings within a consistent integrative-theoretical framework at the end of this first division of his thesis.

The term *foundational* refers to the requirement that the student should relate the integrative theory about his specific topic of spiritual life to a broader comprehensive-theoretical view of the human dimension of Catholic spiritual life and to the foundational concepts involved in that broader theoretical framework. Of course, he will later on in the development of his thesis relate his findings in the first dimension to the basic concepts of Fundamental Catholic Spirituality as a whole.

Finally, the demand that this foundational division of his thesis, as the rest of it, be *communicative* points to one of the purposes of thesis writing in this field, namely, to prepare the student for an effective communication of his knowledge in an attractive, clear, and convincing style insofar as the topic makes this possible.

Differentiation of the Study of the Human Dimension of Catholic Spirituality from other Fields of Study

Having considered the object, objectives, and

methods of the study of the human dimension of Catholic spirituality, we may now proceed to differentiate this study from other types of study which at first glance may seem similar.

First of all, we may ask ourselves in what respect the study of the human dimension of Catholic spiritual life is different from that of natural theology, a theology based on the prerevealed knowledge man can reach about God and his moral life as related to this naturally known God.

We can distinguish a natural theology or "theodicy" and a philosophical ethics from a theology based on Christian revelation or a moral theology rooted in the same. Certain aspects of a philosophical "theodicy" and ethics would be quite relevant to the study of the human dimension of Catholic spiritual life insofar as they are related to a philosophical anthropology of the human person as a spiritual being or insofar as they may contain descriptions or analogies of basic spiritual experiences that are in principle possible in all men, irrespective of their religious belief.

To be sure, the various theologies of different religions and denominations frequently contain considerations and phenomenological analogies that are not exclusively characteristic of the specific doctrine of the religion concerned but rather of the spiritual life of all men. Such basic tenets about the life of the spirit are often submerged in the descriptions and explanations of specific Eastern or Western religions, as expounded in their theologies or ascetical-mystical treatises.

It is one of the tasks of the student of the human dimension of Catholic spiritual life to extricate the description or explanation of a general spiritual aspect or possibility of spiritual growth for man from this specialized context; in so doing one should be careful to focus on the object of study, namely, the concrete development of the spiritual life. Otherwise the student may digress from his specific topic and end up in a quite different field such as that of philosophy of religion.

It is possible, therefore, to study the theologies of Eastern and Western religions and denominations from the viewpoint of the study of the human dimension of Catholic spirituality. In this case, one studies spiritual writings or theological systems to become acquainted with the spiritual tenets to which people of a certain faith are committed. One may do this from the viewpoint of the study of the human dimension of Catholic spirituality for two reasons.

First of all, as we have said, he may do so in order to discover the general aspects of spiritual experience to which theological or religious description points. Secondly, he realizes that people usually live their spiritual life within the framework of one or the other concrete religion. Therefore, after learning what the members of a certain religion or denomination are basically supposed to believe, he shifts his attention to other questions that are more directly relevant to the study of the human dimension of Catholic spiritual life.

For example, the student asks himself such questions as: How is the proposed theology and spiritually lived, expressed and concretely experienced? How does this experienced and lived theology and spirituality affect the development of personality and social life? How is this lived-theology or spirituality related to the fundamental natural dimension of spirituality in the human personality? Can the same theology or spirituality be lived, experienced, and embodied in a way of life which would be more conducive to a wholesome development of the spiritual life?

In other words, the study of the human dimension of Catholic spirituality can deal with the spiritual, social, psychological, psychiatric, cultural, historical, and anthropological aspects of the teachings of any religion. It can deal also with the relationship of these factors to the wholesome development of the human personality and society as a preparation for the life of revealed and graced spirituality. This kind of study is important because of the fact that the concrete history of spiritual development in the individual and society is usually linked to the development of concrete religions and denominations. Therefore, the latter may be storehouses of insights for the study of the human dimension of Catholic spiritual life.

We may now ask ourselves in what way fundamental human spirituality ties in with the art of spiritual direction or counseling. Fundamental human spirituality can provide a basis for wholesome spiritual direction insofar as it can prepare the spiritual director or religious counselor for a wise understanding of the natural psychological and social dynamics that underlie the spiritual development of any religious person and community regardless of religious outlook. This knowledge can then be related to the art of Catholic spiritual direction, illumined by Revelation, graced by God in a special way, and enriched by the insights of Catholic spiritual masters.

A similar approach may be taken to pastoral psychology, which studies the relevance of psychology to pastoral practice as it is usually linked to the theology and spirituality of one specific religion or denomination. In fact, the basic theory of the spiritual life developed by fundamental human spirituality can be one source of insight for a sound pastoral psychology. This discipline can only remain such a source if it is faithful to its own objective and does not limit itself to pastoral psychology. By the same token, existing pastoral psychologies of various religions and denominations may be studied from the viewpoint of fundamental human spirituality in order to determine how much they are in tune with contemporary insights about man's spiritual nature; they can also be studied to discover explicit or implicit findings made by these pastoral psychologies that may be relevant for the deepening, expansion, or differentiation of the basic comprehensive theory of the spiritual life.

Finally, we have to distinguish the study of the human dimension of Catholic spiritual life from the study of the sciences on which it draws and which themselves may have developed a specialty in the field of religion. We know already of such specialties as psychology of religion, sociology of religion, cultural anthropology of religion, and history of religion. While some findings of these disciplines can be related to the study of spirituality, they cannot be identified with this field of study.

The differences between the sciences of religion and the comprehensive study of human spirituality as a preparation for the study of Catholic spirituality are striking. First of all, the other sciences do not claim or attempt to be integrative-comprehensive studies of the spiritual life, gathering together the contributions of the arts and sciences in light of an integrational theoretical frame of reference. On the contrary, each specializes in the study of one specific and limited aspect of the religious personality such as its psychological, ethnic, sociological, cultural-anthropological, economical, historical, political, educational, or aesthetical manifestations.

There is not only an essential difference in the object of study of these special fields but also in the methodology. Each of these disciplines tends to follow the scientific research methodology proper to its own field. This usually means that they concentrate on the scientific study of predominantly factual manifestations of spiritual life in society. If possible, they use methods of measurement and experimental validation. Unlike the comprehensive study of the human dimension of the Catholic spiritual life, their empirical research is not primarily directed towards the experiential illumination of fundamental structures of the spiritual life and their embodiment. The results of their studies, however, can be important for the integrative study of the human dimension of Catholic spiritual life. Some of their findings offer material for theoretical reflection on the concrete development of the spiritual life, its conditions and consequences.

Finally, the sciences of religion do not always pay attention to their implicit philosophical assumptions; neither are they primarily concerned about the development of a theoretical frame of reference that is partly rooted in such assumptions; nor is their guiding question the praxis of spiritual living.

As we have said, certain findings and insights of the sciences of religion may be of value for the integrative study of the human dimension of Catholic spiritual life. We have to add the opposite also, namely, that the basic spiritual anthropology emerging from this Catholic study can be enlightening for the experts in the social sciences of religion.

Ranking the Order of Allied Sciences

It may be advisable to say a few words about the rank or hierarchy of relevance of the arts and sciences to the study of the human dimension of Catholic spiritual life. The study of literature and of psychology, more specifically, the psychology of personality, of human development, and of motivation have obviously a priority of interest for the student of the human dimension of Catholic spiritual life. The spiritual person as disclosed in literature and personality theory stands in the center of his study.

Next in order of precedence come sociology and cultural anthropology insofar as they disclose the social and cultural dimension of the human personality without which the person cannot be known as he lives within the context of humanity.

Immediately after this, the student of fundamental human spirituality finds himself interested in psychiatric, psychoanalytic, and clinical studies of personality and society since they make him aware of the numerous ways in which the human person can deviate from wholesome development.

Historical, cultural, economical, political, educational, medical, biophysical, and nutritional studies follow in importance insofar as each of them may contribute some insight or finding that is relevant to his topic of specialization in studies of the spiritual life.

Finally, the student involved in the study of the pre-revealed dimension of Catholic spirituality is interested in the fields of counseling, guidance, psychotherapy, and communication in that they help him to become initiated in attitudes and techniques that may facilitate the effective communication of his findings to individuals and communities.

Transition to the Study of the Revealed Dimension of Catholic Spiritual Life

The knowledge of the human dimension of Catholic spiritual life is a modest but basic beginning of a full knowledge of this life. The study of this dimension can never substitute for that of the revealed and graced dimension. It is difficult to understand the concrete dynamics of the latter without a knowledge of the former.

The central dimension of the study of Fundamental Catholic Spirituality is the practical living of the revealed and graced dimension. This central dimension is infinitely different, for it speaks of the undeserved miracle of the graced spiritual life of the divinely elevated man. It does so in light of an equally undeserved Divine Revelation. Yet this central dimension is closely allied to the human dimension of Catholic spirituality, for the Church holds that grace does not destroy human nature but complements and perfects it. Therefore, no human knowledge about the life of the spirit is lost; no right knowledge of the human dimension of the spiritual life is useless. A student of Fundamental Catholic Spirituality should master the knowledge of the human dimension of the Catholic spiritual life as a preparatory and supportive knowledge of his main study, research, teaching, and spiritual direction. It is for this reason that the elements of a study of the human dimension of Catholic spiritual life should be integrated in any program of Fundamental Catholic Spirituality.

Because the study of the practical living of the revealed aspect of Catholic spiritual life is central we devoted most of the chapters of this book to that aspect, referring wherever possible to the human aspect. We hope that this chapter, given over as it is to considerations about the study of the importance of the human aspect, may insure a balanced approach to both the human and the revealed and graced dimensions of spiritual living.

XI

RESEARCH IN FUNDAMENTAL
CATHOLIC SPIRITUALITY

We have reached the end of this book, a book meant to be an introduction into some possible ways of studying and formulating the fundamentals of a practical spirituality. It was by necessity a limited tentative initiation, touching only some of the features of this newly emerging field. No matter how limited this discussion has been, it may be clear by now what the scope and complexity of a fully worked out study of these fundamentals of practical spirituality would entail. Indeed, such a study would be as complex as life itself, as far ranging as the continuously expanding cultural and scientific insights and findings about the praxis of the good life and about the structures, dynamics, and conditions this praxis has to take into account. The development of a Fundamental Catholic Spirituality, relevant to daily living in all its dimensions, would thus imply a never ending research task of scholars and students in this field.

In the Center for the Study of Spirituality, we have tried to organize a modest beginning of this enterprise. One of the projects of the faculty, students, and graduates of this Center is to engage themselves in the research necessary to devise a first tentative outline of a fundamental spirituality. This research to date has resulted in well documented theses on various topics related to this tentative overall outline of the foundations of a practical spirituality. At the end of this book, the interested reader will find a selected listing of these already completed studies, together with the proposal of a thesis on the topic of "Originality and Spirituality." These concrete examples may tell better than the considerations of this book how research in this field proceeds.

Growing interest in this area of study and praxis has prompted many requests to publish at least a schematic review of the methodology used in this kind of research. This final chapter, in combination with the previous one, is partly an answer to these requests. Readers less interested in the bare bones of a research method and its rationale may still profit from this final chapter. It may deepen their insight into the study and meaning of fundamental spirituality as well as throw new light on what has been discussed in other chapters of this book.

Outline of Fivefold Division of Research

In the foregoing chapter, a first step in research in fundamental spirituality was explained in detail. We proposed there that a study of any topic of Fundamental Catholic Spirituality should deal first with the human dimension of the topic of spirituality we are researching.

The full study of a topic of interest to Catholic spirituality could be developed in five consecutive divisions. They are illustrated in the thesis proposal in Appendix One at the end of this book. It is advisable to read this proposal first in order to obtain a concrete view of what follows.

1.   *The extra-revelational dimension:* The human dimension of Fundamental Catholic Spirituality dealt with in the previous chapter.

2.   *The pre-revelational dimension:* This division of the study could deal with the human dimension of spirituality insofar as it is religiously oriented towards at-oneness with the transcendent in any type of organized or non-organized religion. To the degree that this religious orientation is compatible with the Christian revelation, we may consider it a preparation for Fundamental Catholic Spirituality. This possible dimension of research too was in some measure dealt with in the last chapter; it will need more elaboration in this chapter.

3.   *The post-revelational content dimension:* This could be considered the central dimension of any study in Fundamental Catholic Spirituality. This dimension could deal with fundamental spirituality as enlightened and transformed by the Christian revelation, communicated in Church Doctrine and related to the spiritual life by the Church's acknowledged spiritual masters, scholars, and students of spirituality.

4.   *The post-revelational presently lived dimension:* This is an investigation of the way in which present day Catholic Christians or a specific segment of them, such as priests, religious, married people, single persons live or should ideally live Fundamental Catholic Spirituality in today's world.

5.   *The post-revelational applicative dimension:* The implications of the research done so far would be applied to the spiritual initiation and direction of Christian Catholics or a specific segment of them as re-

searched under dimension four. This application could be researched in light of studies and literature on spiritual initiation and direction that are relevant to the specific topic of study chosen.

We want first of all to clarify how and why the third, post-revelational dimension of this suggested possibility of research would be considered central and how this central dimension would relate to the other possible dimensions of this structure of research. After this clarification, we can reflect on some possible ways of articulating this third dimension

The Central Position of the Post-Revelational Dimension

The post-revelational dimension of spiritual life refers to the life of the spirit as lived in light of the Christian revelation.

Spiritual life as revealed and graced by our Lord is not merely an activity of the mind; it is the permeation of my whole existence by my growing personal union with the God of Revelation; it is the lived experience and praxis of my life as uniquely called by Christ.

Personal life, far from being a static given, is an on-going history of dialectical interactions with continually changing appeals and challenges in daily life. Personal life is a "having to be," a task, a challenge, a project to be worked out in perspective of a value I choose to be the ultimate guiding light of my life. For the man of faith, this ultimate value is unity of love with the Divine to which he knows himself invited. Christian spiritual life is the unfolding of one's life in response to this divine call.

Research in the third, post-revelational dimension of spirituality deals with man's response in faith to the unique call of God in Christ. It does so in relation to the topic of the research concerned. It asks itself: how does this faithful creative unfolding of life as discovery of and response to the life call in Christ relate to some specific aspect of life, such as leisure, work, originality, communication, leadership, bodily care, humor, trust, friendship, to name only a few possible topics.

The ground of the Christian spiritual life is faith in the living, creating God. The origin of our faith is God Himself. He Himself moves us inwardly to surrender ourselves in faith to His offer of salvation, revealed in Christ. He is the inspirer of our faith, already active in us before we confess our faith to Him. Faith is our total response to this offer of redemption and personal intimacy. Faith, therefore, cannot be merely an act of the mind. The dynamic presence of the Divine in us is not such that it touches only our intellect. Faith, as the source of our Christian spiritual life, is our presence to a God who reveals Himself as the One who wants to be our life partner, who calls forth our total person. This God who calls us asks for the assent of our will. With my intelligence I acknowledge Him as the one who wants to be for me a redeeming and uniting love, and with my will I assent and surrender to this love.

This insight teaches me that He wants me totally, not only my intellect, but also my heart, my feelings, my whole spiritual, psychological, and bodily life, all my actions. I cannot reserve any dimension of my life for myself. He calls the whole of me.

This total calling suggests already the importance of the human dimension of Christian spiritual life. A balanced understanding of who I am in all the dimensions of my being, as seen in the light of human experience and of the insights offered by the arts and sciences, can be a facilitating factor in the purification and transformation of my whole personality to make it more ready for union with God in faith.

We live our faith presence in and through our surrender to Christ. Christ is the visible personification of the divine initiative of salvation for man. Christ is our Brother, image of our calling, prototype of the new man, the new Adam.

Faith, at the heart of my spiritual life, calls for the surrender of my whole person to the living God. I do not and cannot see the face of the living God, to whom I must surrender myself. He is hidden, unknown, unintelligible. He is not a given I see clearly before me. Faith at the heart of my spiritual presence has to search for the loving God of revelation; faith has to discover the traces of His presence in the midst of daily life. If God allows my faith to find Him, this finding can only happen in and through my human experiences in this world.

The center of Christian spiritual presence—faith—does not unfold itself in a privileged dimension of myself. My self is radically rooted in this world; it emerges from this earthly and cultural reality that surrounds, permeates, and carries me. My faith cannot unfold itself outside this world and culture from which I emerge. My whole life is already interwoven with this cultural reality. I am worldy through and through. To live a Christian spiritual life can never mean removing myself totally from this world I participate in already. Faith means for me a new way of looking at this world; it is seeing people, events, and things from a viewpoint that transcends us all. It grants me the wisdom to interpret all in a new way.

The life of faith is a life of enlightened perception.

Faith enables the spiritual person to uncover gradually new meanings in the human knowledge of life and world, meanings unknown to a merely human vision, no matter how sophisticated.

The life of faith grows thus by discovery; it cannot be understood as a static possession, a property locked away somewhere in heart or mind, as we lock our valuables in a safe. The spiritual life of faith must unfold itself in the midst of the daily world from which the human self emerges by participation. Faith must actualize itself over and over again in confrontation with what this world offers us as the matrix of self-emergence and as the matter of participation.

Therefore, the Christian spiritual life is animated by a searching faith that is tested out by human wisdom and knowledge, attractively and convincingly offered by science and culture. This necessity of growth in the spiritual life of faith, through a new presence to the world with which we are interwoven, explains the function of a first division of study in Fundamental Catholic Spirituality.

We study a specific aspect of life, such as experiencing and living spatial surroundings, time, commitment, leadership, discipleship, womanhood, change. Before man lives such aspects of life in light of faith, he may already be living them unwittingly in light of his genetic endowment, his childhood experience, his culture, his education. Therefore, the student's first research is a search for how man in his culture is already living—or may be invited by his culture to live—such aspects on an extra-revelational level. He researches his own self-experience in this regard, the experience of others as described by fellow men, by literature, by the human sciences. He searches not to condemn but to correct and complement in his study what has already been discovered, pointing out in the process how the same aspects can be experienced and lived in light of faith.

The spiritual life of faith lived in Christ and the spiritual life lived in accordance with human wisdom are not two competing lives. Present day culture has emancipated itself from the Church in a way medieval man could have never dreamt possible. Each Christian today is born and raised in this emancipated culture; he is touched by it daily. He cannot escape it; he unwittingly emerges from it; it is no longer something outside of himself.

Spiritual life in faith implies a gradual metamorphosis of the human way of the spirit already implicitly lived by man in some measure. This spiritual transformation has to take place in Christ. Culture did not wholly accept the wisdom of Christ. The human vision of living the life of the spirit has often rejected the vision of faith. Because of this rejection, the arrogance of a merely human view has been condemned by God; but condemnation is not His last word. The cross of Christ is a cross of reconciliation. The relation between divine and human vision is not one of exclusion but of dialogue. The "no" of God to mere human wisdom is contained within a wider divine affirmation. The divine "no" remains only in force insofar as human wisdom is not yet transformed in accordance with the wisdom of Christ. The risen Christ integrates in His new wisdom all true human wisdom about the life of the spirit.

In Christ the promise has been given that God will be all in all. Because of this divine promise, the student of Christian spirituality studies respectfully all human wisdom that can be related to the spiritual life in faith. He studies it so that he may transform it into the wisdom of Christian spirituality in the central division of his study.

Insofar as his own life has been unwittingly permeated already by human wisdom, the new insight he is gaining will help him to ready his own life also for the divine transformation of his self as pervaded already by the wisdom of this world.

This transformation of his emergent self in Christ is not an eradication of all that he already is and knows; it is an enrichment and deepening by his faith-orientation of all that is good in human spiritual knowledge. The student of Catholic spirituality is moved by the dynamics of the eschaton; he tries to bring to light and to live what, in the eschatological future, will be true for all in accordance with the promise given in Christ.

The Church has the mission to integrate all human knowledge about the life of the spirit in the Revelation of Christ. It is part of the mission of the Church to proclaim that all human understanding of the good life should be elevated and transformed by the wisdom of our Lord. This transformation implies not only a condemnation of certain false spiritual views; it implies also an elevation of compatible spiritual wisdom to the fullness of a spiritual wisdom in Christ.

The student participates in this aspect of the mission of the Church. In and through his study, he helps man to see that Christian spiritual life is not a flight from findings and insights rendered by the arts, sciences, and accumulated experiences of humanity.

Christian spiritual life in faith is not the cultivation of an individualistic or exclusive spiritual relation to God, in which the search of humanity for the life of the spirit has no part to play. Christian wisdom is not insulated from the spiritual wisdom of humanity, waiting in splendid isolation for the parousia of Christ and the fullness of revelation. On the contrary, Christian spirituality is a knowledge that emerges also in participation in any sincere search for a fuller human and spiritual life.

The student of Christian spirituality, in and with the Church, must participate in the accumulated wisdom of mankind, not to dominate it but to serve and help forward the spiritual search of humanity.

Therefore, we suggested that, in the first two divisions of his study, the student research what human knowledge and the wisdom of other religions and denominations may have to offer for possible transformation by the traditional wisdom of Christian spiritual life. He should do so in respectful openness to what representatives of searching humanity really tried to communicate. It may be advantageous first to summarize fairly, without premature comment, what relevant theorists, scientists, artists, and representatives of various religions have said about topics that may be in some way related to his own chosen topic of spiritual research. Only then may he, in subsequent reflections, respectfully ponder the relevance of their contributions to his study; and only later, in the third division, may he try, in the light of faith, to elevate and transform this human wisdom without diminishing or distorting it.

The resulting familiarity of the student with the human expression of man's search for the life of the spirit will enable him also to foster spiritual growth in men and women of good will, not yet ready for a fuller revelation of Christian spirituality. His promotion of their spirituality will necessarily be oriented by his acquaintance with the Christian message he himself is studying and living. His communication with them will be influenced also by his growing understanding of how any compatible human wisdom is already implicitly related to the gift of Christian wisdom. Therefore, his fostering of human spiritual growth is already an initial, preparatory, and indirect proclamation of the wisdom of the Gospel.

Such indirect illumination of the spiritual life of humanity does not imply a betrayal of the identity of Christian spirituality; it does not hide this identity; it merely does not proclaim it fully. Similarly, Christ did not, from the very beginning and all at once, reveal the fullness of His Godhead to all who listened to Him.

To be sure, the student himself has steadily to nourish his own Christian life of faith by Word and Sacrament, by prayer, reading of Scripture and spiritual masters, reflection and meditation. Otherwise he may be overwhelmed by the mere human wisdom of the writers, thinkers, and scientists he is exploring.

All of this reminds us of the custom of the ancient Church to exclude the not yet baptized catechumens from the second part of the Holy Mass, the singing of the Creed and the Eucharistic Meal. The Church spared not yet sufficiently prepared people full confrontation with the mysteries of the faith. At the same time, the Church made sure to nourish its faithful with Word and Sacrament.

Similarly the student of spirituality lets himself be nourished by the Church. At the same time he knows how to restrain the fullness of Christian spiritual knowledge from those who are not yet ready for this confrontation. His research in the extra and pre-revelational dimensions of the spiritual life helps him to find ways to reach contemporaries not yet ready for the fullness of Christ's message.

After discussing the central place of this third dimension in the totality of a study on Catholic spirituality and seeing its relationship to the first two dimensions, it is not so difficult to show how this third dimension is related to the fourth and fifth.

In the fourth dimension we look at present day Catholic Christians or a segment of them in the light of what we have discovered about the human and transformed dimension of spiritual life. In that light, we research ways in which this population lives in relation to what we have discovered and what the special difficulties are that this population must face in growing in Christian spiritual life. This research may make us aware of new aspects of the problem at hand that may have escaped us in the former three phases of our research.

Then, in the fifth and final division of this study, we apply the results of what we have found so far to spiritual direction and initiation in regard to our specific topic of study and the particular segment of the Catholic population we want to apply it to. This part of the research project stresses the practical dimension of the theoretical-practical science of spirituality; it may give rise to new insights that can in turn enlighten the former phases of our research and compel us to integrate such findings within these former divisions.

We have already spoken about the first dimension and its methodology in the previous chapter on the human dimension of Fundamental Catholic Spirituality. Some of the more general principles of research in fundamental spirituality, such as its comprehensive, experiential, theoretical, and foundational characteristics, apply equally to the four other dimensions we proposed for study. We might recommend here actual study of the theses already completed by graduates of the Center for the Study of Spirituality and contained in the bibliography of this book.

We turn now to an explanation of the general meaning of the four other dimensions of the research project we propose. Let us first reflect on the central third dimension, whose position in the total structure of our suggested project we already attempted to clarify.

The Structure of the Post-Revelational Content Dimension

The study of the revealed and graced aspect of the spiritual life could—as one main possibility—be structured effectively around a consideration of the three theological virtues of faith, hope, charity and a consideration of grace and prayer. How much attention should be given to each of these categories, or whether these categories would be useful at all, may partly depend on the character of the topic under study and the personal intent of the student. Let us look briefly at each one of these categories to see how they can present one possible means to place our findings on the extra and pre-revelational levels within the light of grace and revelation.

Faith

Discussing the central place of the post-revelational dimension, we highlighted the fact that the divine gift of faith is the core of our Christian spiritual life. Faith is more than an intellectual assent to doctrinal statements; it is a total surrender of my whole person in Christ to the living God. We stressed that this faith should grow and realize itself in confrontation with daily experience. To this living faith we may relate the topic we are studying. We may ask ourselves how the specific topic of our study, for example, silence, recollection, obedience, trust, gentleness can be lived as a facilitating condition for the spiritualization of our life by the divine gift of faith. We may ask ourselves also how faith can help us to see, experience, and live these human virtues and conditions in a new way.

Finally, faith may help us to realize that we are essentially pilgrims on this earth without a lasting home, always living in the expectation of our real home with God.

Hope

Faith teaches us that all spiritual attainments in this life are only means and roads to a loving union with God that will come to full flowering in the hereafter. Faith is in some way a first beginning of eternal life. Faith, therefore, gives rise to hope. Hope is characteristic of people who truly believe that an as yet unknown ultimate self-unfolding in Christ is awaiting us. We belong already in Christ to a new creation. The fullness of this creation will be revealed to us in the unknown future. We can only hope for it. The ground of our hope is the mystery of Christ's life, His passion, death and resurrection. Our hope is oriented toward the future where the mystery of Christ will find its final fulfillment: His glorious return to humanity that will bring out the ultimate effectiveness of salvation, taking away the ambiguity of sin and the human situation.

Our faith in God's fidelity to us vitalizes our hope. Our hope becomes then a dynamic force in our Christian spiritual life. It enables our spirit to put all people, events, and things in a wider, ultimate perspective. The dynamism of hope is an effective force in our daily spiritual life. It makes us realize that the future glory of redeemed humanity must be given some visible form here on earth to celebrate what has already begun in us by grace and also to foreshadow the splendid reality we are hoping for. The imperfection of what we realize in this world stimulates us to improve as much as we can the human reality in order to symbolize better what we are hoping for.

Charity

The object of our hope is the transcendent fulfillment of our humanity in Christ. On basis of our faith in God and His revelation, we may realize that this fulfillment can be none other than a lasting intimacy with God in love. This intimacy begins already in us through the divine gift of faith. Faith is a real beginning of the eternal life of union with God in us. God Himself moves us inwardly to believe in Him, trust in Him, to unite with Him in love. He is the source of our faith, out of which our Christian spiritual life grows and unfolds itself.

Faith is the revelation of God in the hidden core of my being as the One who calls me to a unique intimacy of life and love with Him. This divine gift of faith gives rise to my recognition of God as my destiny, my fulfillment, as the One who will grant me everlasting joy. Such is His offer of love and intimate lasting friendship. It is God Himself who effects in us our friendship for Him. Love and friendship require a certain alikeness; therefore, God elevates us to His level. He makes us partners who can become His real frineds.

In Christ this friendship between God and man received an irreplacable and ultimate form. In the Lord, the divine love for us is made visible. The love of the man Jesus for God is the most adequate response to the offer of love of the Father.

This love for Christ in us for His Father in Heaven, that we call charity, is the third dynamic force in our Christian spiritual life. In and with Christ we have to live this love out by doing the will of the Father. God asks us to respond in obedient love to the values we discover in this world. We hear in these values the appeal of God Himself. We realize them in love for our fellow men whom we love with the love with which Christ loves us. Therefore, the charity of Christ extends itself in and through us to all people, independent of their personal attractiveness.

This charity of Christ, at the heart of the Christian spiritual life, makes us creative; it compels us to create room on this earth for goodness, truth, and beauty. In this effective love for our fellow men, our spiritual life unfolds itself precisely because it is God's love itself acting in us. Our total activity, our thinking and feeling, our interaction with others receive their orientation from God's effective presence in us. It is God himself who sanctifies us in our obedient love for Him, a love that receives its concrete form in our interaction with others in the way in which Christ loved us.

Grace

From what we have said about our life project of faith, hope, and charity, it may be evident by now that this project is only possible to the degree that we leave the initiative to God. God offers Himself to man as the object of a faith, hope, and love that transcends human nature. It is the same God who gives man the possibility to appreciate Him as such. This gift of God to us is grace. It is God Himself who offers Himself to man as gift, as salvation, as intimate friend. In surrender to this gift, man becomes for the first time his true and deepest self.

Only in this participation in divine life do we discover our deepest spiritual identity. Living in grace means discovering by divine illumination our deepest self in God and with God's loving assistance realizing this identity in life. This life of grace cannot emerge from any human culture, no matter how sublime. The life of grace is only possible when we make the center of our self-emergence not culture or nature but God Himself. We leave the initiative to Him; the other centers of our personality become subordinated to God as the gracing center of our new existence in Christ.

This grace of God enters our emergent self not as an alien force. Divine grace accommodates graciously what has been given to us by culture and nature insofar as it is compatible with the hidden spiritual identity in Christ God has given us from eternity. Nevertheless, graced growth should not be understood as a mere outgrowth of what a person already possesses because of natural and cultural endowment. Graced growth is a drawing out by God's love of human possibilities that could in and by themselves never reach the same height as now effected by the power of grace.

The grace of God assumed in human history a visible appearance in the person of Jesus of Nazareth. God shows us in Christ the meaning and destiny of His offer of union with Him. The death and resurrection of Christ is the paradigm of our graced spiritual life.

The reality of our graced spiritual identity is only given to us in faith. Faith implies, as we have seen, that we cannot yet fully understand what it means to be graced or to participate in the life of God. Therefore, living in grace is always also a prayerful search for the hidden God, an attempt to come to know Him. To be faithful to the intimations of grace in our life, a constant ascetisicm is demanded of us—an asceticism of daily life that affects all our actions, perceptions, styles, and customs.

Prayer

We have seen that the graced presence of God in our lives is the depth dimension of our existence. Our graced spiritual identity can articulate and incarnate itself only in this concrete world of people, events, and things. Spiritual life, therefore, cannot be a life isolated from our every day existence. The articulation of our graced spiritual identity before God does not take place in some isolation chamber locked away in our soul.

Spiritual living in the Christian sense is the graced spiritualization in faith, hope, and charity of our whole life in all its dimensions, articulations, modes and modalities. The divine presence in our being is an all permeating presence.

At certain times, we feel the need to emphasize, to make explicit in our attention, to thematize, this presence of God in our lives. We want to be explicitly present to the Presence. We focus our attention on the Presence itself that pervades our graced spiritual identity and its many incarnations. This worshipful concentration is called praying. Prayer is possible because of the faith we have that our graced identity is hidden with Christ in God. Graced prayer is God's initiative in us. Prayer singles out the deepest meaning of everything in our life: the divine meaning. Prayer thus cannot be totally isolated from our life; it demands, however, a certain distancing from everyday involvement. We want in this distancing to experience as figure what in daily spiritual life is given as an always present ground.

One could compare this situation with that of love between husband and wife. When husband and wife truly love one another, they are somehow present to one another in all they feel, think, and do. They take each other implicitly into account. Their love for one another is a hidden dimension of their lives even when they are away from one another, working in a school, office, or factory. Real lovers are never totally absent from one another. Still they create special moments of loving togetherness in which all the tasks and preoccupations in which they incarnate their love recede in the background. The rest of their lives is not totally absent during such moments of intimate togetherness; their loving presence cannot be isolated from the ways in which they express this presence in their daily lives. Without such moments of explicit loving togetherness, the love dimension of their daily lives would diminish and in the long run disappear.

Similarly, we have to restore periodically the depth dimension of our daily spiritual life by moments of explicit presence to God. Here, too, prayerful presence should not be isolated from the presence to God that should permeate our daily lives.

In and through prayer, we renew our graced spiritual presence to the situations in which we are involved. The moments of concentrated and explicit presence to God help us to see daily events as meaningful revelations of the Divine Will, as divine challenges, as questions to be answered by us in Christ.

Conclusion of the Third Dimension of the Research Project

In this third and central dimension of our study, we try to revise and understand anew what we have described in the extra and pre-revelational phases of our study.

We can conclude our considerations of the graced and revelational dimension of this study by saying that Christian spiritual life is a life of grace that takes up and transforms all human meanings in the light of God's revelation. This dimension enkindles in us the awareness that it is God alone to whom belongs the initiative in regard to the graced transformation of the attitudes, customs, experiences, and styles we have explored as lived on the human level. This phase of our study helps us to realize that it is only God's grace and revelation that gives a sacramental meaning to all good attitudes, insights, people, events, and things we meet in this world or reflect upon in our studies about the spiritual life.

This central part of our study helps us also to realize the relativity of the human goodness we discover in this world. Our life is oriented in faith, hope, and love toward what already has begun in us and toward the eschatological future where God will bring us home in a union of love with Christ our Brother.

The Pre-Revelational Dimension

This division of study takes up the human dimension of spirituality, researched in the first division. In this second division, the student may ask himself which concrete religious orientations this human dimension may have received in various organized or non-organized religions. In the previous chapter on the human dimensions of Fundamental Catholic Spirituality, we reflected already on some aspects of this general religious dimension as present in various religions and denominations and as studied by different sciences.

Here, in connection with the pre-revelational dimension, we want to add to considerations thus far an outline of the three essential dimensions of the experience of God. Insight into these three dimensions may help us to structure the second phase of our research, because different religions may stress in varying degrees one or the other of these three dimensions.

The Three Essential Dimensions of the Experience of God

Our encounter with the Divine has three essential dimensions. To clarify the meaning of these three dimensions, I must repeat here the analysis of the fundamental structure of encounter I presented in my book *Personality Fulfillment in the Religious Life.*

Many approaches may lead to an understanding of the experience of divine encounter. One which seems helpful is to reflect for a moment on the word *encounter* itself. It is made up of two words: *en* and *counter.*

Going back to the Latin, I find that *en* is related to the Latin *in* and refers to the experience of being in, being identified with, being at one with: in short, the experience of *in-being.* On the other hand, the English *counter* is related to the Latin *contra,* which has the opposite meaning of *in-being.* For *contra* means against, being opposed, being different, not being totally identified with. It is interesting to note that the word encounter was initially used—among other things—to describe a hostile meeting with enemy troops in battle.

Presently, encounter has a third meaning that combines in a higher synthesis the two seemingly opposed meanings of "being in with another" and at the same time "standing over against this other." Encounter in this sense implies the emergence of a certain intimacy between persons who experience and respect each other as unique and, therefore, different. This intimacy is rooted in a deeper dimension of being they somehow have in common. The experience of intimacy combines the two experiences of being alike and being different in an experience of freely chosen togetherness that transcends and integrates the two components of sameness and uniqueness.

True encounter is a more or less intimate meeting with another that transcends and at the same time keeps alive within their intimacy a polarity of in-being and counter-being. All three experiences—"in-being," "counter-being," and "transcending intimacy"—are essential constituents of a full grown, loving, or friendly encounter between mature self-reliant people.

These three experiential dimensions of mature encounter seem necessary also in man's encounter with the Divine. I need to experience, first of all, in-being with God. This is the necessary ground for any possibility of feeling at home with Him. This experience of in-being has to be moderated, however, by the experience that He is totally Other, that I am not absorbed in God, that I am not God myself. Encounter is only possible when I discover not only my being-in with God but also my not being God. Both the experience of in-being and the experience of infinite transcendence created by the experience of counter-being must be surpassed by an experience of gratuitous personal intimacy: an intimacy offered to me by the Infinitely Transcendent One in Whom I find my ground by in-being.

In our spiritual experience of God, we can thus have "in-being experiences" with the Divine because the Divine is at the root of our being. The experience of God's immanence can be so deep that spiritual men and women may never go beyond this experience of in-being. We see this in certain Eastern nature mystics who feel so "in" with the Divine that they no longer know who is I and who is Divine. The awareness of one's spiritual identity before God seems lost. Christians, too, may have moments in which this awareness of total in-being is experienced.

Another dimension of the experience of the Divine makes us experience God as Transcendent, as "counter-being;" we experience God as the Totally Other, the Most High. Such an experience of God as person seems more possible in an undistorted way if He as Person is pro-claimed by a religion like that in the Old Testament. In general, man seems more inclined to distort God's image when in counter-being he experiences Him as Person, somewhat like himself. In the experience of counter-being, we go beyond seeing God as identified with nature and ourselves as part of this nature. We see Him somehow as a person like we ourselves are persons with an identity of our own. This view is open to distortion in the same way we so often distort the image of other people around us. We project our own fantasies onto God if we are not protected by a clear proclamation of a church or religion in regard to who God is. It is difficult to move beyond the experience of immanence without a projection of human characteristics onto the gods, as we find in Greek mythology, where gods fought, murdered, and performed all too human acts.

The basic intuition of the total counter-being of a personal God is right. However, when He as Person is not proclaimed, as in the Old Testament or in Moham-medanism, people have to make up their own minds about what God would be like as a person. This attempt to describe God as a person leads easily to a falsification of God's image by human projections.

Personal Intimacy

Only when we experience both in-being and counter-being is the stage set for the possibility for personal intimacy. An infant cannot have a personal relationship with his mother until he can experience that she is different from him as a person. When the adolescent discovers his parents as other, he often resists them. Later on, when mature, he can relate to his parents in a personal, dignified way, for there can develop a balance of in-being and counter-being between them by means of a growing relationship of respectful personal intimacy. Some people do not go beyond the experience of in-being. Others remain in the stage of experience of counter-being, such as often happens to the frightened or rebellious adolescent. Others grow beyond the former two stages to the experience of intimacy. The same happens in spirituality.

Intimacy in Spirituality

The phase of personal intimacy in spirituality is one typical of Christianity. God is proclaimed in Christianity as a loving Father—so loving that we in Christ become one with Him, for in Christ we are His adopted sons. In Christianity, we find the fullness of all three dimensions of spiritual experience. We can have the experience of a mystical at-oneness with the Omnipresent and Eternal who fills the universe. He is also revealed to us as the personal, totally other God who stands over against us and infinitely transcends us. Yet He is also given to us as a God who loves us personally in Christ and pursues a loving encounter with us, respecting the unique spiritual identity He granted us.

This last phase of personal intimacy is totally dependent on a revealing proclamation. We cannot know by our own human knowledge alone that God is offering us a life of personal intimacy with Him. Outside Christianity, we do not find the same awareness of God as

intimate lover of man. We may find Eastern mystics who
live deeply "in-being experiences," who feel totally at one,
for example, with nature or cosmos experienced as the
whole and Holy; they have a natural mystical experience,
but, without grace, they cannot reach the experience of
graced intimacy with a personal God that may be given to
the Christian.

Because of their belief, such mystics will not easily
speak of a personal love relationship between God and us.
They refer mainly to a being at one with the whole. Christian mysticism and spirituality always express themselves
in terms of personal loving intimacy. The prevalence of the
graced aspect of intimate love in Christian spirituality does
not imply that Christian spirituality can neglect the experiential dimension of in-being, of divine immanence. In some
mysterious way, by creation and ceaseless preservation,
God is always in us, keeping us in being, carrying us, permeating us. This experience of at-oneness with the Divine
is the ground dimension of all spiritual encounter with the
Divine, also in Christianity. As we said earlier, the experience of in-being is a basic ingredient of any experience of
encounter, also of an encounter with God.

In-being, counter-being, and personal intimacy form a
three dimensional unity of the fully unfolded spiritual encounter with the Divine. These three dimensions are interrelated in any experience of God's Presence. The more we
begin to live the liberating experience of this three
dimensional relationship to the all pervading Holy, to the
personal almighty God, and to the intimate eternal Lover,
the more that experience begins to radiate and reverberate
in our whole self.

From these considerations, a possible structure of the
pre-revelational divison of our study emerges. If the

specific topic lends itself to it—which may not always be the case—one could first investigate how the topic studied has received a religious orientation in spiritualities of religions that are mostly interested in the experience of in-being. This research could extend to those authors in religions that are less oriented to in-being, but which nevertheless highlighted this dimension of a full spiritual experience. The same can be said about people outside organized religion, who described spiritual experiences of in-being they tried to foster in themselves and others.

In this second part of the structure of this division—dependent on his topic and interest—the student could perhaps concentrate his research on religions such as Judaism and Mohammedanism that give rise to a pronounced experience and description of the dimension of counter-being in spiritual experience. This examination could be expanded to include literature of other religions and of people outside organized religion insofar as it focuses on this dimension of spiritual experience.

Finally, the student may explore how various non-Christian religions called forth spiritual men and women who tried to come to a personal intimacy with God, a relative intimacy that can be seen as a foreshadowing of the graced and revealed intimacy offered to man in and through Christ.

Christianity itself has taken on many forms. In some of these, we may find particular ways of trying to realize the graced and revealed life of intimacy with God in Christ. While we are here already on the level of Revelation, we may examine the approaches of non-Catholic Christianity at the end of this division on pre-revealed approaches. The results of this examination could be added, perhaps as a subdivision. For, while other forms of Christianity take into account the Revelation, they may not give the full and orthodox explanation of it. It is understood, of course, that the student explores these three dimensions of spiritual experience only in relation to the specific topic he is studying, should his topic lend itself to such use.

The Post-Revelational Presently Lived Dimension

Following his research on the extra, pre, and post-revelational levels, the student is ready to ask himself, in light of the results of his research, questions about the concrete spiritual life of present day Catholic Christians or a specific segment of them. He may examine how they live the attitude, experience, or style he has researched so far. Such an investigation may teach him about the special obstacles they meet in realizing this specific attitude in their lives. This insight will be helpful for the later fifth and final dimension of his study, which will deal with the problems of spiritual initiation and direction of such Christian Catholics in regard to the topic researched.

As we have seen, in Chapter VI on spiritual identity and its modes of incarnation, people live their unique spiritual call in a variety of life forms and tasks. We concluded there that no style of life, no vocational and professional style, would be appropriate for everyone as the only possible way of spiritual living. We mentioned also, as we did more extensively in our book *Religion and Personality,* that man tries to unfold his life in response to certain values that appeal to him and motivate him. This value appeal is ultimately an appeal of the spirit, which makes man spontaneously resonate with precisely those values offered by the culture that are in tune with his unique spiritual identity.

This human living, oriented towards the realization of values that are uniquely appropriate, is not changed by the fact that we try to live a graced Christian spiritual life. Christian spiritual life does not mean that we begin to devise our lives in a way totally different from the value affinity we already experienced in ourselves spontaneously. If anything, the graced spiritual life helps us to discover what our most unique value affinity is and to correct any false value orientations that are at odds with our deepest self. Spiritual life, therefore, does not give rise to a life style or life form adjacent to the human style and form we are already invited to assume in keeping with our individuality and unique spiritual identity. Christian spiritual life enables us to recognize these value appeals as personal invitations of God to enter into loving communion with Him in and through the life style, life form, vocational and professional styles, to which we are called uniquely.

We realize in faith that God inserted us in His world, in history and culture, as free and autonomous persons. Our life situation is the domain of our free responsibility; it is assigned to us as our field of activity, an activity in and through which we are called to enter into His Kingdom. Faith, at the heart of our Christian spiritual life, does not make us believe falsely that God will intervene miraculously to do our task for us, to solve the problems we have to cope with, to straighten out the married life He may have called us to. God respects the freedom and responsibility of the spiritual man. What faith makes us see is that this responsibility and this challenge comes from God, that it lies embedded in our creatureliness, that our life form or task is an assignment, a challenge posed by God Himself to our life here on earth. Christian spiritual life implies the wholehearted acknowledgement and acceptance of this divine call underlying any life form and task. In our chapter on spiritual identity, we used the phrase life call to express this divine depth dimension of daily reality to which we respond with commitment and consecration.

Christian spiritual life means the growing awareness that we are already within God in all we are called to do and realize in this life. In God is already hidden our daily unfolding of world and culture. Therefore, in a certain sense, we can call this daily cultivation of world and humanity through our task a divine culture or divine cultivation. In light of the faith given to us, we believe that there runs a thread through the history of mankind. Christian spiritual life in the world is rooted in the conviction that the end of human history has become manifest in one historical figure, Jesus of Nazareth. Christ is the ultimate end, the manifestation of the eschatological reality, the absolute norm of our participation in the unfolding of mankind and culture. Jesus is the revelation and manifestation of the Father *in* history. God offered man an intimate communion of love with Him. This union of love between God and unfolding humanity was historically realized in the man Jesus. This loving at-oneness was not only realized in our Lord as representative of all humanity; also in and through Him this intimacy became a concrete possibility for each individual person.

Insofar as this intimacy between God and man becomes realized in a Christian spiritual life, we may say that we have a sacramental anticipation of the ultimate end of human history. The most convincing sign pointing to this ultimate end of history is the Christian love that unfolds itself within the spiritual life of each Christian. In the measure that our spiritual life reveals and creates love, it points in a sacramental way to the eschaton. In loving we actualize the golden thread that makes history one in its tending towards the final destiny of humanity.

This integrating orientation of history has already been realized in Jesus' reconciliation of man with God. The grace of salvation becomes historically visible for the world in the spiritualized life of Christians. In and through this love that animates their spiritual life, Christians contribute—each one in his own way—to the divine project for humanity. Effective spiritual life is thus a participation in the salvation of humanity by Christ. The Christian's cultural activity is assumed with him in Christ and therewith in God's project for the salvation of mankind and world.

Christian spiritual life implies the development of a life style, life form, vocational and professional style, which enables the spiritual man to help world and mankind unfold themselves in accordance with that orientation towards the ultimate divine destiny of humanity, the eschaton, as it appeared in Christ. The humanization of mankind and man is thus by no means a task to be left to non-believers involved in arts, sciences, and other cultural activities. On the contrary, it is the deepest assignment of any spiritual man who lives a Christian spirituality to involve himself in this humanization in and through his life style, life form, vocational and professional style.

This spiritual vision clarifies immediately in which sense the Christian spiritual life is essentially apostolic. Apostolate is not only sought after in extracurricular activities that manifest at first glance a more pious appearance than one's daily task in family, office, school, laboratory, or factory. The apostolate of the spiritual man is achieved, first of all, in the way he lives his chosen life form and in the various modes of human labor to which he is called by his life situation.

In a pluralistic society, the same life form is lived, and the same cultural labor is performed, by people who are not Christians and do not live the Christian spiritual life. These same labors are the domain of the first apostolate of the Christian. In our books on *The Vowed Life* and on *Personality Fulfillment in the Religious Life,* we called this apostolate one of "value radiation in the culture." We explained that this value radiation within one's daily task is the primary apostolate of the married or single Christian in the world as well as of the participative religious who finds himself engaged in one of the various tasks meant to help mankind grow towards its ultimate destiny in Christ.

As we explained in Chapter VI on spiritual identity, life form and daily task can be lived in a variety of styles. For the Christian spiritual man, this style is modulated by his presence to Christ, by the faith, hope, and charity implanted in him by God's grace. This Christian style of spirituality is not isolated from the various acceptable styles in which people live their life form or task within a specific culture or cultural period. Because Christian spirituality is essentially an incarnated and incarnating spirituality, it is sensitive to historical changes in styles of living, in human sensitivities. Hence the style of Christian value radiation is flexible, open to reorientation in light of newly emerging sensitivities of people; it is always ready to accommodate humanity by restructuring itself in more compatible historical forms.

The Christian spiritual man sees every true and creative articulation of culture as an effect of God's influence on man, even if such realizations are merely humanistic and not motivated by the Christian faith. Because the Christian believes that God works in this way in human history, he is gladly willing to cooperate with such human realizations and to dialogue with them in function of the emergence of his own Christian spirituality. In regard to such dialogue, we have already demonstrated the dialectical method used by the student of spirituality to interact with the findings and insights of the arts and sciences. In this dimension of the research project, we are speaking about Catholic Christians who have to do something similar in their lives within the life form and tasks they are called to. On basis of the Christian's life communion with God that was initiated in him by grace and that actualized itself in his life of faith, hope, and charity, this Christian shares in some measure God's vision of the world, to the degree that he lives a Christian spiritual life. This divine vision enables him to live a life of value radiation, to focus human attention, by the example of his own life, on the deeper sacred dimension that he knows in and through his faith to be present in the various domains of life.

The Threefold Path

Living my life form and daily task in a style of spiritual value radiation is an essential aspect of the graced Christian life. Research in any topic of spiritual living should, therefore, include research in how this topic is related to the daily life style of the spiritual person.

We shall reflect now on one of the possible ways in which this dimension of the research project may be articulated. The structure of the threefold path, as developed in our book *The Vowed Life,* has often proved helpful for the articulation of this dimension of the research project.

The threefold path is a pathway of respectful openness to God's hidden Presence in the world. This pathway differentiates itself in three ways of respectful openness in accordance with three main horizons of meaning in this world. This world reveals God's Presence in three different kinds of creatures, namely, in events, things, and people. Openness in faith, hope, and charity to each of these three specific self-manifestations of the Divine in this world and its history demands three different appropriate approaches of the graced spiritual person.

Obedience

In regard to events, man can only become what God wants him to be in Christ by living in an attitude of surrender to anything that may manifest itself as truly God's will for him. This readiness to follow any true manifestation of the divine orientation of this world and its history implies a steady openness for the possible speaking of God in the events of daily life so that life may be reoriented, if necessary, in accordance with what seems to be God's holy will.

Ready to surrender wholeheartedly to God's self-manifestation in any event, the spiritual person is humbly open with his graced spirit and intelligence, his feelings and intuitions, his experience and learning; with his prayerful, scientific, practical and poetic attitudes; with his eyes and ears, his sense of touch, his body, hands, and feet.

Like Jesus and Mary, he is a ready listener to the will of God. This obedience of the spiritual person is dynamic; his graced ability to listen in surrender to the hidden divine meanings of natural, cultural, and historical events is never closed but ever ongoing and expanding. This expanding openness is rooted in the essence of obedience, the readiness to follow the divine pleasure no matter how hard this may be in one's personal and vital life as it has developed so far. When this readiness to surrender diminishes, the person becomes less open, for he is afraid that he may be confronted with a divine command that is at odds with the complacent life he has begun to live.

Obedience is a sharing in the obedient listening of Christ to the manifestations of the will of His Father in all events. Obedience helps us to find and realize the appropriate response to all things God allows to transpire in and around us. The heart of this listening in faith, its very essence, is our readiness with Christ to say, "Yes, Father," at every moment that it becomes clear to us what the divine will entails for our lives.

In order to listen to the Father's will for us as hidden in all that we encounter in our daily life situation, we need the grace of enlightenment; this grace will help us to transcend the needs and compulsions of our vital and personal life. It is given to us by the spirit of our Lord, who is always with us, ready to purify our ways of sensing and knowing by means of His gifts.

As we have seen, the Christian incarnates his love for Christ in his fellow man by personal participation in humanity and culture. Obedience in this life setting implies that the Christian keep in tune with the ever changing society of man. He engages himself in the attempt of mankind to listen to all the revelations of reality. His faith, hope, and charity make him look for the will of the Father behind these revelations.

For the spiritual man, the will of the Father for his

life and for his participative endeavors is not revealed in some closed off interiority or in some far out abstract concept of humanity or world; it is revealed in his concrete life situation in which he daily labors and listens. The spiritual person realizes also that the spirit of Jesus may speak not only to him but potentially to his fellow Christians and to other men of good will. Through each one, the Spirit may reveal some aspect of the divine will, adapting itself to the limited abilities and perspectives of each unique person. Each spiritual person sees the situation of the culture and its hidden divine demands from a different perspective, for each is blessed with his own spiritual identity, task, character, temperament, education, and affinity. Accordingly, each one receives his own inspiration to the degree that he allows the Holy Spirit to illumine and deepen his limited perspectivity.

The original and at times divinely illuminated perspectivity of each spiritual person leads to the fortuitous fact that different aspects of the cultural situation will be revealed to different Christians and others of good intent. This revelation occurs when they are truly open and listening to reality in and through Jesus, who is present in each one in a unique way. The humble awareness that the Lord is not the exclusive partner of any one spiritual person alone but that He is present in all enables each person to listen respectfully to the other. Ours is a mutual listening in the hope that the divine will may manifest itself to us through one another—a listening inspired by the willingness to live the essence of obedience: conformity to the divine command that may come to us in this listening. Faith in Christ's presence and His possible speaking in all may thus give rise at times to respectful dialogue between people who share the same life form or are engaged in the same task.

Obedience in Christ implies also a listening to the Church, which, in a privileged way, listens to the will of God and communicates this holy will to us. Again the listening of obedience is not simply an intellectually interested listening; it is a committed listening, a listening that is in advance committed to realize in life what will be heard as God's will.

The Church is like a master-listener who, under the guidance of the Holy Spirit, binds many partial views together in a unifying wisdom regarding the desirable general way of acting of all Christians. Listening to and with the Church as master-listener may help to foster in all spiritual people true unique participation in the culture without diminishing their rootedness in the Church which, through Word and Sacrament, protects their initimacy with Christ. In other words, obedience to the will of the Father implies obedience to the possible manifestation of His will in one another and in the Spirit-enlightened Church as master-listener.

The more every spiritual person is ready to listen to the word of the Church in surrender, the greater may be the opportunity for free expression of insights, feelings, and inclinations. The certitude that everyone will abide by the word of the Church, spoken in dialogue with its members, guarantees that the unity, peace, and serenity of Christianity may be maintained without detracting from the possibility of candid disclosure of opposed feelings and ideas. An atmosphere of mutual respect may then prevail in which every member of the Church can feel at home and in communion with the Lord, who is the source and inspiration of the abiding respect for each person's unique spiritual identity in Christ, a respect that characterizes the authentic Christian life.

The attitude of obedience invites the spiritual person

to participate in the unfolding of history as flowing from the Divine Logos. Disobedience would isolate him from the Logos, as the center of the true cultural unfolding of humanity. To the degree that he gives into this temptation, he will experience isolation from history and culture, from mankind and society, and their transcendent meaning.

Poverty

The world I have to be present to is not homogeneous in appearance. We have distinguished events, things, and people as three different manifestations of the Divine Presence in this world, each one demanding its own approach. Obedient listening implies a spiritual approach to events. Poverty describes the proper spiritual attitude towards the natural and cultural things we find around us or interiorized within us.

Things in my life space are gifts of God. I feel called by the Holy Spirit to perfect and use them in a way which respects their deepest meaning, a meaning that they received in and through the Word, for in and through Him everything came to be. The Holy Spirit inspires the spiritual man to use things in a way which respects the spiritual identity of himself and of other persons for whom things are utilized. The spiritual man is able to abide in such respectful presence only when he distances himself repeatedly from the surface dimension of things.

This spirit of distancing from the superficial meanings of things in order to deal with them wisely and respectfully in accordance with their deepest and divine meaning is called poverty in the Christian tradition. Such distancing creates room for the emergence of my true self or spirit; it frees my vision for the perception of deeper meanings and of possibilities to be realized in the respectful use of culture and nature in accordance with the divine destiny of human history.

Hope directs us towards the eschaton, the new creation in Christ to which we belong already and which will be manifested in us in a future still hidden from our sight. Hope teaches us that this world and all the goods it can offer is not a lasting place and will never fulfill our deepest yearnings. If hope loses this orientation towards the mysterious beyond, we are tempted to replace the eschaton by the idle expectation of a world here and now that will totally satisfy us. This expectation makes us cling to cultural and natural things inside and outside ourselves as if they could fulfill us totally. It is in the light of the divine gift of hope that we are pried loose from the things on which we are fixated. By the same token, hope helps us to deal with things respectfully insofar as they can be used to build a world of limited goodness willed by God here and now for redeemed humanity, a good society that fore-shadows the world to come.

This limited goodness of the things of this world can then be seen as a revelation of God's own goodness. Our Lord Himself was filled with tender respect for nature. His sensitivity vibrates in His words when He speaks in parables about lilies of the field, dressed so beautifully by the Father, and about little sparrows cared for so deeply by Him that not one falls without His knowing it. Jesus asks men to base their trust in the Father at least partly on the fact that He manifests such great care for all other things in nature. In numerous ways, He shows how the gifts of nature and culture should be used respectfully and lovingly by man.

Visiting a wedding party, He makes available in a wondrous way the finest wine so that the guests may be joyful and make merry. He multiplies the loaves and the fishes so that the crowds following Him can still their hunger and regain their vigor. When His apostles are not able to fill their nets with fish, Jesus is there to fill them to the breaking point. When Mary Magdalene, in a beautiful gesture of respectful presence to Him, pours fragrant and expensive oils over His feet He appreciates it deeply and tells the other guests that she did the right thing. He reprimands them when they murmur that this precious oil should have been sold and the money given to the poor, for their complaint reflects a onesided and materialistic view of poverty.

This respectful attitude toward the gifts of culture and nature became such a hallmark of Jesus' life that one of the main attacks on Him was that He was a drinker of wine, a man without asceticism, who allowed His disciples to eat the corn of the field on the Sabbath. On the other hand, it was clear that His presence to the gifts of the Father was only possible because of His ability to distance Himself from the mere material meaning of things. He never became enslaved to them, but strove always to discover and celebrate their deeper meanings and possibilities in accordance with the life situation.

Poverty thus gives rise to the free and liberated use of things. Jesus was so free from things that He could honestly say He did not possess a stone on which to lay His head. This does not mean that He never found a place to sleep, for He often stayed in the homes of his friends like Mary and Martha; it only serves to emphasize that He kept Himself free from onesided concern for such things. His example does not mean that the people who consecrate their life to God within the fundamental life form of marriage, for example, should not care about food, shelter, and clothing. It only means that they should do so in His spirit of poverty so that they will not be absorbed by these preoccupations.

The practice of poverty should be somewhat different for each person because each person is unique. Each one differs in life call, life style, and life form in physical health and strength, in sensitivity, insight, and interest, in need for a certain amount and kind of recreation, in background, preparation, and task. True Christian poverty takes all of these factors respectfully into account. What is the wise and respectful use of things for one spiritual person may prove to be an unwise and disrespectful use of things for another.

In short, there is an infinite variety in the individual practice of poverty. It varies from person to person and even from one period of life to another in the same person. For the person changes and grows and the practice of poverty has to change accordingly. Most important are not the details of this practice but the spirit of Christ in which this practice is lived.

The practice of poverty should never become rigid and inflexible, isolated from the growth of the Christian personality as a whole. True Christian wisdom in regard to the wise and respectful use of things is always an openness to all the changes in one's own personality and in the situation in which one has to use things in the best interest of his spiritual growth.

The spiritual person, freed from mere possessiveness, may find God in a sunset, in the smile of a child, in a painting, in a sip of mellow wine, a crust of bread, an evening of good company. Everywhere in culture and nature, the mystery of the Divine is waiting to reveal itself to the spiritual man, no longer burdened by the need to possess things disrespectfully. Unfortunately, man is tempted to forget the most fundamental tending of Christ in him toward the Father, to see only the glass of wine, the lovely face, the house in which he lives. Our inclination is not to go beyond the shell of things into the mystery they contain. We easily fall away from our innermost calling, from the message of a God-filled reality, and from our mission to live and radiate this meaning. By our anxious and possessive preoccupation with things in isolation from their deepest ground, we may lose our joyful presence to things in poverty.

Chaste Love

A last specific manifestation of God's love in the world demanding a special approach is the human person. People differ from events and things. To understand people, I need to empathize with them, to feel at one with them, to love them. The same is true for myself. I have to love my deepest hidden identity as a precious gift of God. For the spiritual man, the love of people and of himself is a practical expression of the divine gift of charity. The most fundamental reason why he loves himself and others is his love for God in himself and others, whom he knows present because of the gift of faith and whom he reaches in himself and others by the divine gift of charity.

We call this love respectful or chaste love. The meaning of the word "chaste" is related to that of the verb "to chasten," which means "to refine," "to purify." A chaste love is a love purified from egocentric impulses which threaten to use self-love or love of others as a means of manipulating self and others, or of violating the integrity of self and others spiritually, psychologically, or physically. While obedience tends to restore man to unity with unfolding reality, respectful love tends to heal the break between man and man. Disobedience as a force of isolation, fragmentation, and closure alienates us from the cultural-religious unfolding of life. So, too, lack of respectful love is another source of disintegration, which alienates us from mankind and man as flowing from God. If we reflect upon lack of loving respect as a disintegrating force in person and society, we may be able to view chaste love as a fundamental healing attitude which restores man to an abiding respect for the Divine in himself and others.

When I lose respect and love for myself, I also lose respect and love for the other. I am neither able to harmonize my own personality nor to live in harmony with my fellow men. A decrease in self-respect decreases in me the possibility of self-integration and integration with society.

Chaste or respectful love means that I accept myself wholeheartedly as emerging from the Holy in dialogue with my unique life situation. The height of loving self-respect implies the deepest possible humility. True self-love and true humility go together. The most profound act of humility is that of full acceptance of the limited gift which I am; humility calls for surrender to the mystery of my personal unfolding within the successive limited life situations allotted to me.

The healing power of Christian love in the culture should not be understood in a narrow way. A narrow attitude would restrict such freeing love to its most ostentatious expressions, such as the immediate relief of certain concrete needs of my fellow man, by giving him food, nursing his wounds, and building his house. These are praiseworthy manifestations of Christian love; a great many people are called to this excellent incarnation of Christ's love for humanity. Yet some people may be called to other perhaps less spectacular incarnations of charity, which may be even more beneficial to their fellow man.

When I am called as a Christian participant to incarnate my healing love for mankind and its unfolding by serving scholarship, artistic creation, or scientific experimentation, I—together with my colleagues—may accomplish more for mankind than by feeding a certain number of hungry people or teaching a small number of children a certain amount of practical knowledge. By means of my contribution to such scholarly fields, I may hasten the moment in which a new insight is born. This birth of new knowledge will not only benefit one small class of school children or one small group of poor people. Untold millions may profit from it.

Possibly a certain technical and scientific development may remove the very causes of poverty for an entire population. It may also be that the emergence of a new expression in art may bring many to the threshold of a deeper humanization. Mine may be a talent and ability to incarnate my Christian love effectively in a contribution that would sustain indirectly common cultural efforts to relieve the needs of all mankind. In that case, it would be foolish, perhaps even sinful, to spend my time solely relieving the concrete immediate needs of a small group of children in my community, even if I enjoy doing so and deeply love those who need my care. I shall leave this task to the admirable people who are called to it.

I may dread the thought of embodying my Christian love in the tedious service of mankind by means of study and research. There are no immediate rewards, no grateful voices and warm sympathy awaiting me; there may be no experience of concrete success. I may die long before the cultural enterprise in which I am participating as a teacher or expert grows to a moment of sudden victory over human needs—a victory which will be possible only because numerous men and women have spent years of quiet dedication, experimentation, research, and teaching in this unique field of service to mankind. I may be called to become one of these persons. If so, my Christian love for mankind should free me to pursue this loving contribution.

The awareness that the Word was made Flesh and is dwelling among us gave a whole new and unsuspected divine dimension to human love for self and others. Jesus Himself told us that whatever we do to the least estimated persons on earth, we do to Him. He described how at the end of time people will ask Him in surprise when did we clothe you, give you to drink or visit you in prison, and the answer was that anything done to the least of His brethren has also been done to Him.

Christian love thus implies respect for myself and the other because of the redeeming love of Christ for each of us. The coming of the Light into the world in the person of Christ makes possible and infinitely fosters our growth from crowd and collectivity to true human communion and community.

Conclusion

After our considerations of the threefold path, we may ask ourselves in what way is this path valuable for the fourth dimension of the research project we are describing.

We can study how present day Christians concretely live out obedience, poverty, and love in their contemporary life situations. Where does their Christian obedience, poverty, and love fail or how is their meaning misunderstood? What can we do in service of the unfolding of the spiritual life of the present day Christian to foster the right kind of Christian obedience, poverty, and love? Is the topic we are studying related to the fostering of this threefold path in a Christian sense? How would the attitude, style, or custom I am concentrating on in this study be enhanced or deepened by the exercise of the threefold path? It seems that in many cases obedience, poverty, or chaste love present three helpful perspectives from which to study the revelance of the topics considered in this fourth dimension of the research for a specific population.

The Post-Revelational Applicative Dimension

As we explained in Chapter II on the science of spirituality, our discipline can be defined as a theoretical-practical science. All theoretical research in spirituality is ultimately oriented towards the praxis of spirituality. It seems advisable, therefore, that the student in this field finish his research with this final fifth dimension in which he explores how the insights and findings about a specific attitude or praxis of the spiritual life can be applied to the population he focused on in the fourth dimension of his study. He must examine existing literature and research on spiritual initiation and direction that may be relevant to his specific topic of study and the particular segment of Christian Catholics he has chosen.

He may have chosen as his population people who are on a certain level of spiritual development. He must then carefully investigate sources that deal with this specific stage of their spiritual development. Undoubtedly, a study of classical or more recently formulated phases of spiritual growth would be helpful in many, if not all, studies about the application of the results of specific research to concrete people trying to grow in the spiritual life, for human and spiritual growth always happens in stages. Here we present some general considerations about this fifth and final dimension of the research, its meaning and rationale.

Spiritual Initiation and Direction

The person who lives a Christian spiritual life is moved by grace to radiate his divine gifts of faith, hope, and charity in the world. He does so in a basic style of obedience, spiritual poverty, and respectful love. These virtues give rise to a whole set of other virtues, such as wisdom, prudence, courage, strength, gentleness, zeal, dedication, that gradually transform not only his life style but also his vocational and professional style of being in the world. In and through this new style of Christ-like living, he changes his world and, in the process, he grows daily in his own life as an expression of his spiritual identity in Christ.

This way of Christ-like presence to humanity is the usual way in which the Lord shines forth in every Christian who lives the life of the spirit. It is not the only way. At times, every spiritual person may be called by the Holy Spirit to be more directly and intimately involved in the promotion of the deepest spiritual growth in himself or in his fellow men. This direct fostering of the spiritual life is called spiritual initiation and spiritual direction.

Spiritual initiation refers to the experiential and practical beginning of the spiritual life. Spiritual life is, in principle, present in the baptized Christian and is essentially nourished in the Church by Word and Sacrament. When we speak about spiritual initiation, we focus mainly on the practical ways in which we may assist a person in initiating the growing experience and praxis of this graced life in the Lord. We presuppose thus that this life is already begun, that it is steadily nourished by Word and Sacrament and protected by a moral way of life in consonance with the general norms of Christian living as promulgated by the Church.

Spiritual direction refers to special animation and guidance during one's growth in the life of the spirit. A person can apply what he has learned about his spiritual life to his own situation. In that case, spiritual direction becomes self-direction. Similarly, a person may try by means of spiritual reading and meditation to initiate himself in some measure into this more intimate experiential and practical life of union with God; spiritual initiation becomes self-initiation. Because of the many pitfalls on this path of spiritual initiation, this proceeding by oneself alone is not advisable in the beginning, except in special cases. On the other hand, once one is going in the right direction a certain amount of spiritual self-direction becomes necessary.

The results of one's particular study of spirituality can be applied also to the spiritual initiation and direction of others in regard to this specific topic. Each of us may be called at times to be a momentary light for a fellow man who tries to walk the path of the spirit. At times, we are the receivers of spiritual animation and insight; at other moments, we are the donors of spiritual encouragement and inspiration. Each of us can be called as an occasional spiritual animator of a person in need of spiritual help. For example, parents are called to inspire the spiritual life of their children; husbands and wives, who try to live the life of the spirit, become an inspiration for one another. The same can happen among friends, engaged couples, or between doctors or nurses and their patients, teachers and their students.

A few people are called to spend a considerable amount of their time in the spiritual initiation and direction of others. They become spiritual directors or directors of initiation. We spoke about spiritual direction in Chapter IX and about initiation in Chapter VIII of this book.

All spiritual donors, temporary or permanent, answer the call of Christ to help bring out the hidden spiritual identity in others. In giving to others, they receive, for they can only give insofar as they receive from the Lord. Whether or not they utilize in their own life the spiritual wisdom they receive for others depends on their own free decision. Usually their beneficial influence increases when they themselves try to live up to the inspiration that has been given to them.

Sometimes the person who fosters spiritual values in others is called a spiritual father or mother. At other occasions, they are described as spiritual masters, teachers, or directors. Such metaphorical expressions are of limited use; they can be misleading when taken literally. Such images point to the fact that spiritual direction has something in common with parenthood and education. We shall reflect on these various forms of initiation to highlight certain dangers implied in their similarity.

Our parents were the first ones to initiate us in a

world of human values. The first values they introduced us
to as small infants were vital ones. They nourished us, took
care of our little bodies, and created an environment that
protected us against influences that could harm our health.
Later on, they also initiated us in cultural values that could
enrich our emergent personality. At the same time, they
functioned as spiritual parents by communicating
transpersonal values that would make us aware of our spiritual identity in Christ.

Their first and main influence was of a vital nature.
The first strong bond that resulted between them and their
children was rooted in this vital influence that directly
touched upon the child's survival. This binding may have
been so overwhelming that some people need a lifetime to
cope with it, to find the right respectful attitude towards
their parents or substitutes without regressing to the
dependency of childhood or the rebelliousness of adolescence. All later relationships to any person or institution
that is experienced as giving values may somehow be
modeled by the recipient after this first model of vital
giving and receiving. This reality makes us aware of
potential problems inherent in the relationship between a
spiritual donor and his recipient.

The parents communicate also cultural values to their
children. Part of this task of value communication is shared
by teachers and clergymen, educators and trainers in
academic, artistic, athletic, and other skills. In this sense,
we could call them cultural parents. Along with the child's
natural parents, they foster personal values in him by helping him appropriate the values of human living that prevail
in his society.

Finally, there are people who share with parents the
communication of spiritual values; they are spiritual

animators who in one way or another communicate to them the transpersonal values of the life of the spirit.

As we have already seen, the relation between cultural parents and their pupils is influenced and sometimes distorted by the impact that vital parents had on their children. The relationship between the spiritual parent and his followers may be distorted by both former models of encounter, namely, by the relationships that existed between vital parents and children and cultural parents and their students. It is important to realize that the responsibility of a spiritual director or teacher toward his disciples differs from the responsibility of parents for their children and of teachers for their students. In other words, there is an essential difference between vital, cultural, and spiritual parenthood.

As spiritual director in Christ, the person is called to foster primarily not vital or personal but transpersonal values. That the spiritual animator is not first of all called to foster the vital life of the directee may be self-evident. He will usually speak only about vital values insofar as they facilitate the life of the spirit. For example, he may point out that a certain diet and certain exercises enhance the readiness of a person for spiritual experience and for a vigorous participation in the unfolding of humanity toward the divine destiny of history. What may be less clear is the fact that it is not his primary task at the moment of spiritual inspiration to promote personal and cultural values as such. The spiritual director and initiator represents the transpersonal or transindividual realm of the Divine. He stands for that Kingdom where all graced citizens are discovering their unique identity in Christ that goes far beyond a personal-cultural view of self.

Transpersonal does not mean impersonal. The transpersonal realm needs our personal life to incarnate itself in the world. The spiritual person is not impersonal; rather he is a person who lives his personal life in light of a transcending inspiration, of what God wants him to do uniquely with his life.

Our use here of the words "personality" and "personal identity" is in keeping with present day parlance, as distinguished from a philosophical explanation of these same terms. In the realm of spirituality, and especially in that of concrete spiritual direction, we are in the midst of daily praxis. Life as daily lived is influenced by words as they are used in everyday communication. In present day terms, the word personality is mostly used to indicate the totality of effective interactions with the world on the individual, functional, social, and aesthetic levels. Often a self-consistent pattern of interaction on these levels is guided by social self-interest and not by the realm of the spirit. A person in this society learns how to adapt his individual needs in such a way that he remains an effective, skilled, and well accepted member of his culture. The more he succeeds in that adaptation the more he is praised as a fine personality. This is all for the good, provided that the person does not close himself up in this personalism; on the contrary, he ought to bring this pleasant personal identity under the influence of his spiritual identity in Christ. The spiritual initiator, director, or teacher is there to help him in his transition from an exclusive personalistic life to a personal life open to transpersonal inspiration. This necessity of transition to the transpersonal creates a special kind of relationship between the spiritual master and his disciple.

The respect of the disciple for the spiritual master should not be rooted in the personal charm, skill, and learning of the master, though these elements may facilitate their mutual communication. The hunger and thirst of the directee should be for spiritual enlightenment. The spiritual director should not attach the person to himself but to God whom he represents. The directee should be fascinated not by the personal but by the spiritual identity of the director. He should experience a spiritual bond with this graced and gracious donor, who is called to be a mediator in and with Christ between God and the spiritual recipient. We are not implying that the spiritual animator in Christ should be depersonalized; we mean only that his personality should be a flexible means of incarnation of this spiritual mediatorship in Christ. This transcendent relationship to the spiritual master may help the directee to overcome his inclination to relive, in regard to the master, the vital and personal attachments he may have experienced in relation to his parents and to some of his friends and teachers.

The spiritual director, therefore, should be cautious to be personal but not personalistic. Personalistic means that the personal dimension of the emergent self has become absolute, exclusive, and dominant and is not subordinated to the spirit self. To be sure, we will never reach a stage in which we are no longer tempted to fall back in personalism. Therefore, the spiritual director and teacher should always be on the watch in a relaxed way lest personalism take over in his spiritual direction. Spiritual persons who are called momentarily to function as spiritual animators of others should exert the same caution.

Let us now see why the temptation to personalism is so strong for a director in the Western culture.

Our society tends to be a levelling one, as we

described in our book *Envy and Originality*. The highest wisdom is often that of the "regular guy," that unobtrusive member of a collectivity, crowd, gang, or club. The well adapted personality may even be described in those terms. As long as a person tries to develop only a self that accommodates itself to others, he cannot discover his deepest self, his unique spiritual identity. Transpersonal spiritual values are, on the contrary, an appeal to go beyond mere accommodation to one's fellow man.

Spiritual direction and animation imply, therefore, the duty to challenge the directee's blind immersion into crowd and collectivity. The spiritual director may fear the trouble or responsibility this painful process may bring. He realizes more and more that the task of spiritual direction and animation means tremendous growth as well as suffering and pain. Understandably, he may be tempted by the desire to leave others alone and to be left alone himself, to fade into the wallpaper like so many others in his culture, to lose himself in the homogenizing society. This may be one of the reasons why it is so difficult to find people today who want to take on the responsibility of vital, cultural, or spiritual fatherhood. The paradox is that much protest of young people is an expression of unconscious rebellion against the absence of true parents, who do not try to escape the responsibility of leadership.

Another reason for the temptation to personalism is the functional bent of our civilization. Our society is inclined to exalt adaptive and functional intelligence at the cost of the wisdom of the spirit, of prayerful presence to God, of a kind of living that teaches us facilitating conditions for this presence. The spiritual director may become the victim of this exaltation of mere cultural and functional knowledge. The novice master, for example, may be awed by the intellectual discussions of newly entering novices, fresh from college and able to quote glibly an astonishing number of famed authors. What the novice is doing is showing off, which is one of the means he may use to impress others as a sophisticated personality. If the director of novices falls for this game and tries to show off his own intellectual assets in turn, he may be lost. He may have a hard time to move out of this competitive approach into the more spiritual way. From the first day on, he should make clear to the novices that this year is meant to awaken the spirit. Personalistic intelligence should be calmed down so that the spirit may live.

The director himself may have interiorized unwittingly the personalistic pressures of his society. He may be vulnerable to the subtle challenges of his novices to make this a pleasant year of personal instead of spiritual initiation. As long as he himself is impressed by the glamour of being a personality in the cultural sense, he will be sending out "secret messages" in that regard. The novices pick them up preconsciously; they sense his vulnerability and begin to play on it spontaneously.

Paradoxically, the same society may overreact in a vitalistic way against the overstructuring of life that has marked Western civilization during the last century. The ideal personality then becomes the disorganized, floating, slightly hysterical type. Initiates, impressed by that image, may in the beginning perceive the director of formation as a "super-square" when he rightly insists on faithfulness to a certain program. Here again the greatest enemy of an insecure director may be the false values he himself interiorized in his need to conform to the ideal personality image his society seems to demand at this moment of cultural history. His inner fear of not being in with the latest in the culture is the most powerful ally of the novices in their unconscious attempt to sabotage his appeal to their inner conversion. Only when the spiritual director has overcome this personalistic fear in himself will he be able to diminish the same fear in those who come to him for enlightenment.

The spiritual director should avoid the worldly style of showing off, of name dropping, of one-upmanship. If he observes that a directee is involved in this personalistic style, he should tell him in no uncertain terms to cut out this game that he is unable to play, since it would destroy the possibility of his true initiation and direction.

Another personality image fostered by present day society is that of aggressive and competitive authority. In the spiritual director, personal authority should be mellowed by the spirit. His authority should be rooted in the spirit and his spirit should be rooted in God. His directee should experience that he authors or fosters the life of the spirit in the name of God from whom his mild but assuring authority should flow.

The personalistic society ranks the authority of people in light of possession, status, and position. It asks, for example, what people have done successfully, what degrees they have, how much money they make, the people of name and income who are their friends and acquaintances. The authority in a personalistic sense, in order to be ranked as such, must not only show measurable achievements but have the skill to enhance cleverly the personal security of others by making them feel important. Spiritual authority, however, is not the kind to enhance superiority feelings and the experience of worldy security in others.

Our Lord Himself as spiritual awakener is a striking example. He surely did not help the Pharisees and Scribes to feel superior and secure in their personality, adapted as it was to the cultural standards of the sophisticated members of the Jewish religion at that time in Israel. In His spiritual direction, He tried to break through that personalism, to find an opening for God.

Directees may be initially upset when they realize that the director does nothing to enhance in a worldly way his own personal authority, that he never drops names, or speaks of his own achievements, or tries to flatter their ego, that he never plays the game of personality competition. After some time, however, his quiet self-effacement may help them to go beyond the personality dimension of their director to the eternal spirit he represents.

To help others to find their spiritual identity in Christ, beyond their merely personal-vital identity in this world and culture, the spiritual director himself must live out of his own spiritual identity before God. Every time that a person is called momentarily, or in a more lasting way, to function as a spiritual animator of others he has a splendid occasion to reassert and deepen his own spiritual identity in Christ.

These foregoing considerations on the nature, meaning, and problems of concrete spiritual direction and initiation may give rise to a useful outline to be followed by the student when attempting to explore applications of his topic to life. He could ask himself: how can the population I am concerned with in my particular study be practically initiated and directed in the specific spiritual attitude, facilitating condition, experience, or praxis I have researched. Because every spiritual Christian can be called upon as parent, friend, teacher, counselor, or colleague to act momentarily as spiritual adviser or animator, no group of Catholic Christians, focused on by the student, would be totally exempt from this possible application. A student may choose also to apply his research to self-direction. Finally, this application can be made either from the viewpoint of the director or the directee or both.

Conclusion

The life of the spirit is each person's search for his spiritual identity, a search that will never be ended in this life. As long as we live, we will discover new aspects of our spiritual identity, hidden for time and eternity in the Divine Word. It is only in the eschaton that this search will be ended, for then we will be fully aware of who we were meant to be from eternity. God Himself will purify us from all sin and imperfection, from all the vitalism and personalism that blinded us to who we were called to be.

FOREWORD TO APPENDIX ONE

We realize that Chapters X and XI on research in fundamental spirituality may be difficult to follow for the reader if he does not have a concrete example that illustrates the use of personal experience and its explicitation, the use of other theorists to expand and correct the conclusions drawn from this personal experience, the concomitant integration of all these factors into an expanding theory of the spiritual self, and the working out of all of this in the five dimensions of research without losing contact with life experience and praxis. The best way of obtaining such an illustration of our two chapters on research would be to order one or more of the theses listed in the bibliography at the end of this book. The next best thing would be to read carefully the following thesis proposal by a student who outlines what she is going to do in the fivefold division of the thesis. While such a tentative proposal cannot be compared with the work of the completed thesis itself, it does give at least some insight in the general structure we have described in the two chapters on research and how some of our suggestions are freely and flexibly utilized in the proposal. If the reader wishes, he can later order the thesis that corresponds with this proposal; it can be found among the other theses listed in the bibliography.

Our rationale for selecting the thesis proposal on the topic of "Originality and Spirituality" is based mainly on the fact that it ties in more directly with the theme of this book, man's search for spiritual identity. Reading this proposal, the reader will become aware of many other devices that we have developed to keep the student of spirituality in touch with his personal experiential life. It may be advisable to read this example before studying the two last chapters of this book.

APPENDIX ONE

A THESIS PROPOSAL IN FUNDAMENTAL CATHOLIC SPIRITUALITY
on the TOPIC of "ORIGINALITY AND SPIRITUALITY"
by Sister Una Agnew, S.S.L.

INTRODUCTION TO THE TOPIC

I. *Concrete, Daily Living of Originality*

To the casual listener in everyday conversations the word originality may simply connote "being different from others." Or perhaps when I hear that someone is original I understand that we are referring to a poet, an artist, or a designer of some kind. However, neither the idea of being different nor that of being highly creative accurately expresses what I mean by originality as I speak of it in this thesis. When I examine the word original I see that it is

derived from the Latin verb *oriri* which means "to rise up as from a source." I
am reminded of the image of a fountain. A certain device placed at the center
of a pool or pond of water causes the water to rise up and take on a new
shape. If I change the shape or construction of the device at the center, I
thereby change the shape, size, and even color of the fountain. And so I can
find fountains of all kinds: tall graceful ones, multi-colored ones which have
lights shining from the center, short bubbly ones and others which barely
break the surface of the pond. In a slightly analogous way each person arises
from a lineage, a tradition, a genetic history, a source of being. When I recall
my own personal history, I begin to realize more clearly what this means.

At one specific moment in time and history, within the limits of place
and civilization, I was conceived into a family whose name I now bear. I grew
up out of my family source, a new shoot in the family tree, imbibing as I grew
the cultural and historical background that was mine by inheritance. I was
Irish, born on the borders between North and South, a native of this island
country which still bears the last remnant of an old Celtic culture and
tradition. Without knowing it, I was developing in a unique way because of the
individual blueprint of my genes. I was perceiving the world in my own way,
differently from others, differently even from the six other children of my
family because I had been a different embryo to begin with. I had my own
unique view of life. Just as I look down upon the valley below me and see the
view from a different vantage point than my friend who lives across from me
on the opposite hill, so each person grows up with a totally new and individual
perception of the world. I emerge from my origins in a unique way and bear
within me the source and root of who I really am.

Unlike the fountain image, which I have used to illustrate to a limited
extent what originality means, I can interact with the world. I can admire the
morning sun, feel its heat, wish that the mailman would bring me a letter from
home, greet a passer-by with a casual word. What I perceive, think, dream, say,
or express is somehow part of me. The wellspring of my responses to the
world is within me. A flower, a jet plane, a British soldier—each evoke a
unique response in me because of who I am and what is originally mine.
Nobody else can see, think, or express exactly what I experience. Neither do I
presume to understand *completely* what another originally experiences. This is
what I mean when I speak of being original. Each person therefore can be an
original self because each one arises from his family, traditional, and genetic
origins in a uniquely irreplaceable way. He is a unique expression of life in the
whole of creation. Originality, therefore, is for everyone, not only for the poet
and artist. It involves being rooted in one's origins and allowing one's activity
to flow from oneself. Being original means simply being and becoming as fully
as is possible—oneself.

Being who I am, then, seems to be the secret of being original. How do
I discover who I really am? Am I not to a certain extent a secret to myself.
Sometimes in a dress store I have caught my own reflection unawares. A long
mirror in an expected spot has caused me to excuse myself to "the lady I
almost bumped into." I had not recognized that "the lady" in question was
myself! Going for a drive, sitting in class, doing the dishes at home, I am
constantly being reminded that I respond somewhat differently to each

situation. My response can "tell" me something about myself. For the most part I live these experiences in a forgetful way, knowing vaguely that this is how life is. However, when I reflect on the events of daily life, I am revealed more clearly to myself as being alike or different from others. I have the power to bend back my own inner eyes upon myself and see the facets of my image that are being revealed to me. Personal reflection helps me to discover the stirrings of my original feelings, emotions, desires. Whatever moves within me is part of myself. It may be a memory of the past, an outburst of anger at an immediate situation, an aspiration for the future—all are equally part of who I am. In my work, as I express myself in whatever cultural field I participate, be it medical, social or artistic, I can also see something of who I am. A word spoken or written, a job well done or carelessly undertaken can reveal to me the secret of myself. What I do is also a reflection of who I am. Thus my activity, when reflected upon, can reveal me to myself and aid me in getting to know myself better. From my interaction with the world, from personal reflection on my experience, and from my various activities in the culture, I discover that I am not a total secret to myself. A concrete example from my lived daily experience will help, I think, to illustrate how on occasion I can penetrate more deeply into the mystery of who I originally am.

One autumn evening as I was returning as usual from school with a friend, we stopped on the brow of the hill near our lodgings to admire the autumn leaves. The hillside seemed to be splashed with color—all shades of reds and oranges, pale yellows and deep flame. The whole scene was aglow with the warm tones of the leaves. We were both silently in wonder, deeply touched by the beauty of the scene. Something was happening for each of us as our eyes perceived the different shades of color, the various species of leaves, the setting, the time of year. . . A separate response was being evoked in each of us. My friend began to pick some leaves; she would make some Thanksgiving cards with them for her friends. I too began to finger some leaves, toying with the idea that perhaps I, too, could learn to make cards. Having picked the first maple leaf, I realized that making Thanksgiving cards had no real meaning or purpose for me. Perhaps I would write home to my family in Ireland and tell my parents about autumn in Pennsylvania. It would be interesting for them to hear that I had seen maple and ginkgo trees in the great steel city of the United States. How different, I thought, from the beech and chestnut trees of rural Ireland. I abandoned the idea of making cards and decided instead to store away the memory. Perhaps I would write about it in my diary, speak about it at dinner that evening, or wait until my summer holiday and tell my family about it along with the other new things that I had seen abroad. Meanwhile, my friend would make her pretty cards and send them off with Thanksgiving greetings to her friends throughout the country. As we moved homeward, my friend with her selection of leaves and me with a memory, the gardener next door was raking up the fallen leaves and packing them into sacks for the garbage collector who would pick them up next day.

II. *Reflection on the Experience*

When I reflect on this experience I begin to be aware of its many facets and implications. I had often walked up this hill before on my way home from school, but this time instead of taking the leaves and ourselves for granted I had become *responsive* to both in a new way. At first I noticed the responses of my friend and me and thought how different they were from the gardener's, whose only thought was for getting his lawns cleared of leaves. The leaves for the garbage collector next day would be just another item for the dumping ground. And yet, when I reflected on the experience a little further, I realized that each response was unique and in no way interchangeable. My friend's movement to pick leaves in order to make cards interested me as being different from anything I had ever thought of doing myself. I moved to imitate her, aware that my education had not emphasized this manual art or artistic expression. I had never learnt how to make cards with pressed leaves. Did I really want to begin to learn this skill now or was I being motivated to imitate for another reason? As I picked the first maple leaf, I foresaw how it would probably lie for weeks, pressed in a book, until I would finally throw it out with the rest of the rubbish at Christmas. Or perhaps I would make a Thanksgiving card after all and send it to. . .to whom? What does Thanksgiving me to me? Have I a sufficient experience of what it means after a mere two years in the United States? A new sense of separateness began to make itself felt. I began to think of the Irish Hallow E'en celebration, a remnant of the old Gaelic festival of Samhain. How could an American ever possibly come to know all that the name of Samhain evokes—the ghost-stories, the roasting of nuts on the open fire, the barn brack. My friend too had a whole history of Thanksgiving from her earliest years. She must have a real feel for it in her bones—the dinners by candle-light, the decorations, the colorful arrangements of fruit, gourds and corn, pumpkin pie—it was all so different. I had a totally other history, a different heritage where the feast of Thanksgiving is unknown. I began to think of the histories that shaped us both. We were both alone in our heritage and yet drawn by a common factor at this moment—a bunch of leaves. Out of our separate heritages, we responded differently to these leaves. If I could have penetrated more deeply into our responses, I should have certainly discovered a different emotional response in each of us: different memories evoked, a different urgency to share the beauty of these leaves with others and to give some form of personal expression to the event.

For a moment I think of the gardener, raking away at the leaves. Perhaps he was angry at the leaves for spoiling his neat lawn, and, as for the garbage man, he may have responded with relief that the large sack of leaves contained only leaves and not some heavier waste material. It was certain that from time to time, my focus was attracted to the different responses of the others to the same autumn leaves. The gardener and the garbage collector had such different responses to the leaves that it was easy to see how uniquely different each one's was. Fortunately, the garbage man felt no attraction for hoarding leaves, nor did the gardener feel inclined to finger each leaf on his lawn. When my attention focused on my friend's response, I began to have a vague feeling of unrest. I watched her wistfully and wondered to myself. This idea that had occurred to her of making cards with the leaves was a beautiful one. I wished I could do this too. Like the child who presses his nose against the window of a sweet-shop and longs for a piece of toffee from the tempting display inside, so I wanted my friend's gift for myself. Meanwhile I had completely forgotten my own initial response to the sight. How can I keep this memory alive and new for myself so that I can share it with others who have not seen it? How could I bring it to mind and savor it once again in years to come when I would recall fall in Pittsburgh? In focusing on my friend's response, I had neglected to express my own unique individual response to the beautiful leaves. How would I describe them? How could I best recapture the scene, the atmosphere, the setting? By refraining from picking the leaves, I was somehow realizing that this was not my way to express my true self. I was betraying my own response for the response of another. By accepting the real "me" contained in my own response to the scene, I chose to be myself, to express myself and in this way to become more myself. The more often I perform acts that are really my own, rising from within me, purified of the desires within me that want to be and possess everything, the more I am becoming who I really am and actualizing myself.

Becoming more fully who I really am, or self-actualization, does not of necessity require that I actualize all the talents I have. Each situation will offer its own unique opportunity to be and become myself. I cannot be everything, but I can at least be myself in each situation of my life. I could certainly have chosen to learn to make cards. I could perhaps have succeeded well but was I sure that this was not merely a way of betraying what was really my own for something which I thought to be more attractive? Perhaps I may have thought that making artistic cards might enhance my image in others' eyes. I can see a fine line of distinction between the genuine desire to learn something new and the mere imitation that comes from envy of another's gift. Many of these points are in the process of clarification as I pursue my thesis work.

What does seem to be clear, however, is that in this to and fro of being responsive to myself and to my situation, I can *discover* more and more who I originally am. The more I grow in responsiveness to the leaves in my unique way, the more I am actually becoming the self that I am. Discovering who I am and becoming who I am seem to mark two important "moments" of this experience. There is nothing definitive about either moment. There is only a partial discovery and always only a partial becoming. At times the focus is on myself, my background, my history, and on a deeper level still, on my emotional and vital response to the sight of the leaves. At other times my focus was on the leaves and the autumn setting that had attracted my attention in the first place. By being responsive to myself and to the leaves in my original way, I am somehow becoming the person I originally am.

III. *Insights Gained from Reflection on Experience*

Some of the insights gained from reflection on the incident already described would seem worthy of consideration in the writing of this thesis.

A. The *world* of people, events, and things calls forth and helps me discover who I originally am.

I gradually become aware that the world reveals me to myself. I live in the world in an active as well as in a passive way so that I can respond to what is going on around me. In my meetings with *people,* I am revealed to myself through the experience of how we are alike and how we are unalike. People evoke in me memories, emotions, aspirations which can reveal to me what is truly mine both positively and negatively. If someone's talent makes me uneasy, I may somehow detect that I am envious and not content with simply being who I am. If someone's tone of voice tends to inhibit me, I may discover that I have unpleasant associations with certain voices or certain accents. I may again discover what can prevent me on occasion from being myself.

Similarly, *things* can call me forth in a special way. An autumn landscape, a special kind of bread, a certain kind of perfume, a particular make of car: all are loaded with memories and evoke emotions and aspirations that can reflect me back to myself like a mirror.

Events can also be revealing to me. A walk in autumn, a baseball game, news of an earthquake: all evoke in me sentiments that are extremely close to myself. I may often be unaware of certain fears and memories within me until an untoward event shows me to myself in a new light. The event simply brings to light something which was obscured until now.

The *world*—people, things, and events—reveals to me and helps me to discover myself as having a past, a present, and a future. The episode I described above, evoked my past history of traditional feasts, some facets of my early education, my present situation as a student overseas, and more immediately still, as a person drawn by the beauty of the leaves. My future is evoked by my urge to concretize the beauty of the leaves in a way that will make the memory live on. I am moved to think of a time when I will no longer be in Pittsburgh or to the summer ahead when I will share with my family, at least in part, the experience of the year overseas.

B. By being *responsive* to myself in relation to my world I can gradually *discover* my original self.

Ordinarily, the interaction between man and his world is lived in a pre-reflective or thoughtless way. I do not set out to discover myself, nor do I consciously think about what the world reveals at every turn. From my experience, I can see that though I had walked home along this road many times before, I had never thought of the leaves in terms of my past, present and future. However, I now see that I *can* move to be responsive to the world around me because as man I have the ability to reflect. The reflection of which I speak has a three-fold movement, and it is this movement that I call *responsiveness.*

The first movement of responsiveness veers inwards towards myself. I become present to myself, to the past that filters out into the situation, to the memories that remind me of other fall days. I become present also to the feeling state which I experience. I feel joy, nostalgia, anger, or perhaps envy. I am drawn even deeper within myself to wonder at the uniqueness of my response; the feelings, the memories, the perceptions that make my response uniquely mine. This inward communing with myself I call *self-presence.*[1]

Moving to self-presence means moving also to a certain kind of private or public expression. I formulate inwardly what I discover by being present to

---

[1]The constructs—self-presence, self-expression, self-affirmation, are borrowed from the unpublished class notes of Adrian van Kaam, Fall Semester, 1972, Center for the Study of Spirituality of the Institute of Man, Duquesne University.

myself. As I catch my initial response to the leaves or to my friend's response, I almost immediately exclaim inwardly or outwardly, "Oh! how beautiful!" or "I wish I had thought of that too." This second movement of responsiveness I call *self-expression*. If I were a gardener, I might have spontaneously sighed at the falling leaves or if I were an artist I might have been moved to rapture.

The third part of the responsive movement is a saying "yes" to what I have been present to and expressed of myself. I say "yes" to my positive vital response as well as to the restlessness of my envious feelings. What has been revealed to me I recognize as mine and move to own this in a responsible way. This component of the experience I call *self-affirmation*.

When the world brings to life something that was lying latent within me, I become aware of a spontaneous response being called forth. It is in this first movement of my self, a movement which has not yet been reflected upon, that I find the key to what is most myself. I discover (dis-cover) in my various responses to the world, aspects of myself which remain hidden from me as long as I live in a pre-reflective manner. By being responsive to the initial upsurge of the self, I can grow in uncovering the unfounded fears, the irrational desires, the blind prejudices that prevent me from becoming who I really am. Responsiveness to myself can also reveal to me my true perception, a sudden insight, and a spontaneous trust that also characterize me as the person I am.

C. By being responsive to the world I gradually grow in *becoming* myself.

As I move inwardly in the initial movement of self-presence, I find the world with which I interact already there. I realize that the autumn leaves I have so much admired are the focus of my inward attention. In this movement of self-presence, self and world are in creative dialogue. Indeed, there could be no dialogue without the leaves. Each new situation, then, offers a concrete way of my becoming a self-presence to the world.

Because I am actively involved in a concrete situation where there are pretty leaves, a gardener, a talented friend, I am reminded that the world invites me to express myself. I may exclaim about the leaves to my friend, rake them into heaps, select some for card-making, prepare a sack of them for the garbage or simply finger them thoughtfully. The movement of self-expression, then, is also always expression in relation to a concrete world.

By expressing myself I learn to recognize my limitations and potentials. By inwardly saying to myself, "I know that I have never learnt to make cards with autumn leaves," I am recognizing a real limitation within myself. Similarly I may recognize myself as limited in the manner in which I do certain everyday chores. While doing the dishes after dinner, I may notice my half-hearted approach or my lack of orderly method. Another may see her meticulous attention to the smallest details. *How* I do things is always a reflection of who I am and what my limitations and potentials are. By *affirming* myself in relation to the situations of life, I embody the unique person that I am and look to what I can become.

The more I begin to be open to what is originally awakened in myself, the more I can begin to accept my limitations and accept myself as I am. I can affirm what I do even while seeing its flaws. To store a memory of autumn or write about it in my diary is not a very splendid form of self-expression. But I can affirm my expression insofar as it is true to my own unique activity, insofar as it mirrors my own creative dialogue with the world. Self-affirmation, therefore, encourages my own original self-expression and guides me towards *becoming* who I am.

The more I focus on the other's talent and lose the flavor of my own unique response, the more I am moved to envy of the other. If I focus in an envious way on my friend's ability to express herself artistically in card making, I seem to covet her gift for myself and thereby abandon my own or at least devalue it. Caught in this envious attitude toward the other, I am doing violence to my own expressive energy and failing to *become* anything but envious.

When I follow my own limited inspiration with due respect to the unfolding of other selves around me, I can be enriched by the values I perceive in the world around me. As I learn to be responsive to the episode of the leaves, I can enjoy the beauty of my friend's cards while being happy also with my own happy memory. I respect the gardener for the beauty of his well-kept lawns and I never fail to be impressed by the cheery smile of the garbage collector as he unfailingly picks up the garbage each week. In my relaxed appreciation of others, I am actually *becoming* more and more myself.

Each act of responsiveness—self-presence, self-expression, self-affirmation—in relation to the concrete situations of my life, whether it be in the kitchen, the classroom, or the art-studio, makes me more myself. I learn to be who I am and do what is me. I come to recognize my own style by imprinting this self on all that I do. By being responsive to myself and to my world I *become* myself.

Responsiveness can guide me to correct the spontaneous *reaction* of the emotional or conventional "me." By being responsive to my spontaneity, I can learn to discipline myself and become who I most truly am. The experience I have described revealed to me that my envious comparison had to be disciplined so that I could find my own inalienable response to the leaves. It would require painstaking discipline on the part of my friend also to translate her initial project of making Thanksgiving cards into a concrete reality.

IV. *Components of the Experience*

The overall dynamic which seems to emerge from a consideration of man viewed in relation to his world, from the point of view of this topic, is that the world reveals man to himself and man becomes himself in relation to his world. The necessary precondition for man's discovery of himself as revealed by his world is that man become *responsive* to his world. By being responsive to himself man *discovers* who he originally is as reflected by his past personal history, by his vital response to the world, and by his deepest spiritual calling to be himself. Each time man responds to a situation he does so in terms of his past personal history, in terms of his biophysical self, and in terms of the unique person he is in the whole of creation. By being responsive to himself man can learn to discover who he originally is. By being responsive to the world in each situation of his life man *becomes* himself.

V. *Statement of Purpose*

This thesis will aim at exploring the dynamic interaction between man and his world by which man gradually, but always only partially,*discovers* the original person that he is. Through his response to the world man *becomes* or *actualizes* himself. In today's world many people interest themselves in palmistry, horoscopes, and handwriting analysis in order to penetrate into one of the most astounding mysteries of all: how each person "works" and what it is that belongs essentially to one person and not to another. By attending to his everyday experience in a responsive way, man can grow in self-knowledge. The more deeply he can enter into his own original self, the more he will discover that life-giving Source from which he "flows." This Original Fountainhead of Being is the Origin of origins who holds the total secret of who each original man is. The aim of this thesis is to explore the dynamic response between man and his world which can guide man towards his own original self-discovery and self-becoming. The ultimate focus of this study will be on the value of original selfhood for the vowed Christian religious. By following man in his continuing quest for originality, it is the aim of this research to bring to light those attitudes, structures, and conditions which hinder or foster man's task of being and becoming himself.

VI. *Statement of Limits*

From my research and reflection so far the notion has evolved that originality has two main requirements: an original person and an original activity. Original activity requires an original source. This means that each person who strives for originality must discover and become the self he truly is. Original activity arising out of original personhood would seem, then, to be the basic thrust of what originality means. In my study of this topic, I intend to focus more on how man discovers and becomes himself through his original activity than on the contribution he makes to the culture in the process of becoming original. The value of creativity in relation to the culture may emerge as part of man's originality, but it will not be extensively dealt with here. An effort will be made to show how originality is to be distinguished from individualism, eccentricity, and either popular distortions of what being original connotes.

VII. *Method of Research*

1. The research is dialectical, interdisciplinary, and integrational, that is, data and insights are derived from research of some of the prominent authors in the sciences of philosophy, psychology, anthropology, sociology, and the literature of relevant spiritual writers.

2. The research begins by describing and reflecting upon an everyday experience of originality. Relevant theory from each of the disciplines is used in order to add depth, scope, and scientific grounding to the phenomena which manifest themselves in the experience. Discussion of the material is done from the subjective pole of reference. This means that research materials will focus on how man can grow in originality—how he can be and become more truly himself in the everyday situation between man

and his world, which, when brought to awareness can aid man in knowing, affirming, and actualizing the self he truly is.
3.   The research is developed in five areas, each succeeding stage of research
being a more specific delineation of the first and broadest area of concern. The following are the five areas of consideration: Man's experience of being and becoming his original self:
a.   on the universal human level;
b.   on the universal religious level;
c.   on the level of Christian spirituality;
d.   on the level of the vowed Christian life;
e.   on the level of initiation into the vowed Christian life.

GENERAL INTRODUCTION

I. *A Personal Experience*

From the experience and reflection already set out in the introduction
to this proposal, I intend to draw out the overall dynamic movement which
will weave itself through the five levels of my thesis, namely, BY BEING
RESPONSIVE TO HIMSELF MAN CAN DISCOVER HIS ORIGINALITY
AND BY BEING RESPONSIVE TO HIS WORLD MAN CAN BECOME
ORIGINAL. Although we can never think of man in isolation from his world,
yet for the purpose of analysis we will look first at man and then at his world.

Man discovers who he is by being responseive to himself. He finds
within himself the roots of his own originality. I propose to show how
responsiveness, which would seem to be crucial to the whole question of
discovering who one originally is, has within it a threefold movement. In order
to be in touch with the original stirrings within himself, man must discover
these through self-presence, self-expression, and self-affirmation. Self-presence
means that man listens to himself and becomes aware of his origins. Man also
expresses himself in thought, word or act and affirms himself and what he
does as the very expression of himself.

Original man is also responsive to his world. By being responsive to his
world, man actually becomes who he is in each concrete situation of his life.
Through *self-presence* he is conscious of how the world calls him forth.
Whatever in the world evokes man belongs to the world but man's response is
his own. He expresses his response in some concrete or symbolic act and
affirms what he expresses as being the unique irrepeatable activity which is his.

When man fails to be originally responsive to himself and to his world,
he may tend to *conform* merely to mass standards of thinking and acting. He
may merely *imitate* others or dissipate his energy by enviously comparing
himself with others. Instead of being responsive to his real self, he may follow
an *ideal image* of himself or respond to an *idealized* world. *Over-activity* may
hinder man from the quiet periods of time which he needs in order to be present to who he is and what the world means for him. If a man represses any
part of his originality, he may stifle also his original self-expression. Self-
affirmation, on the other hand, will foster originality while *envy* will focus attention on the other's gifts rather than on one's own.

II. *A Literary Experience*

In this section of the introduction I propose to examine the experience of the poet Hopkins as expressed in his letters and in Sonnet 34. Nature, he says, mirrors the truth that every creature unfolds in a uniquely original way. Just as each plant, bird, and insect is patterned to express itself uniquely in the whole of creation, so too what each man does is uniquely his and bespeaks his inalienable individuality. As I reflect on Hopkins, I discover that man among all the creatures of the universe can *discover* how he is indelibly patterned. Each person can discover who he is so that he can *be* that person whom he is in interaction with the world. Tom, Dick, and Harry must discover, each for himself, who he originally is and become himself and not an imitation of another. Since each of us is called to be unique and must work at discovering what that uniqueness is, we may ask the question, "Where do I find the key to my originality?" "Where can I look in order to discover who I am?"

III. *The Three Sources of Originality*

In order to show how each person can discover how he can be his original self, I propose to examine van Kaam's theory which points to the existence, for each person, of three sources of originality. The three sources indicated by van Kaam are; historical originality, vital originality, and deepest or initial originality.

Conclusion and transition to Chapter One. In today's shifting and fast-moving society, man is more and more driven to search for the meaning of life and for the deepest meaning of his own identity. Some pose the question by asking the meaning of the world around them while others seek to discover what lies hidden within themselves and what remains with them, though the world moves onwards at its incredible pace of change. The *first* source of originality to which man can look as a key to the mystery of himself is his past personal history or historical originality. In the first chapter of this thesis, we will indicate how man can discover himself in what fate has bestowed on him by way of background, what experience has been his, and how he has coped with life until now.

CHAPTER ONE

Introduction. As I recall that autumn afternoon when my friend and I admired the leaves, I remember that many facets of my past history came into my awareness. The imminence of the feast of Thanksgiving reminded me that I was Irish and not American; the fall reminded me of other falls at home as well as those I had heard described in books by poets who wrote about autumn. The trees reminded me of the chestnut, sycamore, and lime trees that were now changing colors also near my home.

In Chapter One of this thesis, I propose to examine one of the sources of originality which we call our past history. It is the past that has partially made us what we are today. The past includes the familial, traditional, and cultural patterns we inherited as well as our individual perception of these. A Jew who has suffered because he is a Jew will see his historical past differently from the Jew to whom life has been generous and on whom fortune has smiled. Likewise, the person who has been successful in life may see his past differently from one who has known only failure.

Each person in some way resembles an archive. An archive preserves the records of an organization from its beginning. So too with the person. Each person is the perfect archive of his own past. Everything he has experienced, both the pleasant and unpleasant, has been "filed" away in a mostly forgotten past. It is these "files" which we hope to explore in this chapter. Cultures have shaped our thought patterns and families have shaped our attitudes. Traditions have bestowed on us both rich heritages and unwieldly burdens. Man also has learned to cope with his world, to overcome the obstacles that he perceives to be a hindrance to his original development. He has come to have an outlook on the world and to deal uniquely with people in his interpersonal relationships. We will examine in this chapter how man has been uniquely originated by his past history.

As he begins to be responsive to his past, man may discover that he has imbibed his history without personalizing it. He has also perhaps taken on the thought patterns and traditions of his family without healthy criticism. He may discover that he has been mistaken in his attitude towards the world because his "first world" was perhaps over-protective, threatening, or totally rejecting. By being responsive to his past, man can gradually learn to distinguish what is really himself from what has been imposed on him by the collectivities that have shaped him. He may also learn to discover the original view of the world he has adopted, how he has learned to have both prejudices and penchants, and also his own true perceptions of life.

From the more positive standpoint, man can begin to be responsive to the vast heritage that is present in the history that has been given him. He has a history to own whether he be French or American, a Dubliner or a Moscovite. Two people who have grown up in different cultures are obviously different by their origins, but even those who have grown up in the same culture appropriate their culture differently. So too, even two people in the same family grow up in identical surroundings, but each accrues a different personal archive. The fairy-tales, for instance, told by grandmother can be as delightful for one child of a family as they can be boring and tiresome for another. Thus we can see that *how* a reality is perceived by an individual is as important for his development and plays as much a part in shaping his view of life as the reality itself.

Theorists for Chapter One

Adler—the individual and his style of life.
van Kaam—the total past self.
Eliot—the individual and his tradition.
Benedict—the individual as shaped by the culture.
May—freeing oneself from ties with the past.

Minor Theorists

Duncan, Kretch, Smith.

Transition to Chapter Two

In order to come to a deeper level of origination, we move beyond cultural and historical facets of the person to the vital level of man. More personal even than the unique history of each individual is his body. The body, then, is the second source of originality. Each person, be he American, Greek or Jew, is still more individually patterned than his ethnicity and personal history indicates. He is unique by virtue of the original blueprint of his genetic make-up.

CHAPTER TWO

Introduction. As I return to the original experience described in the Introduction to this proposal, I notice that it was through my sensing emotional response to the experience that I became initially aware of myself in the situation. My eyes absorbed the color and my pulse responded to the sight. If I could have penetrated my friend's immediate response, I would have discovered that she had seen a little differently and was evoked by the sight in a different emotional way.

In Chapter Two, I propose to examine how man discovers himself in and through his body. By being present to his vital reaction, his perceptions and intuitions, man gradually discovers how he interacts with the world. Man can discover a great deal about himself by being present to how he is angered, moved to love, fear, resentment, and so on. These feelings are as much a part of himself as are his family name or his nationality.

Each person's basic "moodedness" emerges from a unique organic make-up. Each new perception brings with it all the perceptions of the past. A fall day evokes in me the memory of emotions that have to do with past falls, just as an earache today reminds me that this same ear has hurt before. Similarly smelling, seeing, and sensing are all memory-filled activities, which bring the whole of man into his present involvement.

One of the difficulties man often experiences with regard to his vital originality is that he reasons how he *should* feel before he listens to his feelings. He may even have repressed certain feelings altogether for the sake of polite socializing with others. However, it is not in mere vital reaction to the world that man discovers who he most originally is: nevertheless this reaction is a part of himself to be reckoned with. We wish to demonstrate in this chapter how man's vital make-up is a significant part of his originality.

Man, however, is not only his vital make-up as well as his past personal history. He has a deeper dimension beyond what the past has allowed him to be and beyond what his vital make-up determines. This deeper dimension directs each man's being—his past history and his present vitality—and shapes it into the unique expression of personhood that he is meant to be. Personal history and organic constitution are not denied but rather woven together by the unquenchable voice of man's original call to be that which only he can be. This spiritual source of man's originality will be dealt with move fully on the second level of this thesis.

Theorists for Chapter Two

van Kaam—the involved self—organic and spirit consciousness—the location of
    the self in body and world.
Luijpen—man as a being-at-the-world.
Schachtel—world-openness through activity-affect.
May—learning to feel, to experience, and to want.
Kierkegaard—the life of immediacy.

Minor Theorists

Esliek, Whitehead.

Transition to Chapter Three. Having examined the sources to which man looks
for his originality and having shown how man's task in life is to be responsive
to what he has received biologically, historically and spiritually, I propose in
the next chapter to indicate how man *becomes* his original self in interaction
with his world.

CHAPTER THREE

Introduction. As my friend carefully chose her leaves, intent on the
project of making Thanksgiving cards, I could feel the urge to compete, to
out-do her perhaps in card-making. I felt myself swept along by her idea,
assured by her look of confidence that it was a good one. How should I
respond to a beautiful array of autumn? Perhaps I was waiting to take my cue
from someone else. On the other hand, I was loathe to stand alone and make
my own unique response to the scene. Two tendencies vied with each other
within me, the tendency to *conform* merely to what I thought was expected
of me and to *out-do* the other.

In Chapter Three, I propose to show how man, despite the uniqueness of
his originality, must struggle to maintain and deepen himself in spite of the
tendencies in society that militate against original development. The principal
obstacles that threaten the delicate seed of man's originality are the
competitive spirit and levelling mass-mindedness that permeates the whole
social atmosphere. Under pressure from the crowd mentality of society, it is
difficult to stand in the aloneness of one's originality. The original man evokes
envy and can easily be discouraged by those who resent his self-motivation.
To be able to take one's cues from within oneself means that we must be
inner-directed and not constantly measuring how we will appear in the eyes of
others. The outer-directedness of modern society places accent on efficiency
and achievement so that more attention is given to *what* is done than to how it
is done. When society sets the norms for excellence and rewards those who live
by the norms, it is difficult for man to live and believe in his own original
excellence.

The focus in this chapter will be on man's response to society. We will
see how man's resistance to the destructive forces in society, facilitates,
strengthens, and fosters his emergence as an original man. Man's ability to be

responsive—to be present to, express and affirm the society in which he lives—will be what saves him from the destructive forces that influence him daily as well as provide opportunities for his greater development. While always being a part of the levelling, envious, outer-directed society man can nevertheless protect himself from it and even be enriched by it.

Theorists for Chapter Three

Kierkegaard—levelling in society—crowd-mentality.
van Kaam—envious comparison—the competitive ego society.
Toffler—the modular man.
Riesman—outer-directedness.
Kesey—the individual and levelling authority.
van Kaam—emergence of the self.
Eliot—the society-ridden character of Prufrock.

Minor Theorists

Reich, Bach, Saint-Exupery

Transition to Chapter Four. The world in which man lives is not only a force that threatens to swallow up his originality; it can also be a source of hidden values. These values reside in people, events, and things and are capable of awakening originality in man and of being enlivened by him. By being responsive to his world man is ever being created into the self that he really is.

CHAPTER FOUR

Introduction. In this chapter I propose to show how man becomes original through his contact with values. Values, such as kindness, goodness, sincerity, live within people. It is people who communicate values and it is values that evoke originality. It seems that the power of values lies in their ability to inspire and lead the other to actualize his possibilities. When I reflect on my initial experience, I am struck by my friend's ability to know how she wanted to express the meaning of the leaves in a way that suited her originality. Her assurance was inspiring and led me, in fact, to search for my own original self-expression. At the same time I recall a line from the poet Shelley in his poem *The West Wind.* "Yellow and black and pale and hectic red" went the description of his autumn scene. These were the words he used to express the beauty of another autumn landscape in his own original way. Shelley, too, though present to me in a different way than my friend, inspired me also to seek to be and express myself in this particular situation. Similarly my friend, by being present to me as an American who appreciated her Thanksgiving traditions, inspired me to be aware of my Irish heritage and to value it.

In human relationships man's originality is awakened. In this chapter, I propose to examine friendship as a means of helping man to be true to himself. Similarly, for some people, the therapeutic relationship can be helpful toward growing in selfhood. In both friendship and in the therapeutic relationship, man is given a unique opportunity to discover and become himself through the help of another. Another real relationship, which can be effective in promoting originality, is the relationship to the *things* of nature. Nature invites man beyond the functional relationships of everyday life and invites him to stand in wonder. In this relationship of wonder, man can discover and become himself by realizing areas within him of which he would ordinarily be unaware. By being responsive to nature, man becomes aware of all the levels of his being, his past is evoked by memory; his vital self is stirred at new sights, sounds and odors; his very soul invests his whole self in a stance of gratitude and wonder.

Certain *events* also in man's life bring him in touch with his deepest self. Sometimes when an untoward event occurs, such as a storm, an earthquake, or an accident, man may be called upon to question the deepest meaning of his life. He is drawn beyond the lesser values of his everyday life and brought into contact with what is Ultimate. If man can be responsive to the awesomeness of this experience he can be brought to the very Source and Fountainhead of his life. In awe he stands before the Being who has originated him from all eternity as the unique self that he is. By being responsive to the events of his life man can discover more and more fully who he is, and grow in commitment to the Being who originated him and who is always originating him as the limited being that he is.

Theorists for Chapter Four

van Kaam—originality and values.
Lepp—promotion of existence by friendship.
Rogers—becoming a person in therapy.
van Kaam—dwelling in wonder promotes originality.
Thoreau—growing in personhood in the solitude and company of nature.
Jaspers—marginal situations.

Minor Theorists

Collins, St. Exupery, Maugham.

Transition to the Universal Religious Level. In awe and dread man stands before the Value of all Values. By being responsive to this experience, man can grow in becoming who he most originally is. In this contact with the Ultimate Source of his life, man is brought beyond who he is biologically, functionally, or historically, to discover, in the ultimate source of his originality, who he spiritually is.

UNIVERSAL RELIGIOUS LEVEL

GUIDING QUESTION: HOW CAN I DISCOVER MYSELF AS ORIGI-NATED BY THE ORIGIN OF LIFE AND BECOME THE ORIGINAL SELF THAT I AM?

Introduction. The beauty of the fall scene I have initially described evoked in me a certain longing and nostalgia. I am reminded of the barrenness of the winter which approaches and saddened by the thought that soon all the leaves will be blown down and trodden underfoot. I may perhaps feel a certain yearning for a perpetual autumn or for the eternal quiet of an evening with my friend on the hill. Beyond the immediate, non-lasting feelings evoked by the leaves, I think of the eternal Being in which we all participate, the Designer who fashioned us all so uniquely. Each original genetic pattern, each vastly different history that shapes us—all are foreseen and modeled in the Great Design of Being. Beyond the stirrings of my feelings, the reminders of my past history, I am drawn into a deeper quiet where I see the fall scene, my friend, the gardener, and myself—all of us differently designed and held in being by the Original Hand of the universe. The unique gift that each of us is emanates from the Fountainhead of Being itself. Simply by our being, we are each witness to the Originator of all things; by actively participating in life, as, for example, in our separate responses to the fall leaves, we are each becoming that self we originally are.

On this level of the thesis, I propose to show how I *discover* myself as called into being by my Origin and *become* myself by being responsive to my unique call. When I use the word *call,* I use it in the sense of an already divinely established pattern in my life

I hear the call to be myself in my vital self. My vital make-up determines to a certain extent how I hear the divine call to be myself. I cannot falsify the temperament I have been given: rather it is this temperament which will direct the only way I can authentically respond to my Original Source. Out of my temperamental make-up flows the kind of spirituality that best expresses who I am. Temperament will differ from person to person; so too will the kind of spirituality which each person develops in tune with his individual spiritual life.

I hear the call to be myself in my religious history. The spiritual expression of who I am will also be influenced by my past personal history and in particular by the ideas I have imbibed about the Divine Originator of my life. I may have repressed my real Origin or even suppressed it so that it does not reflect itself as embodied in the original person I am. Just as I have a familial origin, so too I have an Eternal Origin. I am influenced in my spiritual dimension by the ideas I have collected about the Divine Originator of my life. Stories from childhood introduced me to this whole area of my originality; ideas, too, I have gleaned from catechism classes and from courses in theology. These ideas have perhaps falsified the true reality and have become projections that falsify the real Source from whom I flow. It is important, therefore, that I become responsive to my past ideas so that I can affirm what is true and good and set aside what is false. Responsiveness to my past history, therefore, can bring me closer to my Origin and remove the biases in myself that prevent my deepest self-discovery in the Fountainhead of my life.

I hear the call to be myself in my deepest spiritual self. Beyond my pious yearnings for the Absolute and the false projections of God which I have collected along life's way, there is a pure Source of being from whom I flow in my limited wholeness. By doing what I can to be present to this Source and by allowing myself to be drawn to this, my Ultimate Home, I discover who I most originally am as flowing from and partaking in the Fountainhead of my life.

In Chapter Two of this religious section of the thesis, I propose to focus on the importance of integrating my religious identity as a person into my daily lived life. Again responsiveness will be the clue to becoming my original self in light of the Sacred Origin of my life. Through meditative reflection, man can grow in becoming present to himself as a person and to the spiritual dimension of the world in which he lives and works. Through self-presence man discovers the spiritual presence that he is and becomes aware of the obstacles within himself which prevent the perfect reflection of the Divine Presence from shining through the limited presence that he is. The gentleness of man's personal life-style will be an expression of his own acceptance of and regard for the limited person that he is. The realm of ritual and participation in worship that we find in all religions provides a key to man's communal expression of reverence *vis-a-vis* the Divine. The offering of sacrifices and the performing of ritual symbolizes man's offering of himself to the Holy who holds him in being. By expressing himself in this way, man can actually commit his life and all that he is involved in as man to the Sacred Originator of his life. In this way man can return all created things to their original Source. On an individual basis man can grow in awareness that in all he does as part of the ongoing creation of his world, he is co-originator with his Divine Origin. In and through his own original self-expression, man is partaking in Divine Self-Expression.

The third aspect of responsiveness deals with man's own self-affirmation. Here man assents to be the person he is and at the same time affirms the multitude of original expressions of life with which his world is filled. Because all have emerged from the same Original Hand, religious man affirms the Maker of all things while at the same time affirming the work of His Hands. Through self-affirmation, he affirms himself as a spiritual self and affirms the unfolding of others as spiritual beings.

Theorists for the Religious Section of this Thesis

Allport—temperament and desire for religion.
van Kaam—pious emotions as intimations of a deeper reality.
Bloom—being real before the real God.
Strong—projection of a Godhead.
van Kaam—Divine Self-Presence, Self-Expression, and Self-Affirmation.
Durckheim—everyday life as spiritual exercise.

Other Theorists

Eliade, Herrigal, Marcel, Underhill, van der Post.

Transition to the Christian Level

We have discovered how man is rooted in a spiritual Source which he is called to personalize just as in the first section of this thesis we saw that man is called to appropriate his familial, ethnic, historical, and vital origins. We now look at Christian man who has been eternally fathered by a personal God who created him and called him by a special secret name. Man's Christian origins belong to a specific history and are identifiable with the unique person of Christ. In the next section we will try to show how man discovers and becomes his Christian self.

CHRISTIAN LEVEL

GUIDING QUESTION: HOW DO I DISCOVER MYSELF AS A CHRISTIAN
AND BECOME THE INDIVIDUAL CHRISTIAN I AM CALLED TO BE?

Introduction. As I admire the leaves in autumn, I am reminded of a simple though rather hackneyed poem that I learnt in the second grade at school. The poet Kilmer concludes with the lines "poems were made by fools like me/But only God can make a tree." Though the lines jingle a little too much with voices from my schooldays, nevertheless they enshrine a value I have always carried with me. As I return to the autumn scene of my initial description, I can see that the trees also presented themselves as one of the many beautiful expressions of God's creative hand in the universe. By being reminded of the simple poem of my early days at school, I am reminded of a whole Christian tradition from Christ to St. Francis of Assisi to the poets Kilmer and Hopkins—all of whom saw nature as an inspiration for lifting the mind and heart to God in Christian prayer. Recalling the past has reminded me of the Christian traditions and origins into which I have been inserted from my earliest years at home and at school. My response here and now on this autumn evening testifies to the fact that I uniquely express this long history of Christian civilization and that my friend, too, has her distinct originality as a Christian.

As I return to my familial origins in this section of the thesis, I recall the well-worn paths of Christian tradition into which I was inserted at birth by being born into a Catholic family. By being baptized into the Christian religion, I inherited a store of Christian culture. Stories of the saints, heard perhaps with little appreciation in early childhood, bring back, however naively, some of the values of Christian sanctity. Strong though the Christian habits instilled into me by my family and neighborhood are, it was easy to become embedded in the taken-for-grantedness of it all. I was a Christian by inheritance rather than by personal responsibility. It was easy to go to Mass on Sundays because everyone else went. Here we see that custom or habit tended to stifle individual responsiveness to tradition. Christian man can, however, personalize his Christian heritage and become what he already is—the individual responsible Christian he is called to be. In personalizing what he already is, Christian man may temporarily reject what is originally bestowed on him. He may pass through a crisis of faith before he is ready to be "born again of water and spirit" and reappropriate what he owns. It is often in the reappropriation of what he already owns that man discovers for himself in a more clearly defined way, the small "word" that he uniquely expresses as spoken by the Father.

By being responsive to the Holy Trinity in his daily Christian life, man can become his original Christian self. Responsiveness to the Father involves growing in self-presence. This means that I grow in awareness of the unique expression of God's creative hand which I represent and of my ability to be, in my turn, a small creator in the universe. By incarnating my efforts at participation in the culture, I gradually *become* the small "word" that I was originally called to be. Rooted in the sustaining love that binds Creator and

Created in a mysterious union, I allow my little love to imbue both who I am and what I do. Thus, presence to the Father helps us to know better who we are: identification with the Son helps us express ourselves better: and union with the Holy Spirit helps us to love and affirm ourselves and others as we are. It is the delicate balance of these three aspects of Christianity—self-presence in the Father, self-expression in the Son and self-affirmation in the Holy Spirit—that Christian man can come to the fullness of his Christian originality.

Theorists for the Christian Level

Kierkegaard—becoming a Christian in Christendom.
Clark—Christian civilization.
van Zeller—the current of Christian spirituality.
Eliot—conversion as an avenue to deeper faith.
van Kaam—the small "word" in the Word.
van Kaam—explanation of the Trinity in terms of a theory of the self.
Huxley—the place of the Trinity in Christianity.
Dewey—imitation of and identification with Christ.

Transition to the Vowed Religious Level

Having indicated how I can *discover* the unique expression of Christianity that I am and how I can *become* this small incarnated "word" by being responsive to the Trinity, I now discover that man may be inspired to a deeper level of commitment to his God in the vowed religious life. Here he adds a further layer to his originality by adopting a specific form and style of life designed to awaken more fully the original spiritual dimension of his living. He thus attempts to deepen the transcendent dimension of his life by entering into a new and distinct way of life which has had a history in the Church down through the ages.

VOWED RELIGIOUS LEVEL

GUIDING QUESTION: HOW CAN I DISCOVER MY ORIGINAL PLACE IN THE COMMUNITY TO WHICH I AM CALLED AND BECOME MY ORIGINAL SELF IN THE LIFE OF A PARTICIPATIVE RELIGOUS?

Introduction. We were not an unusual sight, my friend and I, as we walked back from our classes at the university. The neighbors would have been quite accustomed to the sight of two religious sisters walking up the hill, one in a brown habit, the other in a blue one. The external factor of the differently colored habits pointed to the fact that each of us belonged to a different vowed religious "family" in the church. My friend wore the century old brown of St. Francis and yet her identity was not only Franciscan. She embodied the tradition of St. Francis in her own unique way, out of her own personal history and vital make-up, out of the spirit of her Franciscan community. Franciscan poverty might be expressed by her in her economy of making her own Thanksgiving cards while another of her community might buy her cards at the store and thereby save time for other things. Each one expresses her common Franciscan heritage but in uniquely different ways.

In this section of the thesis, I propose to show how the religious maintains and deepens her original self in the center of value radiation to which she is drawn by the individual call of her vocation. Each religious community presents a uniform way of life expressed often in the external symbol of a uniform religious habit. The life form presents structures, rule books, and traditions which preserve a certain spirit and which each religious is called to personalize in her own unique way. The individual religious personalizes these uniform structures, according to her vital make-up from which emerges her temperament and talents. Her past personal history may dispose her to conform to the new way of life or, on the other hand, to flaunt authority. She will personalize the new also in terms of her deepest spiritual calling to be the original person that she is. In the first part of this section of the thesis, I propose to show how the structures of a community need not level the originality of each sister. While taking on the way of life of the group, each person has a duty to discover her original niche in the community—how she can be herself and yet be a witness to her religious traditions at the same time. While owning in its essence the spirit of the community, she nevertheless remains truly herself.

By being responsive to the three vows which represent a significant part of the way of life she has adopted, the sister can grow in the deepest original dimension of her life. The three vows can help bring to greater harmony those original aspects of her nature that may hinder the expression of her deepest original self. By gradually detaching herself from the immediate pleasures of life, she will aim at bringing her mind and heart and will into congruence with the mind, heart, and will of her Spouse. The greater the congruence, the greater will be her possibility of discovering her deepest originality.

By participating in the cultural activity of the community in whatever form it may take, the sister is urged to find her original rhythm of detachment and involvement in work. This is necessary so that vitally as well as spiritually she may respect her own originality. Originality, in religious life, while respecting the uniqueness of each person with due attention to the talents and vital rhythms of each, nevertheless fosters the common heritage each religious shares as a member of the group. This shared originality need not destroy or be destroyed by individual originality.

The danger of envious comparison is one that could easily threaten the unfolding of originality in the closeness of religious community. The proximity that can foster mutual admiration and respect, can also foster envy among those who are less secure and who have not discovered their own originality. I propose to show how respect and solitude as well as creative recreations can help alleviate a climate of envy and promote the respectful supportive atmosphere which encourages original self-expression. Times of retreat are also times of renewal which can lead to a deepening of the level of original living. In these times apart, the religious through greater reflection, may be helped to recover her original spiritual orientation.

Theorists for the Vowed Religious Section

van Kaam—centers of value radiation—levelling in religious life—envy and originality—inwardness and originality—creative living.
Tournier—true fellowship and creative solitude.

Haughton—the importance of others in fostering mature living.
Leclerq—asceticism as a preparation for spiritual transformation.
van Kaam—detachment and involvement—the experience of noughting—cultural participation in religious life.

Transition to the Level of Initiation.

In order that the sister may live her religious life in tune with her originality, a careful initiation is necessary. Brought to a new way of life the initiate will be guided by the directress of initiation to personalize, according to her own uniqueness, the traditions which present themselves as a part of her new life.

THE LEVEL OF INITIATION

GUIDING QUESTION: HOW CAN THE DIRECTRESS HELP THE NOVICE DISCOVER WHO SHE MORE DEEPLY IS AND ORIENT HER TOWARDS BECOMING THE UNIQUE RELIGIOUS SHE IS CALLED TO BE?

Introduction. As I stood looking at those leaves on that Fall evening, aware of the tremendous spatial distance that separated me from my home in Ireland, I realized that I was here in Pittsburgh for a special reason. I had not come all the way from Ireland to admire Fall in Pennsylvania; I was preparing to become a directress of formation in a well-known center for the study of spirituality. Likewise my friend too was preparing to take part in the work of formation in her Franciscan Community here in the United States. Our separate tasks would bring us into the work of initiating others of various backgrounds, personal histories, and vital originalities into the structures and traditions of our communities. It would be our separate tasks to guide each initiate towards personalizing her new way of life in a manner which would be in tune with her originality and the original spirit of the community.

The focus in this section will be first on the candidate during her pre-entrance program and then on the initiate during the novitiate year, which is the core-year of initiation. In the pre-entrance program, attention might be directed to the natural original foundations on which the spiritual life can be built. If there are any psychological problems which seem to obstruct spiritual development, then the time of the pre-entrance program would seem to be a suitable time for therapy. At the same time direction for the deepening of the transcendent dimension of her life will be given to the initiate. Spiritual reading might also be assigned; conferences on prayer and the fundamentals of basic Christian living could also benefit the candidate for religious life. Efforts may be made to make the candidate more aware of her Christian heritage and perhaps reappropriate her faith in a more personal way. Some of the insights already discussed on the first three levels of this thesis might be of help in aiding the candidate for religious life become aware of and discover the dignity of her unique originality before she enters the community as a postulant. The task of bringing this originality into dialogue with a new and structured way of life will be the goal of the postulancy. When the postulant has learned to live the structures of religious life in a personal and fruitful way, she may be admitted to the novitiate year.

The novitiate year might be designed to bring the novice to a greater degree of responsiveness both to herself and to her religious life. Quiet times of reading and reflection will be set aside in order that the novice may grow in self-presence. She will be aided by spiritual direction to remove those obstacles within her which hinder the deepening of her spiritual life and the fuller awakening of her original self. The use of a spiritual and reflective journal might be seen as a means to encourage her self-expression and responsiveness to the novitiate experience. The novice will be taught to ground her reflection in everyday experiences, in her attitudes to prayer, work and the common ways of the community. Opportunity for artistic and other forms of self-expression may be part of the novitiate experience so that the novice may have a variety of incarnational situations in which to embody her spiritual growth.

The relationship between directress and novice can be seen as one in which the novice can grow in her originality. The directress, by her appeal and inspiration, might aim at calling forth the originality of each individual novice so that each can unfold as herself and grow in becoming the original person that only she can be.

Theorists

van Kaam—mourning in the novice—spiritual direction in private and in
     common.
Maes—the stepping aside experience—the use of a journal for reflection.
van Croonenburg—the individual in the community.
Muto—the art and discipline of spiritual reading.
Gratton—evoking the freedom of the novice.

BIBLIOGRAPHY

BOOKS

Adler, Alfred. *Social Interest: A Challenge to Mankind,* trans. John Linton and Richard Vaughan. New York: Capricorn Books Edition, 1964.

_____. *The Science of Living,* ed. Heinz L. Ansbacher. New York: Anchor Books, Doubleday and Company Inc., 1968.

Allport, Gordon W. *Becoming.* New Haven: Yale University Press, 1968.

_____. *The Individual and His Religion.* New York: Macmillan, 1970.

Anastasi, Anne (ed.). *Individual Differences.* New York: Wiley, 1965.

Andreach, Robert J. *Studies in Structure: The Stages of the Spiritual Life in Four Modern Authors.* London: Burns and Oates, 1964.

Ansbacher, Heinz L., and Rowena R. Ansbacher (eds.). *The Individual Psychology of Alfred Adler: Systematic Presentation in Selections from his Writings.* New York: Harper Torchbooks, Harper and Row, 1964.

Anthony, Metropolitan (Archbishop Anthony Bloom). *Meditations on a Theme: A Spiritual Journey.* London and Oxford: Mowbrays, 1972.

Arabaugh, George B. and George E. Arabaugh, *Kierkegaard's Authorship.* Rook Island, Illinois: Augustana College Library, 1967

Argyris, Chris. *Personality and Organization: The Conflict between System and Individual.* New York: Harper Torchbooks, 1970.

Bach, Richard. *Jonathan Livingston Seagull.* New York: Macmillan Company, 1970.

Barron, Frank Xavier. *Creative Person and Creative Process.* New York: Holt, Rinehart and Winston, 1969.

_____. *Creativity and Personal Freedom.* Princeton, New Jersey: Van Nostrand, 1968.

_____. *Creativity and Psychological Health; Origins of Personal Vitality and Creative Freedom.* Princeton, New Jersey: 1963.

Beckett, Samuel. *Waiting for Godot.* London: Faber and Faber Ltd., 1956.

Benedict, Ruth. *Patterns of Culture.* Boston: Houghton Mifflin, 1959.

Bennett, J.G. *A Spiritual Psychology.* London: Hodder and Stoughton Ltd., 1964.

Bergson, Henri. *The Two Sources of Morality and Religion,* trans. R. Ashley Audra and Cloudesley Bereton with the assistance of W. Horsfall Carter. New York: Doubleday Anchor, 1935.

Bloom, Archbishop Anthony. *Living Prayer.* London: Darton, Longman and Todd Ltd., 1966.

_____. *School for Prayer.* London: Darton, Longman and Todd Ltd., 1970.

Boros, Ladislaus. *God Is with Us,* trans. R. A. Wilson. London: Burns and Oates, 1970.

_____. *Meeting God in Man,* trans. William Glen-Doepel. London: Burns and Oates, 1968.

Bronowski, Jacob. *The Identity of Man.* London: Heinemann, 1966.

Bugental, J. F. T. *The Search for Authenticity.* New York: Holt, Rinehart and Winston, 1965.

Burland, C. A. *The Arts of the Alchemists.* London: Weidenfeld and Nicholson Ltd., 1967.

Carnell, Edward John. *The Burden of Soren Kierkegaard.* London: The Paternoster Press, 1965.

Chang, Chung-yuan. *Creativity and Taoism.* New York: The Julian Press Inc., 1963.

Chiang, Hung-Min and Abraham H. Maslow (eds.). *The Healthy Personality: Readings.* New York: Van Nostrand Reinhold Company, 1969

Cole, Preston J. *The Problematic Self in Kierkegaard and Freud.* New·Haven and London: Yale University Press, 1971.

Collins, William J. *Out of the Depths: The Story of a Priest-patient in a Mental Hospital.* Garden City, New York: Doubleday and Company Inc., 1971.

Cornwell, Ethel F. *The "Still Point": Theme and Variations in the Writings of T. S. Eliot, Coleridge, Yeats, Henry James, Virginia Woolf and D. H. Lawrence.* New Brunswick, New Jersey: Rutgers University Press, 1962.

Crom, Scott: *On Being Real: A Quest for Personal and Religious Wholeness.* Wallingford, Pennsylvania: Pendle Hill Publications, 1967.

Crowne, Douglas P. and David Marlowe. *The Approval Motive: Studies in Evaluative Dependence.* New York and London: John Wiley and Sons, Inc., 1964.

Cuzzort, R. P. *Humanity and Modern Sociological Thought.* New York and London: Holt, Rinehart and Winston Inc., 1969.

Dabrowski, Kazimierz. *Personality Shaping Through Positive Disintegration.* London: J. and A. Churchill Ltd., 1967.

_____ . *Positive Disintegration.* London: J. and A. Churchill Ltd., 1964.

Drucker, Peter F. *The Age of Discontinuity: Guidelines to our Changing Society.* London: Heinemann Ltd., 1969.

Dubos, René. "Biological Determinants of Individuality," *Individuality and the New Society.* ed. Abraham Kaplan. Seattle and London: University of Washington Press, 1970.

Durckheim, Karlfried Graf Von. *Hara: The Vital Centre of Man,* trans. S. M. von Kospath and E. R. Healey. London: Allen and Unwin Ltd., 1962.

_____ . *The Way of Transformation: Daily Life as Spiritual Exercise.,* trans. Ruth Lewinnek and P. L. Travers. London: Allen and Unwin Ltd., 1971.

Eliade, Mircea. *The Forge and the Crucible,* trans. Stephen Corrin. New York: Harper and Brothers Publisher, 1962.

_____ . *The Quest: History and Meaning in Religion.* Chicago and London: The University of Chicago Press, 1969.

_____ . *The Sacred and the Profane.* New York: Harper and Row, 1961.

_____ . *The Two and the One,* trans. J. M. Cohen. London: Harvill Press, 1965.

Eliot, T.S. *Four Quartets.* New York: Harcourt, Brace and World Inc., 1971.

_____ . *The Complete Poems and Plays.* London: Faber and Faber, 1969.

_____ . *Selected Poems.* New York: Harcourt, Brace and World, 1934.

Fernandez, Ronald (ed.). *Social Psychology through Literature.* New York: John Wiley and Sons Inc., 1972.

Fordham, Frieda, *An Introduction to Jung's Psychology.* Middlesex, England: Penguin Books, 1966.

French, R. M. (tr.). *The Way of the Pilgrim.* New York: The Seabury Press, 1968.

Friedman, Maurice. *To Deny our Nothingness: Contemporary Images of Man.* London: Macmillan Company Ltd., 1958.

Frings, Manfred S. *Max Scheler: A Concise Introduction into the World of a Great Thinker.* Pittsburgh: Duquesne University Press, 1965.

Fromm, Erich *Man for Himself: An Enquiry into the Psychology of Ethics.* London: Routledge and Kegan Paul Ltd., 1949.

_____ . *The Revolution of Hope: Towards a Humanized Technology.* New York: Bantam Books, 1968.

_____ . *The Sane Society.* London: Routledge and Kegan Paul Ltd., 1956.

Gardner, John W. *Self-Renewal: The Individual and the Innovative Society.* New York: Harper and Row Publishers Inc., 1963.

Gardner, W. H. (ed.). *Poems and Prose of Gerard Manley Hopkins.* Middlesex, England: Penguin Books, 1953.

Gates, John A. *The Life and Thought of Kierkegaard for Everyman.* London: Hodder and Stoughton, 1961.

Gide, André. *La Porte Entroite.* Paris: Livre de Poche, 1966.

Glen, Duncan. *The Individual and Twentieth Century Scottish Literary Tradition.* Preston, England: Akros Publications, 1971.

Goffman, Erving. *The Presentation of Self in Everyday Life.* New York: Doubleday, 1969.

Goldbrunner, Josef. *Individuation: A Study of the Depth Psychology of Carl Gustav Jung.* Notre Dame, Indiana: University of Notre Dame Press, 1964.

Hall, Calvin S. and Lindzey Gardner (eds.). *Theories of Personality.* New York: John Wiley and Sons Inc., 1970.

Happold, F. C. *The Journey Inwards.* London: Darton, Longman and Todd, 1968.

Haughton, Rosemary. *On Trying to be Human.* London and Dublin: Geoffrey Chapman, 1966.

Herrigel, Eugen. *Zen and the Art of Archery.* New York: Vintage Books, 1971.

Heschel, A. J. *Who is Man?* Stanford California: Stanford University Press, 1965.

Hesse, Hermann. *Demian: The Story of Emil Sinclair's Youth,* trans. Michael Roloff and Michael Lebeck. New York: Bantam Books, 1968.

Horney, Karen. *Neurosis and Human Growth.* New York: Norton, 1950.

Huyghe, Gerard. *Growth in the Holy Spirit,* trans. Isabel and Florence McHugh. London and Dublin: Geofrey Chapman, 1966.

Ibsen, Henrick. *Peer Gynt*, trans. Peter Watts. Middlesex, England: Penguin Books, 1966.

Isherwood, Margaret. *Search for Meaning: A Book for Agnostics and Believers.* London: Allen and Unwin Ltd., 1970.

Jacobi, Jolande. *The Way of Individuation.* New York: Harcourt, Brace and World, 1967.

Johnson, William. *Christian Zen.* New York: Harper and Row, 1971.

_____. *The Still Point: Reflections on Zen and Christian Mysticism.* New York: Fordham University Press, 1970.

Jourard, Sidney. *Disclosing Man to Himself.* Princeton: Van Nostrand, 1968.

_____. *The Transparent Self.* New York: Van Nostrand Reinhold Company, 1971.

_____. *Personal Adjustment: An Approach through the Study of Healthy Personality.* New York: Macmillan Company, 1958.

Jung, Carl Gustav. *The Undiscovered Self,* trans. R. F. C. Hull. Boston: Little, Brown and Company, 1958.

Kahler, Erich.*The Tower and the Abyss: An Inquiry into the Transformation of the Individual.* New York: Braziller, 1975.

Kaplan, Abraham (ed.). *Individuality and the New Society.* Seattle and London: University of Washington Press, 1970.

Kesey, Ken. *One Flew Over the Cuckoo's Nest.* New York: Viking Press, Inc., 1962.

Kierkegaard, Soren. *The Concept of Dread,* trans. W. Lowrie. Princeton: Princeton University Press, 1969.

_____.*Journals and Papers,* Vol. II, trans. H. E. Hong. Bloomington, Indiana: Indiana University Press, 1967.

_____. *The Point of View of My Work as an Author,* trans. W. Lowrie. New York: Harper Torchbook, 1962.

_____. *Purity of Heart is to Will One Thing: Spiritual Preparation for the Office of Confession,* trans. Douglas Steere. New York: Harper Torchbooks, 1956.

Kraft, William F. *The Search for The Holy.* Philadelphia: The Westminster Press, 1971.

Krech, David, Richard S. Crutchfield, and Egerton L. Ballachey. *Individual in Society: A Textbook of Social Psychology.* New York: McGraw-Hill, 1962.

Leclerq, Dom Jean. *Alone with God,* trans. Elizabeth McCabe. New York: Farrar, Straus and Cudaky, 1961.

Leggett, Trevor. *The Tiger's Cave.* London: Rider and Company, 1966.

Lepp, Ignace. *The Ways of Friendship,* trans. Bernard Murchland, New York: The Macmillan Company, 1966.

Levi-Strauss, Claude.*The Savage Mind,* trans. George Weidenfeld and Nicolson Ltd., Chicago: University of Chicago Press, 1966.

Luijpen, William A. *Existential Phenomenology.* Pittsburgh, Pennsylvania: Duquesne University Press, 1962.

Macquarrie, John. *Paths to Spirituality.* London: SCM Press Ltd., 1972.

Marcel, Gabriel. *Being and Having.* London: Fontana Books, 1965.

Martin, Philip M. *Mastery and Mercy: A Study of Two Religious Poems.* London: Oxford University Press, 1957.

Maugham, W. Somerset. *The Razor's Edge.* Middlesex, England: Penguin Books, 1963.

May, Rollo. *Man's Search for Himself.* New York: The American Library Inc., Signet Books, 1967.

McConnell, Theodore A. *The Shattered Self: The Psychological and Religious Search for Selfhood.* Philadelphia: A Pilgrim Book, 1971.

McLuhan, Marshall. *Counterblast.* London: Rapp and Whiting Ltd., 1970.

Mead, George H. *Mind, Self and Society: From the Standpoint of a Social Behaviorist.* Chicago: University of Chicago Press, 1938.

Mead, Margaret, Theodosius Dobzhansky, Ethel Tobach and Robert E. Light (eds.). *Science and the Concept of Race.* New York and London: Columbia University Press, 1968.

Miller, David L. *Individualism: Personal Achievement and the Open Society.* Austin and London: University of Texas Press, 1967.

Missildine, W. Hugh. *Your Inner Child of the Past.* New York: Simon and Shuster, 1963.

Montessori, Maria. *The Absorbent Mind.* New York: Dell Publishing Co., Inc., 1967.

Moustakas, Clark E. *Creativity and Conformity.* Princeton, New Jersey: Van Nostrand Company Inc., 1967.

Mullahy, Patrick (ed.). *A Study of Interpersonal Relations: New Contributions to Psychiatry.* New York: Science House Inc., 1967.

Mumford, Lewis. *The Transformations of Man.* New York: Macmillan, Collier Books, 1962.

Muto, Susan Annette. *Approaching the Sacred: An Introduction to Spiritual Reading.* New Jersey: Dimension, 1973.

O'Doherty, E. F. and S. Desmond McGrath (eds.) *The Priest and Mental Health.* Dublin: Clonmore and Reynolds Ltd., 1962.

O'Doherty, E. F. *Religion and Personality Problems.* Dublin: Clonmore and Reynolds Ltd., 1964.

Platt, John Rader. *The Step to Man.* New York: John Wiley and Sons Inc., 1966.

Price, George. *The Narrow Pass.* New York: McGraw-Hill Book Company, 1961.

Rogers, Carl. *Client-Centered Therapy.* Boston: Houghton Mifflin, 1965.
_____. *On Becoming a Person.* Boston: Houghton Mifflin, 1961.

Reich, Charles A. *The Greening of America.* New York: Random House Inc., 1970.

Reisman, David. *The Lonely Crowd,* New Haven: Yale University Press, 1961.

Ruitenbeek, Hendrik M. *The Individual and the Crowd.* New York: Mentor Books, 1965.

Saint-Exupery, Antoine de. *The Little Prince,* trans. Katherine Wood. New York: New American Library, 1964.

Schnapper, Edith B. *The Inward Odyssey: The Concept of the Way in the Great Religions of the World.* London: George Allen and Unwin Ltd., 1965.

Schachtel, Ernest G. *Metamorphosis: On the Development of Affect, Perception, Attention and Memory.* New York: Basic Books Inc., 1959.

Schoeck, Helmut. *Envy: A Theory of Social Behavior,* trans. Michael Glenny and Betty Ross. London: Secker and Warburg, 1969.

Schrag, Oswald. *Existence, Existenz and Transcendence: An Introduction to the Philosophy of Karl Jaspers.* Pittsburgh: Duquesne University Press, 1971.

Scott, Nathan A. Jr. *The Broken Center: A Definition of the Crisis of Values in Modern Literature: Symbolism in Religion.* New York: George Braziller, 1960.

Shakespeare, William. *The Complete Works,* ed. B. Hodek, London: Spring Books, n.d.

Smith, Betty. *A Tree Grows in Brooklyn.* New York: Stratford Press Inc., 1943.

Steere, Douglas V. *On Being Present Where You Are.* Wallingford, Pennsylvania: Pendle Hill Pamphlets #151, 1967.

Strong, Frederick J. *Understanding Religious Man.* Belmont: Dickenson Publishing Company, 1969.

Thoreau, Henry David. *Walden and Civil Disobedience,* ed. Paul Sherman. Cambridge, Mass.: The Riverside Press, 1957.

Toffler, Alvin. *Future Shock.* London: Bodley Head, 1970.

Tournier, Paul. *A Place for You: Psychology and Religion,* trans. Edwin Hudson. London: SCM Press Ltd., 1966.

_____. *Escape from Loneliness,* trans. John S. Gilmour. London: SCM Press, 1962.

Underhill, Evelyn. *Mysticism: A Study in the Nature and Development of Man's Spiritual Consciousness.* London: Methuen and Company Ltd., 1949.

_____. *Practical Mysticism.* New York: E. P. Dutton and Company Inc., 1943.

van Croonenburg, Bert. *Don't be Discouraged.* New Jersey: Dimension Books, 1972.

_____. *Gateway to Reality.* Pittsburgh: Duquesne University Press, 1963.

Van der Post, Laurens. *The Lost World of the Kalahari.* Middlesex, England: Penguin Books, 1962.

van Kaam, Adrian. *The Art of Existential Counseling.* Wilkes-Barre: Dimension Books, 1963.

_____. *Envy and Originality.* New York: Doubleday, 1972.

_____. *A Light to the Gentiles.* New Jersey: Dimension, 1963.

_____. *On Being Yourself: Reflections on Spirituality and Originality.* New Jersey: Dimension Books, 1972.

_____. *Religion and Personality.* Garden City: Image Books, 1968.

_____. *The Vowed Life.* New Jersey: Dimension Books, 1968.

van Kaam, Adrian, Bert van Croonenburg and Susan Annette Muto. *The Emergent Self.* Wilkes-Barre: Dimension Books, 1969.

Van Zeller, Dom Hubert. *The Current of Spirituality.* Springfield, Illinois: Templegate Publishers, 1970.

_____ . *The Inner Search.* London: Sheed and Ward, 1956.
Von Hildebrand, Dietrich. *The New Tower of Babel.* London: Burns and
    Oates, 1954.
_____ . *The Sacred Heart: An Analysis of Human and Divine
    Affectivity.* Dublin: Helicon Press, 1965.
_____ . *Transformation in Christ: On the Christian Attitude of Mind.*
    Baltimore, Maryland: Helicon Press, 1948.
Watts, Alan W. *The Book: On the Taboo Against Knowing Who You Are.* New
    York: Collier Books, 1967.
Weil, Simone. *Attente de Dieu.* Paris: Edition Fayard, 1966.
White, Winston. *Beyond Conformity.* New York: The Free Press of Glencoe
    Inc., 1961.
Williams, Margery. *The Velveteen Rabbit.* New York: Doubleday, n.d.
Williams, R. J. *Biochemical Individuality.* New York: John Wiley and Sons
    Inc., 1956.
_____ . *You are Extraordinary.* New York: Random House, 1967.

PERIODICALS

Eslick, Leonard J. "Existence and Creativity in Whitehead," *Proceedings of
    the American Catholic Philosophical Association,* (1961), 151–163.
Kirkendall, Lester A. and Peter B. Anderson. "Authentic Selfhood Basis of
    Tomorrow's Sexual Morality,: *Pastoral Psychology,* XXI (November
    1970), 19–32.
Schachtel, Ernest G. "On Creative Experience," *Journal of Humanistic
    Psychology,* XI (Spring, 1971), 26–39.
Shaw, Franklin J. "The Problem of Acting and the Problem of Becoming,"
    Journal of Humanistic Psychology, I, (January, 1961), 64–69.
_____ . "Laughter: Paradigm of Growth," *Journal of Individual
    Psychology,* XVI (November, 1960), 151–157.
Shine, Daniel J. "The Analogy of Individuality and Togetherness," *Thomist,*
    XXXIII (July 1969), 197–218.
Shostrom, Everett L. "A Test for the Measurement of Self-Actualization,"
    Educational and Psychological Measurement, I–II (1964), 207–218.
Stack, George J. "Kierkegaard's Concept of Possibility," *Journal of American
    Catholic Philosophical Association,* XLVI, (Spring, 1972), 256–273.
van den Berg, J. H. "What is Psychotherapy?" *Humanitas,* VII (Winter, 1971)
    321–370.
van Kaam, Adrian, "Spiritual Originality," *Envoy,* VII (March, 1970), 43–48.

UNPUBLISHED MATERIALS

Gratton, Carolyn. "Spirituality and Development of the Self." Unpublished
    class notes, Center for the Study of Spirituality of the Institute of Man,
    Duquesne University, 1973.
Maes, Charles. "Religious Development through the Common Ways," Unpub-
    lished class notes, Center for the Study of Spirituality of the Institute of
    Man, Duquesne University, 1972–73.

Muto, Susan Annette. "Art and Discipline of Meditative Reflection and Spiritual Reading" Unpublished class notes, Center for the Study of Spirituality of the Institute of Man, Duquesne University, 1972.

van Kaam, Adrian. "Religion and Personality." Unpublished class notes, Center for the Study of Spirituality of the Institute of Man, Duquesne University, 1971–1973.

* * * *

1. SELECTED AUTHOR'S BIBLIOGRAPHY, 1958–1975

BOOKS BY ADRIAN VAN KAAM

The Third Force in European Psychology. Greenville, Delaware: Psychosynthesis Research Foundation, 1960. Also published in Greek by the Psychosynthesis Foundation, 1962.

A Light to the Gentiles. Pittsburgh, Pa.: Duquesne University Press, 1959. New editions: Milwaukee; Bruce Publishing Co., 1962; Denville, New Jersey: Dimension Books, Inc., 1963.

The Vocational Director and Counseling. Derby, New York: St. Paul Publications, 1962.

Religion and Personality. New York: Prentice-Hall, 1964. (Also in French and Italian).

Religion and Personality. Garden City, New York: Doubleday & Co., Inc. (An Image Paperback), 1968.

Religion et Personnalité. Casterman-Paris-Tournai. Editions Salvator, Mulhouse, 1967.

Religione e Personalita. Brescia: Editrice La Scuola, Officine Grafiche La Scuola, 1972.

Existential Foundations of Psychology. Pittsburgh, Pa.: Duquesne University Press, 1966.

Existential Foundations of Psychology. Garden City, New York: Doubleday & Co., Inc. (An Image Paperback), 1969.

Personality Fulfillment in the Spiritual Life. Denville, New Jersey: Dimension Books, Inc., 1966.

The Demon and the Dove: Personality Development through Literature. Pittsburgh, Pa.: Duquesne University Press, 1967.

Personality Fulfillment in the Religious Life, Volume 1, *Religious Life in a Time of Transition.* Denville, New Jersey: Dimension Books, 1967. (Also in Vietnamese and Japanese).

The Art of Existential Counseling: Denville, New Jersey: Dimension Books, Inc., 1966.

Encuentro e Integracion. (Spanish) Ediciones Sigueme, Apartado 322, 1969.

The Vowed Life. Denville, New Jersey: Dimension Books,Inc., 1968.

The Emergent Self. Denville, New Jersey: Dimension Books, Inc., First American Edition, 1968, Second and Revised Edition, 1968. (Also in Japanese).

The Participant Self. Denville, New Jersey: Dimension Books, Inc., 1969.

On Being Involved. Denville, New Jersey: Dimension Books, Inc., 1970. (Also in French).

Dynamisme du Quotidien: Sherbrooke, Quebec: Les Editions Paulines, 1973.
    Paris VIe: Apostolat des Editions, 1973.
On Being Yourself. Denville, New Jersey: Dimension Books, Inc., 1972.
Envy and Originality. Garden City, New York: Doubleday & Co., Inc., 1972.
Spirituality and the Gentle Life. Denville, New Jersey: Dimension Books, Inc.,
    1974.
In Search of Spiritual Identity. Denville, New Jersey: Dimension Books, Inc.,
    1975.

ARTICLES BY ADRIAN VAN KAAM

"Assumptions in Psychology," *Journal of Individual Psychology,* Vol. 14
    (1958) pp. 22–28.
"Education and Human Motivation by Harry Giles," a review in *The Catholic
    Educator,* January, 1958.
"Freud and Anthropological Psychology," *The Justice,* Brandeis University,
    May, 1959.
"The Nurse in the Patient's World," *The American Journal of Nursing,* Vol. 59
    (1959), pp. 1708–1710.
"Phenomenal Analysis: Exemplified by a Study of the Experience of 'Really
    Feeling Understood'," *Journal of Individual Psychology,* Vol. 15 (1959),
    pp. 65–72.
"Clinical Implications of Heidegger's Concepts of Will, Decision, and Responsi-
    bility," *Review of Existential Psychology and Psychiatry,* Vol. 1, No. 3
    (Fall, 1961), pp. 205–216.
"The Fantasy of Romantic Love," in *Modern Myths and Popular Fancies.*
    Pittsburgh, Pa.: Duquesne University Press, 1961.
"The Impact of Existential Phenomenology on the Psychological Literature of
    Western Europe," *Review of Existential Psychology and Psychiatry,* Vol. 1,
    No. 3 (Fall, 1961), pp. 63–92.
"Counseling and Existential Psychology," *Harvard Educational Review,* Fall,
    1962. This article was later published in *Guidance–An Examination.* New
    York: Harcourt, Brace and World, 1965.
"Religion and the Existential Will," *Insight,* Vol. 1, No. 1 (Summer 1962).
"Review of the Divided Self by R. D. Laing," *Review of Existential
    Psychology and Psychiatry,* Vol. II, No. 1 (Winter, 1962), pp. 85–88.
"Commentary on 'Freedom and Responsibility Examined'," *Behavioral
    Science and Guidance, Proposals and Perspectives,* ed. Lloyd-Jones and
    Westervelt. New York: Teachers College Columbia University Press, 1963.
"Existential Psychology as a Theory of Personality," *Review of Existential
    Psychology and Psychiatry,* (Winter, 1963), pp. 11–26.
"A Psychology of the Catholic Intellectual," in *The Christian Intellectual,* ed.
    Samuel Hazo. Pittsburgh, Pa.: Duquesne University Press, 1963.
"A Psychology of Falling Away From the Faith,"*Insight,* Vol. 2, No. 2 (Fall,
    1963), pp. 3–17.
"Sex and Existence," *Review of Existential Psychology and Psychiatry,* Vol.
    III, No. 2 (Spring, 1963), pp. 163–181. Reprinted in *Insight,* Vol. 2, No. 3
    (Winter, 1964).

"Existential Theory and Therapy" with Rollo May. *Current Psychiatric Therapies*, Vol. III, 1963.

"Together in Obedience," *Envoy*, Vol. 1, No. 1 (June 1964).

"Together in Celibacy," *Envoy*, Vol. 1, No. 2 (July 1964).

"Reflections on Confession," *Envoy*, Vol. 1, No. 3 (August 1964).

"Thoughts on Love," *Envoy*, Vol. 1, No. 4 (September 1964).

"Religious Life and Presence–Part I," *Envoy*, Vol. 1, No. 5 (October 1964).

"Religious Life and Presence–Part II," *Envoy*, Vol. 1, No. 6 (December 1964).

"Religious Counseling of Seminarians," *Seminary Education in a Time of Change*, ed. James Michael Lee and Louis J. Putz. Notre Dame, Indiana: Fides Publishers, Inc., 1965.

"Motivation and Contemporary Anxiety," *Humanitas*, Vol. 1, No. 1 (Spring 1965).

"Religious Life and Presence–Part III," *Envoy*, Vol. 1, No. 7 (January 1965).

"Reality and Life Situation–Part I," *Envoy*, Vol. 1, No. 8 (February 1965).

"Reality and Life Situation–Part II," *Envoy*, Vol. 1, No. 9 (March 1965).

"Reality and Life Situation–Part III," *Envoy*, Vol. 1, No. 10 (March 1965).

"Discipline and Detachment–Part I," *Envoy*, Vol. II, No. 1 (April 1965).

"Discipline and Detachment–Part II," *Envoy*, Vol. II, No. 2 (May 1965).

"Discipline and Detachment–Part III," *Envoy*, Vol. II, No. 3 (May 1965).

"Discipline and Detachment–Conclusion," *Envoy*, Vol. II, No. 4 (June, 1965).

"The Field of Religion and Personality or Theoretical Religious Anthropology," *Insight*, Vol. IV, No. 1 (Summer, 1965)

"Religion and Existential Will–Part I," *Envoy*, Vol. II, No. 5 (September 1965)

"Religion and Existential Will–Part II," *Envoy*, Vol. II, No. 6 (October 1965).

"Religion and Existential Will–Part II," *Envoy*, Vol. II, No. 7 (November 1965).

"Humanistic Psychology and Culture," *Journal of Humanistic Psychology*, Vol. V, No. 3 (Fall 1965).

"Existential and Humanistic Psychology," *Review of Existential Psychology and Psychiatry*, Vol. V, No. 3 (Fall 1965), pp. 291–296.

"The Addictive Personality," *Humanitas*, Vol. I, No. 2 (Fall 1965). Reprinted in *Insight*, Vol. IV, No. 2 (Fall, 1965) and in *Phenomenology of Will and Action*. ed. Erwin W. Straus and Richard M. Griffith, Pittsburgh, Pa.: Duquesne University Press, 1967, pp. 141–154.

"Religious Presence and the Fullness of Life–Part I," *Envoy*, Vol. II, No. 8 (December 1965).

"Religious Presence and the Fullness of Life–Part II," *Envoy*, Vol. II, No. 9 (January 1966).

"Religious Presence and the Fullness of Life–Part III," *Envoy*, Vol. II, No. 10 (February 1966).

"Obstacles to Religious Presence," *Envoy*, Vol. III, No. 1 (March 1966).

"Addiction: Counterfeit of Religious Presence," *Envoy*, Vol. III, No. 2 (April 1966).

"The Threefold Path to Religious Presence," *Envoy*, Vol. III, No. 3 (May 1966).

"Social Formation of Personality," *Envoy*, Vol. III, No. 4 (June 1966).

"The Questioning of Religious Life," *Envoy*, Vol. III, No. 6 (October 1966).

"Encounter and Its Distortion in the Religious Community," *Envoy*, Vol. III, No. 7 (November 1966).

"Community and Structure: Some Fundamental Concepts," *Envoy*, Vol. III, No. 8 (December 1966).

"Anthropological Psychology and Behavioristic Animal Experimentation," with I. V. Pacoe, in *Festschrift Dr. Straus,* ed. R. M. Griffith and W. Von Baeyer. Berling Heidelberg, New York: Springer-Verlag, 1966.

"Differential Psychology," *The New Catholic Encyclopedia.* Washington, D.C.: The Catholic University of America, 1966.

"The Goals of Psychotherapy from the Existential Point of View," *The Goals of Psychotherapy,* ed. Alvin R. Mahrer. New York: Appleton-Century-Crofts, 1966.

"Structures and Systems of Personality," *The New Catholic Encyclopedia,* Washington, D.C.: The Catholic University of America, 1966.

"Francis Libermann," *The New Catholic Encyclopedia.* Washington, D.C.: The Catholic University of America, 1966.

"The Psychology of Falling Away from the Faith," *The Star and the Cross,* ed. Catherine T. Hargrove, R.S.C.J. Milwaukee, 1966.

"Human Potentialities from the Viewpoint of Existential Psychology," in *Explorations in Human Potentialities,* ed. Herbert A. Otto. Illinois: Charles C. Thomas, 1966.

"Religious Anthropology and Religious Counseling," *Insight*, Vol. 4, No. 3 (Winter 1966), pp. 1–7.

"Die existentielle Psychologie als eine Theorie, de Gesamtpersonlichkeit," *Jahrbuch fur Psychologie and Medizinische Anthropologie,* 12. Jahrgang Heft 4, 1966.

"Counseling from the Viewpoint of Existential Psychology," in *Guidelines for Guidance,* ed. Carlton E. Beck, Dubuque, Iowa: Wm. C. Brown Co., 1966, pp. 400–411.

"Counseling and Psychotherapy from the Viewpoint of Existential Psychology," in *Counseling and Psychotherapy; An Overview,* ed. D. S. Arbuckle. New York: McGraw Hill, 1967.

"Sex and Existence," in *Readings in Existential Phenomenology,* ed. Nathaniel Lawrence and Daniel O'Connor. New Jersey, 1967.

"Human Presence and Structure," *Envoy*, Vol. III, No. 9 (January 1967).

"Dimensions of Community Encounter," *Envoy*, Vol. III, No. 10 (February 1967).

"Dimensions of Community Encounter," *Envoy*, Vol. IV, No. 1 (March 1967).

"Community and the Forms of Encounter," *Envoy*, Vol. IV, No. 2 (April 1967).

"Personality Formation and Structure in Religious Life," *Envoy*, Vol. IV, No. 3, (May 1967).

"Culture and Value Radiation," *Envoy*, Vol. IV, No. 4 (June 1967).

"Community and Structure–Irrational Component," *Envoy*, Vol. IV, No. 5 (September 1967).

"Origin and Originality of Participative Religious Life," *Envoy*, Vol. IV, No. 6 (October 1967).

"The Healing Power of Obedience," *Envoy*, Vol. IV, No. 7 (November 1967).

"The Healing Power of Respectful Love," *Envoy*, Vol. IV, No. 8 (December 1967).

"The Healing Power of Celibate Love," *Envoy*, Vol. IV, No. 9 (January 1968).

"The Healing Power of Poverty," *Envoy*, Vol. IV, No. 10 (February 1968).

"Life of the Vows: Polarity Between Participation and Transcendence," *Envoy*, Vol. V, No. 1 (March 1968).

"Life of the Vows: Rhythm of Recollection and Participation," *Envoy*, Vol. V, No. 2 (April 1968).

"Life of the Vows: Unity of Recollection and Action," *Envoy*, Vol. V, No. 3 (May 1968).

"Life of the Vows: Active and Passive Strength," *Envoy*, Vol. V, No. 4 (June 1968).

"Personality Formation of Religious," *Envoy*, Vol. V, No. 5 (July 1968).

"Personality Formation of Religious," *Envoy*, Vol. V, No. 6 (August 1968).

"Life of the Vows: Commitment to Lasting Life Style," *Envoy*, Vol. V, No. 7 (September 1968).

"Obstacles to Religious Living in Western Culture: Utilitarianism," *Envoy*, Vol. V, No. 8 (October 1968).

"Obstacles to Religious Living in Western Culture," *Envoy*, Vol. V, No. 9 (November 1968).

"Obstacles to Religious Living in Western Culture: Specialization," *Envoy*, Vol. V, No. 10 (December 1968).

"Obstacles to Religious Living in Western Culture: Specialization and the Life of the Vows," *Envoy*, Vol. VI, No. 1 (January 1969).

"Obstacles to Religious Living in Western Culture: Functional Homogeneity," *Envoy*, Vol. VI, No. 2 (February 1969)

"Obstacles to Religious Living in Western Culture: Alienation from Personal Experience," *Envoy*, Vol. VI, No. 3 (March 1969).

"Christian Religious Life: The Vow of Obedience," *Envoy*, Vol. VI, No. 4 (April 1969).

"Christian Religious Life: The Vow of Respectful Love," *Envoy*, Vol. VI, No. 5 (May 1969).

"Christian Religious Life: The Vow of Poverty," *Envoy*, Vol. VI, No. 6 (June 1969).

"Christian Religious Life: Christian Celibacy," *Envoy*, Vol. VI, No. 7 (September 1969).

"Christian Religious Life: Celibacy and Celibate Love," *Envoy*, Vol. VI, No. 8 (October 1969).

"Christian Religious Life: Celibate Love for Humanity," *Envoy*, Vol. VI, No. 9 (November 1969).

"Christian Religious Life: Communion and Community," *Envoy*, Vol. VI, No. 10 (December 1969).

"Existential Crisis and Human Development," *South African Journal of Pedagogy,* Vol. III, No. 1 (July 1969), pp. 63–74. Reprinted in *Humanitas,* Vol. X, No. 2 (May 1974) pp. 109–126.

"Assumptions in Psychology," in *The Science of Psychology: Critical Reflections,* ed. Duane P. Schultz, New York: Appleton-Century-Crofts, 1970, pp. 24–29.

"Challenge of Spirituality," *Envoy,* Vol. VII, No. 1 (January 1970).

"Types of Originality," *Envoy,* Vol. VII, No. 2 (February 1970).

"Spiritual Originality," *Envoy,* Vol. VII, No. 3 (March 1970).

"Isolated I-God Relationship," *Envoy,* Vol. VII, No. 4 (April 1970).

"Solitude and Communion," *Envoy,* Vol. VII, No. 5 (May 1970).

"Attitudes of Man as Spirit," *Envoy,* Vol. VII, No. 6 (June 1970).

"Expressions of the Spiritual Life," *Envoy,* Vol. VII, No. 7 (September 1970).

"Faith and Beliefs," *Envoy,* Vol. VII, No. 8 (October 1970).

"Spiritual Direction and Counseling," *Envoy,* Vol. VII, No. 9 (November 1970).

"On Judging People," *Envoy,* Vol. VII, No. 10 (December 1970).

"Education to Originality," in *Psychologia Pedagogica Sursum Barend Frederik Nel,* Stellenbosch/Grahamstad, South Africa: University Publishers and Booksellers LTD, 1970, pp. 214–229.

"Personal Prayer," *Envoy,* Vol. VIII, No. 1 (January 1971).

"Masters of Religious Life," *Envoy,* Vol. VIII, No. 2 (February 1971).

"Envy and Respect," *Envoy,* Vol. VIII, No. 3 (March 1971).

"Self-Envy and Spirituality," *Envoy,* Vol. VIII, No. 4 (April 1971).

"Envy of Originality," *Envoy,* Vol. VIII, No. 5 (May 1971).

"Dealing with Envy," *Envoy,* Vol. VIII, No. 6 (June 1971).

"Envy and Collegiality," *Envoy,* Vol. VIII, No. 7 (September 1971).

"Overcoming Envy," *Envoy,* Vol. VIII, No. 8 (October 1971).

"Wonder and Curiosity," *Envoy,* Vol. VIII, No. 9 (November 1971).

"Living my Own Life," *Envoy,* Vol. VIII, No. 10 (December 1971).

"Originality and Christian Spirituality," *Envoy,* Vol. IX, No. 1 (January 1972).

"Sources of Originality," *Envoy,* Vol. IX, No. 2 (February 1972).

"Spiritual Life and Vital Originality," *Envoy,* Vol. IX, No. 3 (March 1972).

"Spiritual Life and the Family," *Envoy,* Vol. IX, No. 4 (April 1972).

"Union with the Divine Will in Daily Life," *Envoy,* Vol. IX, No. 5 (May 1972).

"Two Kinds of Willing," *Envoy,* Vol. IX, No. 6 (June 1972).

"God's Will and My Original Limits," *Envoy,* Vol. IX, No. 7 (September 1972).

"Original Faithfulness to the Divine Will," *Envoy,* Vol. IX, No. 8 (October 1972).

"Church Doctrine and the Life of the Spirit," *Envoy,* Vol. IX, No. 9 (November 1972).

"The Divine Child," *Envoy,* Vol. IX, No. 10 (December 1972).

"Spirituality and Gentility," *Envoy,* Vol. X, No. 1 (January 1973).

"The Gentle Life Style," *Envoy,* Vol. X, No. 2 (February 1973).

"Gentle Life and Death of Desire," *Envoy,* Vol. X, No. 3 (March 1973).

"Gentleness, At Homeness, and the Meditative Life," *Envoy,* Vol. X, No. 4 (April 1973).

"Listening and the Gentle Life," *Envoy,* Vol. X, No. 5 (May 1973).

"Poverty and Gentleness of Spirit," *Envoy,* Vol. X, No. 6 (June 1973).

"Gentleness and Direction of the Spirit," *Envoy,* Vol. X, No. 7 (September 1973).

"Gentleness and Involvement," *Envoy,* Vol. X, No. 8 (October 1973).

"Spiritual Life and Gentle Reflection," *Envoy,* Vol. X, No. 9 (November 1973).

"Silence and Gentleness," *Envoy,* Vol. X, No. 10 (December 1973).

"Gentleness and Playfulness," *Envoy,* Vol. XI, No. 1 (January 1974).

"Gentleness and Aggression," *Envoy,* Vol. XI, No. 2 (February 1974).

"Gentleness and Anger," *Envoy,* Vol. XI, No. 3 (March 1974).

"Gentility and Emotional Response," *Envoy,* Vol. XI, No. 4 (April 1974).

"Relief of Anger and Growth in Gentleness," *Envoy,* Vol. XI, No. 5 (May 1974).

"Gentleness, Anger and Affective Isolation," *Envoy,* Vol. XI, No. 6 (June 1974).

"Gentleness, Anger and Self-Mastery," *Envoy,* Vol. XI, No. 7 (September 1973).

"Gentleness and Displacement of Anger," *Envoy,* Vol. XI, No. 8 (October 1974).

"Gentleness, Anger, Anxiety," *Envoy,* Vol. XI, No. 9 (November 1974).

"Gentleness, Anger and Despondency," *Envoy,* Vol. XI, No. 10 (December 1974).

"Existential Theory and Therapy," in the *International Encyclopedia of Psychiatry, Psychoanalysis and Psychology.*

"Introspection and Transcendent Self-Presence," *Cross and Crown* Part I, Vol. 26, No. 3 (September 1974); Part II, Vol. 26, No. 4 (December 1974).

II. RELATED SOURCES.*

Muto, Susan Annette. *Approaching the Sacred: An Introduction to Spiritual Reading.* Denville, New Jersey: Dimension Books, Inc., 1973.

_____ *Steps Along the Way.* Denville, New Jersey: Dimension Books, Inc., 1975. (In Press)

_____."Reading the Symbolic Text: Some Reflections on Interpretation," *Humanitas,* Vol. VIII, No. 2 (May 1972)

_____."Mary, A Model for a Richer Humanity," *Our Lady of Fatima Magazine,* Vol. 30, No. 4 (October 1974).

_____."Solitude, Self-Presence and True Participation," *Spiritual Life,* Vol. 20, No. 4 (Winter, 1974).

_____."Richer at Each Awakening," *Cross and Crown,* Vol. 26, No. 4 (December 1974).

van Croonenburg, Bert. *Gateway to Reality.* New York: Herder and Herder, 1971.

_____.*Don't Be Discouraged.* Denville, New Jersey: Dimension Books, Inc., 1972.

UNPUBLISHED MATERIALS

Coulombe, Jeannine. "Presence to Culture: The Implication of Adrian van Kaam's Theory of Counseling for the Pastoral Counselor on an Indian Reserve." Unpublished Master's thesis, St. Paul University, Ottawa, Canada, 1974.

Dunne, Maureen. "Adrian van Kaam's View of Man: Some Basic Aspects of His Theory of Personality and the Implications of His Theory for Psychotherapy." Unpublished Master's thesis, St. Paul University, Ottawa, Canada.

Girard, Robert. "A Study of the Existential Psychology of Adrian van Kaam as Applied to the Ministry of Pastoral Counseling." Unpublished Master's thesis, St. Paul University, Trenton, Ontario, 1974.

Vitaline, Teresa, M.D. "Il Concetto di Presenza nella Teoria del Counseling di Adrian van Kaam e le sue Applicasioni nel Campo della Malattie Psicosomatiche." Unpublished Master's thesis, St. Paul University, Ottawa, Canada.

*

The journals *Humanitas* and *Envoy,* published by the Institute of Man at Duquesne University, can be utilized as resources in this field of study. The tri-yearly publication *Humanitas* offers cultural and scientific articles in relation to specific topics that may be relevant to the human dimension of Catholic Spirituality. *Envoy,* published monthly except for the months of July and August, is more directly revelant to the post-revelational and applicative dimensions of Fundamental Catholic Spirituality.

III. SELECTED THESES COMPLETED BY GRADUATES OF THE CENTER FOR THE STUDY OF SPIRITUALITY.*

Author	Title	Order #	Pages
1969			
Finn, Sr. Mary, HVM	RELIGIOUS AUTONOMY AND THE SPIRITUALITY OF THE NOVITIATE	M-1806	395
Mason, Rev. Gilbert, OMI	THE PERSONAL AND SPIRITUAL FORMATION OF THE RELIGIOUS SEMINARIAN	M-2244	214
Rake, Sr. Johan Michele, CDP	FRIENDSHIP IN RELIGIOUS LIFE	M-1889	392
1970			
Casey, Sr. Bernadette, RSM	OBEDIENCE AND THE AUTONOMY OF THE RELIGIOUS SISTER	M-2560	289
Crosby, Rev. Daniel, OFM Cap.	PERSONAL PRAYER IN CONTEMPORARY RELIGIOUS LIFE	M-2489	505
Hanlon, Sr. Marie Colette, SC	CUSTOM: A WAY OF LIFE—CREATIVE RENEWAL OF RELIGIOUS LIVING	M-2306	449
Helldorfer, Martin, C., FSC	THE PARTICIPATIVE RELIGIOUS AS WORKER	M-2486	406
McKeever, Sr. Clare, SSL	FUNCTIONALITY AND THE SPIRITUALITY OF THE RELIGIOUS SISTER	M-2561	387

*HOW TO ORDER:

Send Name of Author, Title and Order Number to University Microfilms, Xerox Corporation, P.O. Box 1307, Ann Arbor, Michigan 48106. Microfilm: $4.00; Xerography: $10.00 (Make checks payable to University Microfilms). These theses represent the results of three years of research into the structures and dynamics of personal and spiritual living together with the practical application of the student's findings to the situation of religious formation. Besides being an invaluable aid to formation personnel, they will complement any community library. All of these theses were written under the careful supervision of the faculty of the Institute of Man. They are copyrighted by the authors and cannot be quoted without written permission. Note especially, each thesis contains an extensive annotated subject bibliography.

Author	Title	Order #	Pages
1971			
Klein, Sr. M. Geraldine, SHG	COMMITMENT AND PERSONAL GROWTH: IMPLICATIONS FOR THE VOWED CELIBATE RELIGIOUS LIFE	M-3132	307
Kuzmickus, Sr. Marilyn, SSC	AUTHENTIC DETACHMENT IN RELIGIOUS LIVING	M-3179	351
O'Connell, Rev. Anthony, OSM	THE ROLE OF MOTIVATION IN HUMAN LIFE: ITS APPLICATION TO RELIGIOUS LIFE	M-3180	359
O'Toole, Sr. Katherine, SC	PERSONAL RESPONSIBILITY IN HUMAN LIVING: IMPLICATIONS FOR RELIGIOUS LIFE	M-1533	459
Sharpe, Sr. Miriam Joseph, RSM	LIFE FORM AND ITS TRANSFORMING INFLUENCE UPON THE PERSON	M-3367	283
Smurawa, Sr. Elaine, SSJ	LEISURE IN THE LIFE OF THE PARTICIPATIVE RELIGIOUS	M-3178	394
1972			
Breaud, Sr. Barbara, O. Carm.	THE EXPERIENCE OF GUILT: IMPLICATIONS FOR RELIGIOUS LIFE	M-3905	243
Earner, Sr. Mary Agnes, SDR	LIFE AS COMMUNICATION: SAYING, SILENCE, AND THE SPIRITUAL LIFE	M-4368	363
Hageman, Sr. Louise, OP	SUFFERING AND ITS SIGNIFICANCE FOR PERSONAL AND SPIRITUAL LIFE	M-3645	349
Lee, Sr. Shawn, SSJ	THE MEANING OF OUR WOMANHOOD: IMPLICATIONS FOR RELIGIOUS LIVING	M-3904	277
Norton, Sr. Julia, CSJ	THE CHASTENING OF LOVE IN RELIGIOUS LIVING	M-3906	230
Richardt, Sr. Sharon, DC	TOWARDS AN UNDERSTANDING OF HUMAN RECEPTIVITY: IMPLICATIONS FOR RELIGIOUS FORMATION	M-3707	398
Satala, Sr. Mary, DC	COMPASSIONATE LIVING	M-4366	470
1973			
Byrne, Rev. Richard, OCSO	LIVING THE CONTEMPLATIVE DIMENSION OF EVERYDAY LIFE	M-5207	430

Author	Title	Order #	Pages
Fitzgerald, Sr. Bethany, SSJ	HUMILITY: A FUNDAMENTAL ATTITUDE OF RELIGIOUS LIVING	M-5441	273
Gadoury, Sr. Rose Clarisse, SSA	CONVERSION AND LIFE OF THE SPIRIT	M-5321	516
Kelly, Sr. Maureen, SSL	SPIRITUALITY AND HUMAN SPATIAL SURROUNDINGS	M-5208	417
Schaut, Sr. Romayne, OSB	SPIRITUALITY AND THE ROLE OF THE FAMILY	M-5437	339
Sheehan, Rev. William, OMI	THE ONGOING MOVEMENT OF INTEGRATION AND THE SPIRITUAL LIFE	M-5439	360
Sherman, Sr. Sarah Marie, RSM	THE LIVED EXPERIENCE OF PERSONAL CONFLICT: IMPLICATIONS FOR SPIRITUALITY	M-5440	417
Tracy, Sr. Fidelis, CDP	MAN RESPONDING TO CHANGES: IMPLICATIONS FOR SPIRITUALITY	M-5211	408
Warren, Sr. Mary Esther, OP	THE MEANING OF DEDICATION: GROWTH IN SELF-GIFT TO GOD AND MAN	M-5436	494
1974			
Agnew, Sr. Una, SSL	ORIGINALITY AND SPIRITUALITY: THE ART OF DISCOVERING AND BECOMING ONESELF	M-6453	596
Chin, Sr. Marie, RSM	LIVED PRIVACY: AN AVENUE TO TRUE ENCOUNTER	M-6454	352
Gaudet, Sr. Jeanette, OSF	THE EXPERIENCE OF ANXIETY: ON THE WAY TOWARD SERENE RELIGIOUS LIVING	M-6456	301
Gunelson, Sr. Cecile, CPPS	INTERPERSONAL RECONCILIATION: MOVING TOWARD RIGHT RELATIONS THROUGH SPIRITUAL LIVING	M-6457	355
Hustedde, Sr. Germaine, PHJC	SPIRITUALITY AND AGING	M-6459	443
Iacobucci, Sr. Sharon, CSSF	MAN'S SEARCH FOR SECURITY: IMPLICATION FOR RELIGIOUS LIFE	M-6460	266
Jokerst, Sr. Carol Ann, CCVI	ON THE WAY TOWARD A TRUSTING RESPONSE: IMPLICATIONS FOR SPIRITUAL LIVING	M-6461	564

IV. CURRENT RESEARCH IN PROGRESS.

Berrigan, Sr. Elizabeth, CSJ	SPIRITUALITY AND SPIRITUAL DIRECTION
Bindewald, Sr. Andrée, O. Carm.	SPIRITUALITY IN TECHNOLOGY
Blank, Sr. Goretti, SDR	ON THE RELATIONSHIP OF MAN'S BIOLOGICAL ROOTINGS TO HIS SPIRITUAL UNFOLDING
Bomberger, Rev. Ray, SSJ	SPIRITUALITY AND TRADITION
Brissette, Sr. Claire, SSCh	THE EXPERIENCE OF AT-ONENESS: IMPLICATIONS FOR COMMUNITY LIVING
Carfagna, Sr. Rosemarie, OSU	SPIRITUALITY AND EMPATHY
Carboy, Sr. Joan Michael, SSJ	GROWING IN FREEDOM: LIVING AN ATTITUDE OF HONESTY
Chennilath, Rev. Matthew, CMI	SELF-REALIZATION AND FUNDAMENTAL CATHOLIC SPIRITUALITY
Cummings, Rev. Charles, OCSO	SPIRITUALITY AND DESERT EXPERIENCE
Dirkx, Sr. Bernadine, SSM	COMPULSIVE LIVING AND SPIRITUALITY
Dubickas, Sr. Regina Marie, SSC	SPIRITUALITY AND ANGER
Fernandes, Sr. Martin de Porres, OP	THE HUMOROUS MODE OF PRESENCE IN DAILY LIFE
Flory, Sr. Marianne, SCJ	SPIRITUALITY AND NEGATIVITY
Foley, Sr. Sharon, RSM	DISILLUSIONMENT AND TRUTH
Fulmer, Sr. Janice, CSFN	SPIRITUALITY AND CHARITY
Girard, Sr. Charlotte, SCJ	SPIRITUALITY AND KENOSIS
Gorski, Rev. Barnabas, OFM	JOY IN CHRISTIAN VOWED RELIGIOUS LIVING
Geurin, Sr. Ellen Marie, RSM	SPIRITUALITY AND FATIGUE
Harron, Sr. Sheila, RSM	INTIMACY, SPIRITUALITY AND SURRENDER TO THE DIVINE
Hernandez, Sr. Maria del Carman, CCVI	SPIRITUALITY AND GENTLENESS
Hever, Br. Denis, FMS	SELF-AWARENESS AND SPIRITUALITY
Jezik, Sr. Jeanne, OSF	SPIRITUALITY AND FEAR
Jordan, Sr. Grace, SSL	SPIRITUALITY AND LIVED TIME
Keyes, Rev. Paul	THE CARING PRESENCE AND THE SPIRITUAL LIFE
Kruszewski, Sr. Maria, CSFN	SPIRITUALITY AND LIVED INNER PEACE
Laferriere, Sr. Alice, SASV	SPIRITUALITY AND THE EXPERIENCE OF FAILURE
LaMadeleine, Rev. Richard, MS	GRATITUDE AND THE SPIRITUAL LIFE
Lane, Sr. Victoria, OSM	SPIRITUALITY AND AUTHENTIC INVOLVEMENT

Laperouse, Sr. Barbara Nell, O. Carm.	THE SYMBOLIZING MODE OF PRESENCE IN RELIGIOUS LIVING
Leckert, Sr. Mary Therese, OP	CONFORMITY, CREATIVITY AND SPIRITUALITY
Lynch, Sr. Brenda Mary, SSND	SPIRITUALITY AND LIVED PERSONAL DISCERNMENT: THE ART OF DECISION MAKING IN DAILY LIFE
Lyons, Sr. Kathleen, CSJ	UNITY IN DIVERSITY
McKay, Sr. Mary, CSJ	SPIRITUALITY AND THE CALL TO LEADERSHIP
Meissen, Sr. Lucille, CPPS	SPIRITUALITY AND WORSHIP
Mester, Sr. Mary, RSM	A SENSE OF WONDER: IMPLICATIONS FOR SPIRITUAL LIVING
Muggli, Sr. Agatha, OSB	THE ATTITUDE OF DISCIPLESHIP IN SPIRITUAL LIVING
Mulholland, Sr. Gertrude, SCIC	SPIRITUALITY AND LONELINESS
Murray, Sr. Marian, SHG	SPIRITUALITY AND FORGIVENESS
Needham, Sr. Lillian, SSJ	SPIRITUALITY AND THE AGING SISTER
Neely, Rev. Harry, OSA	AUTHORITY AND SPIRITUALITY
O'Reardon, Sr. Mairead, OSF	EXISTENCE IS COEXISTENCE: SPIRITUALITY AND JUSTICE
Pepera, Sr. Gemma, CSFN	SPIRITUAL LIVING AS HOMECOMING
Perring, Sr. Margaret, SSJ	LIFE'S CRISES: IMPLICATIONS FOR SPIRITUAL LIVING
Power, Sr. Kathleen, SSJ	AGGRESSIVE LIVING: OBSTACLE TO THE GENTLE LIFE STYLE
Price, Sr. Mary, SC	ATONEMENT: AT-ONE-MENT
Semple, Sr. Blaise, SSJSM	SOLITUDE AND LIVED SPIRITUALITY
Springer, Sr. Marcella, SSJ	SPIRITUALITY AND CREATIVE FIDELITY
Storms, Sr. Kathleen, SSND	SIMPLICITY OF LIFE AS LIVED IN THE EVERYDAY
Thames, Sr. Celine, FMI	INTERPERSONAL LISTENING: IMPLICATIONS FOR COMMUNITY LIVING
Thompson, Rev. James, OSA	DISINTEGRATION AND DEPRESSION IN THE RELIGIOUS LIFE: A LOSS OF FOCUS
Ulica, Sr. Jeanne Marie, OSF	SPIRITUALITY AND HOPE IN RELIGIOUS LIVING
Viens, Sr. Anita Louise, SSCH	SPIRITUALITY AND LIVED INNER SILENCE
Zeleznik, Rev. Clement, OSB	BE WHO YOU ARE: SELF-ACCEPTANCE AND THE LIFE OF THE SPIRIT
Zimorski, Sr. Christine, SSJ	COMING INTO A LIVED AWARENESS OF MY DEATH: IMPLICATIONS FOR SPIRITUALITY

INDEX

A

acceptance of my unique limitations, 142

achievement culture, 234

acquired presence, 39

active detachment, 39

active life of study, 209

aggressive analytical reflection, 175

à Kempis, Thomas, 24,58

all encompassing Divine call, 169

American Psychological Association, 52-53

anxiety, 113,133

Anxiety and Guilt Feelings, 126

Anxiety of the Spirit, 158-159

apophatic knowing of God, 68

apostolate, 319

       of the spiritual man, 319

       of the Christian, 320

Aquinas, St. Thomas 14,42,46,60,96,155,202,206,209,211,212,216,
    220,276

art and discipline of spiritual self-presence, 177

art and dynamics of formation, 240

art of counseling and spiritual direction, 245

       of integration, 252

       of living the rule, 224

       of the spiritual master, 133

The Ascent of Mount Carmel, 87,99,210

ascetical-mystical life, 87,90

ascetical-mystical treatises, 282

asceticism, 307

       of daily life, 307

atmosphere of equanimity, 176

at-oneness with the transcendent, 292

Attempted Solutions of the Crisis of Spiritual Direction, 254-259

attitude of obedience, 325

       of receptivity, 106

attitudes of psychotherapists, 260

Attuning myself to my Divine Calling, 144-146

Augustine St., 9,96,209

author of *The Cloud of Unknowing*, 39

"authority", authority, 74,105,112,121,124,127,229,231,248,344

authoritarian attitude, 235

authority in a personalistic sense, 344